Library of
Davidson College

THE AUTOBIOGRAPHY OF AN AMERICAN COMMUNIST

Eugene and Peggy Dennis, New York City, 1950.

THE AUTOBIOGRAPHY OF AN AMERICAN COMMUNIST

A PERSONAL VIEW OF A POLITICAL LIFE 1925-1975

BY PEGGY DENNIS

Lawrence Hill & Co.
Creative Arts Book Co.
Westport/Berkeley

Acknowledgments

At the very beginning there was the grant from the Louis M. Rabinowitz Foundation, New York. At the end there was Barry Gifford, author and editor, who brought the manuscript and publishers together, then edited and saw the project to fruition.

In between there was: Dorothy Healey, both enthusiastic and critical in her readings of first draft versions, who was most helpful, as throughout our twenty-five-year friendship, when we heatedly disagreed, forcing me to more clearly delineate my viewpoints.

Rose Perry, friend of many years, who gave fulsomely of her recollections of the 1950s and 1960s, much of which we experienced together.

My sister, Mini Carson Bock, my brother-in-law Albert and my niece Laura, who separately and collectively served as "preview audience" to my first draft chapters, and whose responses sometimes sent me back to my desk to clarify and simplify.

Jackie, who brought me a young woman's unique views on matters political and personal, and during these years transformed a traditional daughter / mother-in-law relationship into a treasured friendship.

And Gene—no longer son alone, now friend and mentor, supportive critic. Patiently he read, criticized, encouraged and edited, demanding I write with candor and without looking over my shoulder. Relentlessly he goaded me through the frequent moments when I almost gave up.

It has been a long and lonely and difficult road back in time. To each of these who have helped, my gratitude.

—P.D.

Library of Congress Cataloging in Publication Data:

Dennis, Peggy.
    The autobiography of an American communist.

    Includes index.
    1. Dennis, Peggy. 2. communists—United States-bibliographical. 3. communist—United States—1917-

I. Title.
HX84.B56A32   335.43'092'4 [B]   77-23607
ISBN 0-88208-081-4
ISBN 0-88208-090-3 pbk.

Copyright © 1977 by Peggy Dennis.
All rights reserved. No part of this work may be reproduced or transmitted in any form by any means, electronic or mechanical, including photocopying and recording, or by any information storage or retrieval system, without permission in writing from the publisher.

First U.S. Edition, October, 1977.

Published by Creative Arts Book Company (Berkeley, California) and Lawrence Hill & Company (Westport, Connecticut).

Manufactured in the United States of America.

To Gene
(1905-1961)

It was the best of times,
It was the worst of times,
It was the age of wisdom,
It was the age of foolishness,
It was the epoch of belief . . .
—Charles Dickens

and
To Mini,
my sister, my friend

CONTENTS

Preface

One: THE BEGINNINGS 13
Family backgrounds — Gene's I.W.W. contact — Joining the Party — Gene and I meet — Full-time revolutionaries.

Two: INTO THE CRUCIBLE 34
1929-1931 — Southern California — Strikes — Unemployed struggles — Union organizing — Arrests and Trials — Underground activity — Fugitives — Soldier of the Revolution — Tim's birth.

Three: WORLD'S EYE VIEW 58
1931-1935 — Life in Moscow — The Comintern — Gene's travels: South Africa, the Philippines, China — My work: School for Foreign Children — Red International of Labor Unions — Lenin School — Travels in Europe and Asia.

Four: SINKING HOME ROOTS AGAIN 88
1935-1937 — Return to U.S.A. — Tim remains in Moscow — Wisconsin party organization — The People's Front — Building the C.I.O. — Aid to Spain.

Five: MOSCOW AGAIN, NOT MADRID 112
1937-1938 — Work at the Comintern — Stalin purges — Browder and Foster in Moscow — Gene-in-the-middle — Back home.

Six: VIEW FROM THE TOP 126
1938-1940 — Life in New York and Washington — United Front — Hitler-Stalin Pact — Break with New Deal Coalition — Underground again.

Seven: **WORLD AT WAR** 138
1941-1944 — Wartime Moscow — Wartime New York — Birth of Gene, Jr. — National Unity policies — Achievements and Mistakes.

Eight: **BROWDER DREAM, TRUMAN NIGHTMARE** .. 159
1945-1950 — Reformist policies — Browder expelled — Gene becomes General Secretary — Issues and Debates — Cold War politics — H.U.A.C. — Smith Act trial.

Nine: **POLITICAL PRISONER/ PRISON WIFE** 184
1950-1955 — Prison — Underground and floundering — The McCarthy Era — Writing and Travelling.

Ten: **UNRESOLVED CRISIS** 219
1956-1959 — Out of prison — Stalin crimes revealed — Internal crisis — Views and analyses — Political consolidation.

Eleven: **THE LAST YEAR** 240
1960 — Gene's Illness — An evening with Khruschev and Gromyko — Meeting with Tim — Alienation — Gene's death.

Twelve: **A WOMAN ALONE** 258
1961-1976 — Influences and Changing Views — Young Gene — Foreign Editor — Travels in the Socialist World — Divisions in the movement — Final Analysis — A new outlook.

Appendix: **LETTER OF RESIGNATION FROM THE COMMUNIST PARTY, U.S.A.** 289

Index 297

Preface

I do not proselytize my Marxist beliefs in this book, nor do I undertake to define or defend them in their theoretical or philosophical aspects. This is the personal story of two very politically involved people, not a treatise on political or economic theory.

Yet nothing that happened to us throughout our lives, nor that we allowed to happen to us, can be understood unless one recognizes the force of the total commitment that my husband Gene and I had to the body of economic, social and political outlook called Marxism-Leninism, and to the Communist Party, which we believed to be the only viable vehicle for that commitment.

Upon joining the Communist Party, my husband at 21 in Seattle and I at 16 in Los Angeles, and for the next thirty-three years together, Gene and I were fulltime revolutionaries whose daily lives were dedicated to the needs and demands (real and imagined) of the Movement and the Party. As Gene in particular rose rapidly into leadership positions locally, nationally and internationally, our personal lives became our political lives. Both were lived against the backdrop of history—as the Party from Moscow to Shanghai to New York interpreted that history.

Although no source data nor footnote impedia have been included, all facts and events dealt with in this account have been verified by intensive research in the libraries and archives of the University of California (Berkeley); University of Wisconsin and the State Historical Society of Wisconsin (both at Madison); the city libraries of Los Angeles and Seattle; the offices of the American Civil Liberties Union and the Library of Social Sciences (both at Los Angeles); also in the reading, in addition, of hundreds of books of differing analyses of the political and economic events during the five decades this book encompasses. All interpretations of these facts are definitely my own.

The year's research served two main purposes—to refresh

my personal recollections of what happened and when it happened; also it evoked vivid memories of personal responses to those events. The scenes and dialogue reconstructed here are rooted in those memories.

My husband's views, decisive to the policies and work of the Communist Party and therefore to our personal lives, are given here on the basis of his prolific writings—reports, speeches, pamphlets, articles; on personal letters which recipients sent to me after his death; on notes scribbled on margins of papers found among his few records; and particularly have I relied upon my intimate knowledge acquired in thirty-three years of living with him, discoursing and often hotly arguing with him. My own views are at all times clearly indicated as being the separate identity they have always been.

The last chapter, "A Woman Alone," capsulizes all too briefly the years 1961-1976. No one is more aware than I that those sixteen years, in their rich complexity, deserve to be the theme of a whole new book. Instead they are offered here in summary to indicate the main influences which compelled me to respond rather drastically, in light of my past, to new circumstances.

—Peggy Dennis
Oakland, California
1977

One:
THE BEGINNINGS

I

We came by car and bus and the hitchhiker's thumb from cities and towns across California, Oregon and Washington state. Five miles out of Woodland, somewhere between Portland and Seattle, the meeting house of the Finnish Cooperative Society was to be home to fifty-four of us for the next six months. The barn-like white building stood on a knoll overlooking the icy Lewis river, surrounded by flat fields and dense forests. An idyllic vacation spot; but we had come for a more serious purpose.

It was June 23, 1928, opening day of the fulltime Pacific Coast Marxist Summer School. For the first hours of our arrival at least, we were each somewhat pompously aware of the honor and responsibility bestowed upon us by committees back home who had selected us as worthy enough to come to school.

In age our student body ranged from 15 to 30. I had come with a very small group from San Francisco, but the large contingent from Southern California and I embraced enthusiastically. We knew each other well, for we had gone through the Communist children's and youth movement together and had joined the Communist Party at about the same time. However, one Angeleno I knew only slightly, and greeted him rather formally. I was inhibited too by the fact that he was not a student like the rest of us, but one of our five instructors.

Dubbed in 1947 by the FBI as "the man with many aliases," among them that of Eugene Dennis, Frank Waldron had arrived in Los Angeles in 1927. A short time later my husband Bill and I were sent by the Party to work in San Francisco. During the brief interim, and from the vantage point of being an eighteen-year-old newly-married woman, I had been amused at the flurry of feminine interest in this young, very tall, lanky, Frank Waldron, our Party's new and rather handsome educational director for Southern California.

Within a couple of days our summer school settled down to the routines of classes, studying and numerous committee assignments. The younger, less politically sophisticated comrades from Oregon and Washington selected assignments in planning sports and Saturday night entertainment. The California sophisticates became wall-newspaper editors and the organizers of nightly discussions on current events. The school was governed by an elected student council responsible to the daily morning assembly. Kitchen duty and sanitation chores rotated amongst all of us, including our teachers.

In our past-curfew exchanges up in the attic which served as women's dorm, I joined the others in expressing respect for quiet-spoken, unobtrusive, but ever-present Oliver Carlson, our school director; but we all voted Gene (or Frank as he was then) the most exhilarating and satisfying of our instructors. I noted once again, as I had earlier in Los Angeles, that the approval was not all objectively academic.

Free of Party clichés and jargon, and with a wry, delightful humor, Gene was different than the Party people I had known. By the time I came to Woodland I was already a lifetime Young Communist who had made many public speeches about Marx, Lenin, and world revolution. In Gene's class on "Social Forces in American History" that summer of 1928 I learned a version and approach to my country's history never taught me before.

Twenty-three years old and only two years in the Communist Party, Gene had us lay claim to the revolutionary traditions of our own country, to not concede that rich history to the misrepresentations of the flag-waving superpatriots. At a time when our Party was based upon reverence for and aping of the German and Russian experiences, Gene taught us that our Marxist movement had to be rooted in the American experience, molded by the American culture.

In style, too, he was excitingly different. In socratic form, he probed us for answers. Outside the classroom, he would appear on the fringes of our study groups as we lay scattered under the trees, sunbathing in the fields, sitting on the rocks at river's edge. With long legs stretched out, a blade of grass or a long, narrow pipe stem in his mouth, he lay on his back listening to our discussions. When someone sought a "correct" answer from him, he countered with questions.

Interspersed with our classes in political economy, Marxism, principles of Communist organization, labor journalism, and Gene's class on American History, we were always organizing athletic events, art festivals, agitprop theater and the weekend dances to which came our Finnish hosts, also oldtime socialists from the logging camps and the shingle weavers and fishermen's unions.

In small brigades we went to Portland and Seattle to speak at union meetings on behalf of mine strikes in the southwest and textile strikes in the east. Each Sunday morning we climbed the soapbox in the city park at Woodland to discourse on current events at home and abroad.

The most exciting highlights in the first weeks were our infiltration of a reserve army camp, and the invasion of our school by town rowdies threatening to wipe out "those Commie bastards," "Jew-boys," and "free-love bitches."

In our labor journalism class we labored over a leaflet exposing U.S. imperialism in Latin America and Asia, calling upon the reserves to "down guns." In our Communist organization class we plotted how to reach the young men in the camp. Pooling our meager "dress-up" supplies, a group of our girls attended a dance at the army camp. We flirted and danced enthusiastically, despite our unease in the presence of so many uniforms. According to plan, at a specified moment a shower of leaflets filled the air. The young men, obviously believing this to be part of the evening's entertainment, reached for them avidly, while we made a quick exit to cars waiting down the road. Two of us were caught and questioned by red-faced, gold-starred officers who, wanting to keep the whole incident quiet and unable to break our stoicism, let us go. Back at school we were triumphant. We had bagged the lion in his den and we hoped that a few young men in camp that night were reading our call to fight imperialism.

When friends from Woodland brought us the news that there was talk in town about threats to destroy our school, long and heated debate at our regular morning assembly disrupted our class routines. No Bolshevik group in Czarist Russia debated the issue of reformism versus adventurism more seriously than did we that summer morning. Lines divided between those who wanted to stand and fight and those who felt that maintaining the school was the primary goal, that we should retreat to Portland or Seattle into some makeshift setup in Party headquarters there.

Under the skillful, unobtrusive influence of Gene and Carlson, we adopted a third alternative. We would try to reason with our intruders while being prepared to do battle if, and Carlson emphasized *if,* we were attacked. Moving to the city was held in abeyance, depending upon the outcome of the confrontation.

We put ourselves on organized military alert. According to Gene's strategy, except for the small group who constituted the persuasion brigade, we were deployed into three divisions: a reserve patrol remained out of sight in the woods; a circle of guards with wooden clubs menacingly surrounded our building; and there were the commandos, some of whom were hidden in the attic with buckets of water, while others of us roamed the grounds clenching bags of pepper and salt mixtures in our pockets.

On the second night they came, seventy young bully-boys itching for a fight, motors revving, exhausts backfiring. Under strict orders to ignore all verbal provocations and fight back only if physically attacked, we apprehensively waited as Carlson and his persuasion group urged the ringleaders inside to talk. Pouring coffee and passing cookies, Carlson quietly discoursed upon our constitutional rights against theirs. Outside the intruders circled around us, taunting and daring us to fight. With sweaty fists clutching clubs and pepper/salt bags, we were grateful for the presence of the seasoned loggers and shinglers who had arrived earlier to aid us.

The persuasion group won no converts that night, but the uncomfortable guests scuffed their way out, and with a gruff "les' go" to their disappointed stalwarts, they piled into their cars and drove off.

We stayed up late that night excitedly discussing the events, each from our particular vantage point. The persuasion group claimed credit for the non-violent outcome, but the rest of us heatedly argued that it was the visible show of physical readiness to do combat that helped make the persuasion effective.

Cars from town continued to harass us; they zoomed onto our road, circled our hall and pup tents where the men bunked, honked horns, shouted obscenities. Our patrol duty continued in shifts around the clock. Our main fear, as we went routinely about our school activities or stood our turn at guard, was a possible gunshot from one of the cars or a fire set in the forest surrounding our building, but nothing serious occurred.

II

In the ordinary course of things, that Woodland summer would have been a worthwhile experience. It became much more than that when suddenly, midpoint in the six weeks session, Gene and I discovered each other in a manner quite apart from the casual flirtations going on around us. One moment we were merely friendly members of our school collective, the next we were in a world of our own.

We became truants from school activities; we wandered off deep into the sun-laced forest; we spent whole afternoons in our private hideaway, forsaken books strewn about us, a cascading waterfall screening us from all else. We stayed on at the river's edge long after the campfire was officially doused, and each night I stealthily climbed the outside safety-ladder to the attic dorm in the early dawn, in violation of curfew rules.

In between long, heart-racing, breathless silences, we talked, probing each other's thoughts and emotions. Sometimes gently, sometimes provocatively, sometimes harshly, sometimes humorously, we probed and challenged each other as man and woman, as revolutionaries, as human beings.

So absorbed was I in this new experience that when on our last day of school Gene asked, "What about Bill?", I looked dazed. I had forgotten my husband. Bill and I had known each other for some years; he had been one of my sister's romantic discards. We had been active together in our radical movement in Los Angeles, and we had gotten married. We were comrades among other comrades, involved in movement activity together, but not deeply, irrevocably involved with each other. I might not have known the difference if I had not stumbled on what Gene and I now had. Now there was no choice. Gene, however, insisted I return to San Francisco before I made a final decision; that I join him in Seattle only if, in the reality of ordinary life back home, I still felt the way I did now. The next three weeks were difficult for all of us. Bill suddenly displayed a sensitive understanding of the lacks in our marriage and pleaded for a new beginning. Mama watched, waited, and said nothing. Papa took me for a walk, cleared his throat, and said, "I don't want you to get hurt, yet you must be ready to get hurt, if necessary, or not leave at all. You should not go to one man with the belief that you can always come back to the first one if it doesn't work out. If you believe this new love is worth losing Bill for even if it should fail, then have the courage to go." This was an unusually long speech for Papa.

On the night before I left San Francisco, Mama broke her silence and said she had something to tell me and my sister. We went into the bedroom, leaving Papa, Bill, and my sister's husband, Al, in the kitchen. She told us of a secret love she had had back in Old Russia with a young leader who had been recently sent to her town to head their illegal Leninist group. Their group was discovered by the czarist police, her love was arrested, and she was ordered to Siberian exile because of her known record as a dangerous revolutionary with many stays in prisons where she had led protest hunger strikes. Hurried arrangements were made to smuggle her out of the country before she was due to report for exile. Papa was a member of an opposing revolutionary group, but he was a friend of the family. He married her to give her a viable passport once they travelled the underground route across the Russian frontier. They made their way slowly to Amsterdam, London, and finally to New York. Clinging to each other, the marriage took emotional root. Yet somewhere in the past there was that young first love, consummated and destroyed in the flame of struggle and repression.

I was not sure what Mama's intent was in telling her story now. Was it to convey the message that I should follow my love? That life was too precarious to give it up? Or perhaps that love comes not just once, and can be satisfactorily replaced. I had always been partial to my father; my growing-up animosities had been directed against my mother. Now I suddenly felt close to her—we were women together.

I arrived in Seattle on September 4, 1928. This was to become our anniversary date because in the thirty-three years we lived together, Gene and I did not legalize our marriage. We had no use for bourgeois institutions and needed no legal papers to sanctify our life together.

My family of aunts, uncles, cousins, and grandmother met Gene five months later. My sister quipped, "He's powerful stuff." Papa warmly smiled as he embraced him. Mama shyly held his large calloused hands, looked up at his over six-foot height and murmured, "The hands of a worker, the face of a poet." My brother-in-law Al was grudgingly non-commital. He resented the break-up of the close foursome my sister Mini, he, Bill, and I had had first in Los Angeles and later in San Francisco. The aunts and uncles were ill-at-ease with this first Gentile to enter our close circle, but everyone was curiously interested.

For his first visit to Grandma, Gene resurrected a few German words and greeted her, "Guten tag, Grossmuter, *vei geitz?*" She beamed and said to the rest of us in the only language she knew, "And they say he's not a Jewish boy. Listen to him, he even talks Jewish, that's more than you do."

The first time he came to our traditional Sunday family gathering, Gene's shy but ready smile and his slow speech got lost in the crossfire of shouting voices that lapsed into Yiddish soon after the first careful use of English for his sake. To his startled question, we laughed uproariously over the steaming glasses of tea and lemon and the piled plates of sponge cake and strudel.

"Fighting? Who's fighting! We're discussing the news of the day!" And to my large, excitable, warm, radical family, the news of the day was its very lifeblood.

III

When Mama and Papa came to America they were not seeking the legended golden mecca. As young Jewish revolutionaries, they knew they were coming to a capitalist America, but at least it was not tyrannical, monarchistic Old Russia. They were not surprised at the sweatshops where they both got jobs, nor at the cold water tenements where they lived, nor even at the cossack police that broke up their strike picketlines on New York's east side.

The 1905 revolution in Russia raised jubilant hopes among the young emigrés, and Mama, pregnant with my sister, made plans to go home. The revolution failed; going-home talk slowly receded, but Mama and Papa and the aunts and uncles did not assimilate into the new country. They rejected the mores of capitalist America. They were critical of those among their emigré circles who adjusted and tried to make it by the exploitative measures needed to succeed. Their goals remained alienated from those of this country. They wore their poverty like a badge of honor, continued to meet in small groups which at least now were no longer illegal as in Old Russia, and talked about the needed revolution.

In 1912, when I was three and my sister six, we took the

long, slow train trip to Los Angeles. Mama had contracted a virulent asthma that made her a permanent semi-invalid and I had some kind of bronchial chest weakness. The West was prescribed for both of us.

Five years later the Russian Revolution changed the course of world history and for the family it was a very personal victory. Mama wept at farewell parties for young Russian and Jewish families going back to help build socialism. It was too late for her, she said. The new socialist state needed young, healthy workers. Her happiest moment, I think, was in 1935 when, upon my return from Moscow, I told her that the Soviet comrades had told me that her original membership in that Lenin group so long ago qualified her for preferential, Old Bolshevik status in the Soviet Union.

Not all radicals embraced the Russian Revolution, and the immediate months and years after 1917 that erupted into sharp clashes within the Socialist Party and its Jewish Arbeiter Ring fraternal order also tore our family apart. Aunts, uncles and friends fought bitterly, dividing into Rights and Lefts; Kerensky versus Lenin; Brest Litovsk peace compromises versus permanent revolution; proletarian dictatorship versus social democratic parliamentarism. Marriages floundered, lifetime friendships were destroyed, and our Sunday family gatherings became embittered explosions. The road to socialism apparently was a single, narrow one for these oldtime revolutionaries; only their own was the correct path.

Through it all we children grew and played in this self-contained, foreign-born, radical community. We were enrolled in the Socialist Party sunday school at the Labor Temple at the time we started public school kindergarten, and the former was more important than the latter. Among my early memories are those of being lifted each week onto a table in stark meeting halls and lisping my way through recitations of revolutionary poems by Yiddish writers my parents and their comrades loved so passionately. Papa coached me at home, explaining the pathos and courage and hope of the words I was to recite.

During our elementary and high school years my sister and I stayed out of school on May First, International Workers' Day of Solidarity and Struggle, and neither we nor our parents would use the easy "she was sick" excuse. It was important to make it very clear to teacher and classmates the socially significant reason for our absence that day.

By the same token we went to school on all Jewish religious holidays, even if we had a cold. Heaven forbid that teacher should think we observed those days. Each year I was mocked for being the only Jew at school on Hebrew holidays, just as I was scolded during the war years for refusing to buy war savings stamps and kept our class from a 100% patriotism record.

But I held my head high, cheeks flaming, and back ramrod straight. I knew that all religion was the opiate of the people and that Wilson's war was a capitalist fight for division of the world. We were belligerently atheist, internationalist, and anti-imperialist, and the narrow-mindedness of our block, our school and our community only made us feel special and superior.

We marched on picketlines in meat strikes and milk strikes organized by a small militant women's movement, in which Mama and the aunts were very active. Our social life revolved around fund-raising concerts for Soviet Russian famine relief, beach picnics for the *Daily Worker,* and dances in support of mine and textile strikes in faraway states.

At school we were good students, cynically giving back to our history and civics teachers the capitalist propaganda we knew they wanted to hear. Our fulsome efforts went into our classes in literature, drama and composition, which we loved. We consumed library books voraciously and from the time we were eight, Papa, with difficulty, won our right to the adult white library card in each new neighborhood to which we moved. Our literary diet leaned heavily to the Russian classics, although later it expanded to include Upton Sinclair, Sinclair Lewis, Theodore Dreiser; in high school years we discovered Michael Arlen and Edna St. Vincent Millay. I had not heard of Langston Hughes, however, until 1928, when Gene gifted me with a slim volume of *Weary Blues.*

Being poor was a natural state and we grew up with no I wish . . . ." hungers. Papa worked as a cloakmaker downtown, as did Mama during the months she was physically well. From time to time Papa opened a small cleaning and pressing shop in the Jewish ghetto along Brooklyn Avenue, or further east where the barrios were beginning to appear, and sometimes on the edges of the Gentile areas along First Street. We lived in the two or three rooms in the back of the store where kerosene fumes permeated our lives. My sister and I were secretly glad each time the shop failed, because then Papa went back to work downtown and we moved into a small cottage. Mama sewed our underwear and dresses, Papa fashioned our coats—all were made out of durable family hand-me-downs lovingly refashioned for us. Only our shoes were store-bought, while our house furniture, as well as the dolls and doll carriages I was given on birthdays, came from Papa's rummaging through Salvation Army rejects. Possessions were unimportant, books and politics were all-important. Money was merely the pennies we gave the green grocer and butcher for soup-greens and bones which became the big pot of soup, our weekly mainstay together with the bucket of oranges bought for fifteen cents off my uncle's fruits-and-vegetables wagon.

The alien world we ignored so completely did intrude in an explosive way that only drove us deeper within our safe counter-community. I was twelve at the time. An angry lynch mob stormed our home in East Los Angeles. With lighted torches and baseball bats, our white, Gentile neighbors stomped onto our porch, trampled our patch of lawn, crushed Mama's carefully tended flower beds. They threatened to burn our house down. They demanded Papa's body. They were furious because we had just sold our modest five-room cottage (which still belonged to the Morris Plan mortgage company) to a Japanese family. At the time anti-Asian feelings in Southern California ran higher in many ways than anti-Chicano feelings, while Blacks were rarely seen out of their ghettoes in the far-off south end of the sprawling city.

Mama locked Papa in the bathroom, over his angry protests. He wanted to lecture the mob about the equality of all races and explain that race hatred was a tool of the capitalist class. But Mama's tactics were more pragmatic and survival-oriented. I was sent out the back door, running breathlessly across empty lots, clutching a nickel in my hand to phone the uncles for help. With my sister at her side, Mama stood on the porch, the front door locked behind her, and she talked against time, the flickering torch flames outlining the shouting, hateful faces milling about her. Late that night, after we had been led to safety and sat huddled and shaken in my Aunt Ida's kitchen, the sheriff phoned. Our home, he reported, had been mysteriously damaged, "by fire, cause unknown."

IV

In 1922, at the age of sixteen, my sister Mini, already a Young Communist League member, organized the first

Communist children's group in Southern California. I was her first recruit and rapidly became that organization's public spokesperson—a fiery, tense thirteen-year-old. In school I was selected to recite James Whitcomb Riley's "Little Orphan Annie" poems at PTA meetings; out of school I made eloquent speeches at Communist mass meetings, denouncing the Rockefeller and Morgan warmakers and urging support of the new children's revolutionary movement as an alternative to school-taught capitalist propaganda. Our organization grew quickly. Within our first year we had a membership of 350 children, centered mainly in the dominantly Jewish Boyle Heights district, with smaller groups meeting weekly in outlying areas and towns.

We grew up unaware of such things as sibling rivalry and other psychological approaches to life relationships. I adored my sister Mini and I conceded to her the accolades of affection and praise she drew since infanthood from doting aunts and uncles and later from admiring comrades and teachers. I was not consciously competitive, but I was emulative as I followed closely on her heels. Over the years I received my share of limelight and admiration in our community of comrades and at school, but there was a difference. Mini worked hard at making herself liked by everyone; she was outgoing, always bubbly effervescent, animated, fun to be with. Only years later did she and I relate her hard-bitten fingernails, her brittle, endless chatter, her avoidance of things unpleasant, to the toll extracted for that popularity.

She was outgoing and glittering, while I grew up self-consciously shy and silent, except in public speaking situations. Where she needed people around to admire her, off the speaker's platform I sought solitude. Where she was outwardly always cheerful because, she said, that was the way people liked her, I frequently exploded into outbursts of anger.

Dark of skin, hair and eyes, I was often mistaken as one of theirs by old Mexican grandmothers as I played in the streets edging the barrio out in East Los Angeles. By the time I was six I learned to glibly reply, *"Yo no comprendo."*

By a quirk that Mama could no longer explain, I was given the very royal name of Regina, a name I was uncomfortable with and never used. Among the brood of cousins for a time I was dubbed "Nigger," a tab I liked and it had no racist connotation in our tensely equality-minded, revolutionary family. At home I was Ginnie (probably because it more easily rhymed with Minnie), or in its more loving and diminutive forms—Ginky or Ginkele.

Throughout school and within the movement I was known only as Reggie by teachers, classmates and comrades alike. The custom of changing one's last name (if not both first and last) upon joining the Party may have had something to do with job and community security in some industrial parts of the country. In New York and Los Angeles, however, in those years it was motivated more by a rather synthetic need to "Americanize" our movement at a time when it was essentially foreign-born. When Mini joined the Party and YCL she substituted Carson for the family name of Karasick. I followed suit, three years later. The small local reputation we built around that name in the early years within the movement became well-known throughout the state as Mini became a popular strike leader, union organizer, and one of the few women in state Party leadership. My Party life led me in other directions. The Carson name, for me, became Ryan in Moscow; Peggy Dennis was created in a New York hotel room in 1935. Unlike my original given and family name, I have been comfortable with these two ever since.

It is perhaps strange that we did not suffer split personality symptoms as we grew up keeping our political and school lives in separate compartments. While the first remained always the more important and real to us, we thoroughly enjoyed becoming popular and active at school.

At Hollenbeck Junior High and then in high school, Mini at Lincoln and I at Roosevelt, we deliberately entered the straight world for the sheer fun of it. We won numerous schoolwide elective positions. We participated in statewide oratorical contests and Shakespearean festivals. We each won the lead in our separate senior plays, and I was an editor of school newspapers at both schools. We went steady with popular athletes and we belonged to the in-groups noted for being intellectual, service-minded, trend-setting. Away from school, on evenings and weekends, we were deeply involved in Communist meetings, Marxist discussions, conferences, organizing new chapters of the children's movement.

My traditional Sweet Sixteen party celebrated too my graduation from high school, my passing from the children's movement into the Young Communist League, and into the Communist Party where my first assignment was that of adult leader of the children's organization.

At sixteen I also reluctantly enrolled in the Teachers College at the University of California. Going to college in those days was not the ordinary thing to do for children of poor families. Mama and Papa, however, were imbued with the Jewish immigrant's respect for Education, even capitalist education. Also, they argued, Mini and I had to have some way of becoming economically independent from whatever husbands we might someday acquire. Becoming teachers made sense to them. Mini stuck it out for three and one-half years and then left the University in her senior year. I stayed only one year. I enjoyed my Freshman Composition class and wrote my weekly essays enthusiastically. I nearly flunked Survey of World History because I was bored with the irrelevancy, to me, of the reign of Charlemagne or the Holy Wars. In the key classes drilling us how to teach children math and reading, I upset my instructors by asking *how* do we explain to children *why* two plus two equals four, and that "b" follows "a". I left in disgust, convinced that Teachers College—no less than grade school or high school—did not teach us the "whys" of the world. Instead I turned to my work with the children's movement.

There the small group of Young Communists met weekly in discussion seminars, exploring ideas of child psychology and methods of learning-by-doing that were unheard of at that time. Through games, songs, skits, picnics and child-prompted discussions, we creatively applied the concepts set by our national leadership in New York:

". . . to help children understand on the basis of their own experiences in school, at home, on the streets, the reasons for their problems, society's responsibility for creating them and to foster a sense of confidence and solidarity derived from the group, from social struggle for common solutions."

Today this approach is practically routine. At that time it was unique.

Although our Communist movement tolerated no revolutionary ideology other than our own—in fact at one point we went about breaking up meetings of social democrats held to denounce the Soviet Union—we defended actively all victims of capitalist repression. Demonstrations and meetings and picketlines were constantly organized in support of the I.W.W. who filled the jails in San Pedro and San Diego; for Tom Mooney and Warren K. Billings and the McNamara Brothers in San Quentin and Folsom state prisons; for the young army men, Paul Crouch and Walter Trumbell on Alcatraz Island; for Sacco and Vanzetti, for whom we stood on the street corners and wept the night they were executed, August 22, 1927.

Less than a year later, after Bill and I had moved to San Francisco into state leadership of the Young Communist League, I came to the Woodland summer school a nineteen-year-old political sophisticate. I had made numerous reports about the need to Americanize our Communist Party. I had helped draw up many plans to send Young Communists into local factories. I had written leaflets exposing U.S. imperialist designs around the world and I had gotten up at dawn to distribute them at factory gates. I had organized children's groups in Southern and Northern California. I had spoken at endless forums on current events and on Marxist theory. But we were still a vanguard far removed from mainstream America, and we were fiercely proud of being different. For public occasions we wore the flaming red, embroidered shirts of the Soviet Russians, our songs pledged our lives to the International Soviet that would free the human race. We were confident that we alone were tapped by history to fulfill its mission for humanity's liberation from exploitation and oppression. We alone had the answer as to how this could be done; and because there was only one socialist state to emulate, the Soviet Union was our blueprint.

We were happy, unconflicted, suffered no identity crises, saw no generation gaps. We lived in isolated security amongst our own kind. The goals and hopes of our parents were ours. We rejected those of society around us; ours was the dream of the Future.

V

During these years Gene was growing up in Seattle in quite a different, more typical American way.

At the turn of the century, his father, Francis Xavier Waldron, then a twenty-five-year-old railroad worker from New Jersey, followed the lure of quick fortune to Alaska where he laid claim to a small gold find, sold it for quick cash, and drifted down to Seattle. In this raw, booming, frontier town grown fat on the exploitation of imported Chinese laborers and the broken dreams of other young Francis Xaviers, the young railroader from New Jersey settled down, married in 1904, fathered a son in 1905, and a daughter one year later.

Taunted by the persistent get-rich-quick lure, he left home again and again, once traveling as far as Shanghai. But all his ventures invariably failed, and he began to sit at home, plotting new plans, becoming morosely weighted with the guilt of failure because wealth, that world's measure of success, eluded him. He resigned himself early to the loser's life on the shabby edges of respectable, lower-class Seattle.

Gene rarely spoke of that early life. I did hear him scoff at what he called his sister's sentimentalized versions of their childhood. He claimed, somewhat caustically, that she had not understood or had blocked out the tensions in that family dominated by a defeated, embittered, hard-drinking father.

In the earlier years they did live comfortably at times when his father's schemes temporarily paid off. Then they'd be poor again and his father sat planning new, sure-thing money schemes. Gene added, as an after-thought, "He was driven by quiet desperation, not by love of the adventure. The come-backs became less and less frequent and he sank deeper into despair, seeing his failures as an indictment of himself as a man and as a family provider."

Gene boasted often of his paternal Irish grandfather, a boilermaker by trade, and he bragged of that ancestor's life as a revolutionary freedom fighter who fled the Old Country with a British price on his head. However, I heard little of the maternal Veigs and practically nothing of his mother, Nora, born on a Minnesota farm after the family transplanted from Norway.

I soon realized that this reticence hid a traumatic hurt at her long illness and death when he was barely eleven. He said once, quietly, "I stopped believing in the power of prayer when she died. I refused to enter church again and dropped out as choir boy," adding in amusement, "much to the horror of my Catholic family blessed with a couple of nuns among the aunts."

Contrary to the Cinderella myth, the speedy advent of a stepmother brought much-needed warmth and love into the Waldron household. Tall, large-boned, with strong facial features, Amelia radiated a supportive love for her new children and her intelligent, humanist social views left an impact on the young Gene. I first met Amelia in 1929 when Gene and I returned to Los Angeles from Seattle. I responded gratefully to her warmth and interest in me as a person in my own right. I admired, too, the fact that, newly-widowed, she was working as a librarian in correctional institutions so that she might be with young people.

Gene's sister Nora disapproved the political direction her

brother's life had taken. She could not understand us nor the lives we led, although her personal idolization of Gene remained constant. I resented that idolization just as I resented his victorian protectiveness of both Amelia and Nora. It was to me a trait totally out of keeping with our own earthy, lusty relationship, which paralleled that which I had known in my own family.

VI

Time magazine, in April 1947, bestowed upon Gene the dubious honor of being their Man of the Week. It was in the backwash of the national publicity glare centered on Gene's appearance before the Un-American Committee. The magazine sported his photograph on its cover and had a long biographical article on the inside. He was described as a young Frank Waldron "who danced and wisecracked his way into Franklin High School's social upper crust" even though "his family was far from well-to-do." They quoted from his graduation book, listing him as leader of the school's crack debating team, manager of the varsity basketball squad and also of the senior play.

The *Time* article did not mention a different side of Gene that sent him on lone camping trips to Mercer Island where, with only his dog as companion, he hiked the woods by day and wrote poetry in front of his campfire by night. Nor did the article explore the home conditions which turned the boy Gene into an early provider for the family whose father receded more deeply into taciturn withdrawal. As newsboy, doing physical combat to protect his street corner rights; pitching manure in the grocer's stable; driving the horse and wagon making home deliveries after school; and working in logging camps where he met his first revolutionaries—the Wobblies.

In the woods, on the chow-line, in the bunkhouse talk, young Gene was drawn to these migrant, rootless workers whose Red Card of Brotherhood in the Industrial Workers of the World welded them into a One Big Union family. He listened avidly to their recollections of the 1916 Everett and Centralia massacres in which Wobblies were imprisoned, tarred and feathered for defending themselves, while deputy sheriffs and goons who had ambushed and shot them went free.

He remembered well the great 1919 general strike when all Seattle was governed for five days by a multi-union strike committee. Now, sitting on the edge of his bunk, he listened intently as oldtimers re-argued I.W.W. tactics of participating in the strike despite official exclusion by the A.F.L. leaders. He heard, from the inside now, how when the strike was over, the employers, the city fathers and the A.F.L. hierarchy once again made the I.W.W. their chief target. Once again their union halls were wrecked, their members beaten on the streets. The cry of solidarity rang throughout the West, and Wobblies converged on Seattle, deliberately filling the jails to bursting and neither threats nor clubs silenced the voices of these singing jailbirds.

Gene's eyes glistened as he sat night after night re-living the courage of the past. During the day he joined the job-slowdowns his older workmates organized to fight for job safety, better food, cleaner bunkhouses.

Time magazine did note that by the time he graduated high school, the young Frank Waldron had become "a serious young man who hung around Seattle's American Federation of Labor temple." He considered himself one with the Wobbly lumberjacks, but back in the city he began to explore other working-class ideas, at the Labor Temple and on the street corners of skid row.

Skid row—the labor college of the early 1920s, and winter bivouac of migrant workers. Into the skid rows from San Diego to Seattle came the servants of God dispensing free soup that temporarily warmed the empty stomach for the low price of listening to promises of plenty in the Hereafter. More popular by far were the political agitators vying for the working man's allegiance. Nightly the street corners rumbled with heated debate on economic and political theory, excelling by far the pallid versions taught in the university classroom from which Gene became a dropout after one semester.

Along Yessler Way the Communist soapboxers debated sharply, humorously, satirically, and dramatically. They hammered at the lessons unfolding in Soviet Russia. They ridiculed the timidity of the reformists, the sellout of the Socialists, the insufficiency of the economism of the I.W.W. They urged the need of a new kind of state power, proletarian power, and a new kind of party, the Communist Party of Marx and Lenin.

These polemics sent Gene to the public library and to the small local radical bookstore. His heart was still with the I.W.W., but his mind began to turn to the Communists. Lenin's polemical writings on revolutionary tactics influenced him greatly, and in later years he said that Lenin's booklet *Left Wing Communism: An Infantile Disorder,* convinced him.

Although written in the heat of debate raging within the Communist movement, this treatise impressed Gene, the political novice. He responded to Lenin's argument against super-revolutionary alienation from the mainstream of working people. He liked the polemic against purist withdrawal into "immaculate, little workers' unions, guiltless of bourgeois democratic prejudice." He accepted Lenin's view that people will act on the basis of their own experience, not by the exhortations of others. He was intrigued with the emphasis placed on the need for serious revolutionaries to "take advantage of every, even the smallest, opportunity of gaining a mass ally, even though this ally be temporary, vacillating, unstable, unreliable and conditional."

Making revolution, Gene began to realize much more than I in my isolated radical splendor in Los Angeles at the time, was more than an emotional hatred of capitalism. It was hard, daily work among people who did not agree with you. It was hammering out a strategy that was effective only to the extent that skillful tactics won people over to struggle with you. Lenin's struggle and polemics against sectism and leftism in the revolutionary movement had a life-long impact on Gene and affected his whole style of activity.

In 1926, he felt he had found the answers he had been seeking and, barely 21, Gene joined the Communist Party. But before he could immerse himself in its activity, he detoured for a year into the Mojave desert, seeking the poor man's self-cure for tuberculosis which both he and his mother, Amelia, had contracted. He hired on as a pick and shovel laborer for the power utility company, silently walking away from the road boss' snide question, "Why is a clean, American boy like you gonna work on the Mex gang?"

Later, fearing for his mother's safety after a couple of violent, knife-wielding outbursts by his father, he took over the operation of the power sub-station at Lone Pine, which kept him close to the cottage where the three of them lived together.

In the desert Gene heard of the angry struggle of the Owen Valley ranchers against the Los Angeles utility over water rights. On his trips for supplies into Bishop and Lone Pine he learned of guerrilla dynamiting of aqueducts and dams by armed ranchers against Water Board agents.

However, in the main, the year was an isolated one devoted to self-healing, reading, long solitary walks, vigil over the high voltage power surging through the station; a year that only intensified the quiet reserve and Lone Wolf self-reliance that marked his complex personality.

The bout with the dread disease that had sent Gene and Amelia into the desert was won. In Gene it left some permanent effects. He suffered recurring pleurisy attacks, and his impaired lungs created a permanent oxygen deficiency that plagued him into being a self-consciously poor public speaker.

The family settled in Los Angeles where Gene supported them working as a structural iron worker, truck driver, and at times as a salesman of sophisticated electrical engineering equipment.

He plunged into local Party activity and his remarkable grasp of Marxist-Leninist theory and tactics, a product of the rigid self-study course he had followed in the desert, qualified him as Southern California education director.

In early 1928 he travelled north to commit his father to the Northern State Hospital at Sedro Wooley. Francis Xavier, Senior, died a few months later, before his fifty-third birthday. In June Gene came as an instructor to the Woodland summer school.

VII

He had gone to Seattle when school ended to get away from a factional situation within the Party in Los Angeles that he could not accept.

Since early 1922, before either of us had joined the Party, sharp differences erupted throughout the national organization. The debates often became abstract, but important issues did exist: formation of an independent, third, labor party versus working within the two-party system; independent, militant, industrial unionism versus working inside the A.F.L.; whether American capitalism was "exceptional" in its strengths or moribund in its contradictory weaknesses. Practical tactics were to be determined by such analyses.

One faction accused the other of sectarianism and that group in turn accused the other of reformism. When I joined the Party in 1925, the battle was raging. Far from New York, to us the names of general secretary Jay Lovestone and Party trade union leader William Z. Foster were just names, but their differing policies and tactics were very real. We vigorously defended and battled behind the programs of one or the other. Our factional loyalties turned all Party meetings into screaming, conniving sessions that often ended in fist fights. Strategy caucuses to outwit our Party opponents became our main activity, the common class enemy was forgotten. I was an ardent Fosterite and became a skillful, if quite young, sixteen-year-old factionalist, enjoying the intrigues and caucusing that went on constantly. After arriving in Los Angeles, Gene became theoretician and polemicist for the Foster group, but he was repelled by the bitter in-fighting and refused to become a part of it.

Los Angeles was one of the very few Foster strongholds around the country. Lovestone adherents were constantly sent in to seize control; therefore the struggle was fierce. In Seattle, however, the Lovestoneites were in firm control; there was no organized Foster group there. For this reason, Gene believed that the Party in Seattle would be involved in mass organization activity, free of factionalism. After Woodland, he went to Seattle, got a job with Puget Sound Power & Light as a cable splicer, and reported to Party headquarters for assignment.

He had miscalculated. The local Lovestonite leadership wanted no Fosterite settlement in their territory. They refused to accept his California Party transfer, as they did mine when I arrived. They would not allow us to apply as new members locally, and so we were ostracized. With the national office in Lovestone's hands it was senseless to appeal to New York.

Gene was incensed and wanted to return immediately to Los Angeles. I pleaded for time. I was too engrossed in this totally consuming, personal, non-political life of ours. I revelled in our nights free of meetings, which we spent talking and reading before the huge stone fireplace in our tiny one-room cottage. The giant old bed that filled our back porch from wall to doorway, the earmarked books of poetry Gene had brought from his bachelor quarters, our singing jaunts in the rain to gather firewood in Seward Park—all this was a far cry from my former routines. I knew the hiatus couldn't last, but for the moment the revolution could wait.

Under Gene's prodding we did start a self-study course, selecting the documents of the recently concluded World Congress of the Communist International. Held in faroff Moscow, that Congress confirmed Gene's final decision to return to Los Angeles. It was my first experience in which political events and shifts were to affect our immediate lives as we moved over the years more deeply into the life of the fulltime revolutionary.

As was its practice until its dissolution in 1943, the Comintern projected sweeping analyses for the entire world movement. That 1928 summer it declared the end of post-World War I stabilization of the capitalist world. It forecast an immediate new era of imminent world economic crises, wars and revolutions which would lead to socialist power in a number of countries. It placed before all Communist Parties the primary task of becoming the sole and undisputed leaders of this revolutionary period. Reformism and social democracy were declared the main enemy because their "lesser evil" support to bourgeois democracy and gradualism aided capitalism.

Whatever one might, in hindsight, think of the specific tactics of the Sixth Congress, its economic analyses were proven valid, although at the time capitalist economists and politicians scoffed. In the U.S. the 1929 stock market crash was little more than a year away. In a short time tens of millions were starving. The jobless roamed the country. Workers lost their homes, farmers their land.

In 1929, convinced of the forecast of the struggles ahead, Gene could no longer accept the local Party leaders' edict keeping him out of the one organization we believed decisive to that struggle. In February we rode the bus to Los Angeles where we immediately found what Gene was looking for, and personally got more than we had anticipated.

Two:
INTO THE CRUCIBLE

I

A special commission of the Sixth Congress, with Stalin personally participating, demanded an immediate end to the factionalism in our American Party. It sharply criticized both Lovestone and Foster for an unprincipled struggle for power. The organization was put in receivership. Lovestone and some of his followers resisted and were expelled. Abruptly the faucet of vituperative recriminations ceased to flow.

In our political naiveté on the West Coast, and being far from the centers of national and international leadership, we younger comrades did not particularly connect our own internal struggle with that which had raged in the Comintern and the Soviet Communist Party. Nor did we realize that the Sixth Congress' decisions and its halt to factionalism was part of Stalin's consolidation of his leadership within the Soviet Party and the international movement, less than five years after Lenin's death. Whatever the reasons, the end of the internal struggle had salutatory effects. In Los Angeles a small but militant young Party core emerged, for the first time attuned to the world around it—the city's eastside barrios, southside Black ghettoes, the downtown hovels of Asian workers, the souplines on skid row.

Four weeks after our return from Seattle, Gene wrote in the national *Daily Worker* of the 90,000 jobless in our city. From official statistics he noted that the majority of Mexican workers in the country were unemployed. He concluded, "with ninety percent of the working class outside the organized labor movement, our burning need is to organize the unorganized, militant industrial trade unionism and class struggle versus class collaboration."

A Chamber of Commerce booklet, however, urged industry to come to Los Angeles, "the home of contented labor" based upon a "30 year principle of the Open Shop." And Britain's Winston Churchill visited Southern California and praised Los Angeles as "a happy city . . . poverty and squalor have never entered its broad avenue of palms."

Gene was now Southern California head of the Trade Union Unity League, a militant Left center organized first in 1922 as a rank and file movement inside the craft union, almost lily-white A.F.L. Now it was shifting, as was the Party, to greater emphasis on independent organization of the unorganized and the formation of new industrial unions outside the A.F.L.

A citywide general strike in the needle trades was Gene's first initiation into his new work. The strike symbolized graphically the multi-aims of T.U.U.L., for it contained four fronts of struggle: the action against the employers; rank and file opposition to the old A.F.L. and Socialist Party leadership within the union; conflicts between the skilled, mainly male, dominantly Jewish craftsmen who were oldtime unionists and the young, unskilled, Mexican women workers new to the union and in their first strike; and the building of the T.U.U.L.'s Needle Trades Industrial Union.

Gene also spent much of his time in the port town of San Pedro some twenty miles away organizing the T.U.U.L.'s Marine Workers Industrial League. Suddenly, overnight, our Party and Young Communist League began to break with the old insulated isolation of past abstract revolutionary posturing. We began to come to grips for the first time with the very real social and economic problems of people around us.

II

From our first weeks in Seattle Gene had pleaded for a child, regaling me with visions of our travelling with babe on our backs from barricade to barricade, wherever the revolution called. But his was a foreign cause. I had been cast in a different mould. As Soldiers of the Revolution, I and my Young Communist comrades had often declared our renunciation of such individualistic frailties. Gene argued this was sectarian nonsense. "We are of the people, not ascetics, not a caste apart." Then he'd plead on more intimate terms and I would vacillate. The ever-changing dimensions of our relationship seemed to continually propel me into unexplored pathways. Now, in March 1929, fascinated yet wary, I became pregnant.

Basking in Gene's excited pleasure, I nervously prepared to break the news to Mama, but made Gene promise to support my claim that it was an "accident." With abortion completely out of our awareness at the time, the act was irrevocable. All I had to contend with was Mama's displeasure. I carefully chose the moment as we rode the Brooklyn Avenue streetcar, so she could not make the scene I expected.

Mama was an intense feminist. She was more the protagonist for woman's unshackled spirit than a sign-toting activist for equal rights. She believed the two to be inseparable, that individually women could live the first while fighting for the second. Frustrated by ill-health and transplanted to a foreign land and alien culture she refused to adapt to, Mama did not personally act on her beliefs, but she was determined that her two modern daughters would.

My sister and I were willing pupils, and we early absorbed Mama's special pride in being female, destined for greater things than merely being some man's wife. We acquired the conviction that personal love was not a sufficient singular purpose in life; that for women, no less than for men, there must be much more to an enriched life. Conventional marriage was the deadly trap and motherhood was the snaplock to that trap door.

Mama scorned housekeeping and cooking; they were unavoidable chores to be disposed of with minimum effort. She knitted, crocheted and sewed beautifully, but she refused to teach us, saying we had more important things to do with our time and abilities—like studying, writing stories, making speeches, attending meetings, planning the revolution.

Papa had been a quiet supportive influence in all this. Slight of build and height, he was gentle and sensitive and there seemed to be no female/male role-playing in our family. He often buffered with good humor and with dance and song Mama's tense moodiness. He washed supper dishes and scrubbed kitchen floors, urging us to go to the library or write the composition due at school. Mama loved us tenaciously, spurring us on to be a credit to womankind. She was eternally grateful she had been given two girls instead of two boys to raise. Papa loved us with a quiet pride that made us put high worth on ourselves as human beings.

When Bill began staying overnight in my bed, Mama kept the fact secret from his parents, for his sake. When we were legally married to mollify his mother, Mama was furious. I was traitor to my Free Spirit. In joining Gene, a year later, I was exercising my courage to go my own way, as they had taught me. Now I was pregnant and I had betrayed twenty years of revolutionary and feminist conditioning.

I could not define to Mama or to myself the changes in me. I was torn with the contradictions between my emotions and my theory. With Gene I had become the classic handmaiden to love, a role blatantly contrary to what I believed in, and yet I was revelling in it.

So on the rumbling, swaying streetcar, I hesitantly broke the news. And somehow as I talked, the beauty and mystery and romance with which Gene had enhanced this new event for me dissipated. I suddenly got a glimpse of myself as just another ordinary pregnant female. Big deal.

There was no scene. Papa beamed, his warm smile embracing me once again in whatever I did. Mama sat silent, looking out the trolley window. Then, without looking at me, she said in a flat voice, "The pity of it is it will change your life, not his."

III

By mid-May my queazy stomach could no longer tolerate the food odors in the B/G Sandwich Shop on Broadway where I worked as part-time waitress; Gene was spending much of his time in San Pedro, and we decided to move there for a few months.

Snatching moments between Gene's longshore job and our separate evening activities, we often walked in the early morning or late at night in Point Fermin Park, a few blocks from where we lived. High on the cliffs overlooking the Pacific we talked of our miracle growing within me and exchanged news regarding our organizing problems.

San Pedro was a tough port town, a tight, anti-union town since the shipowners and vigilantes had broken the militant I.W.W. strikes in 1922-1924. As we walked, I told Gene of the time during the strike when the muckraking novelist Upton Sinclair had come to San Pedro from his Pasadena home. He announced that he was going to read the Bill of Rights outdoors on Liberty Hill. He defied the police to arrest him, and they did. The following week ten thousand people, many of us in trucks from Los Angeles, demonstrated at Fourth and Beacon streets. I recalled it was the first time I had seen speakers chaining themselves to lamp posts, shouting their speeches as police labored to cut the chains and haul them off to jail.

Gene listened intently. I described the night in June, 1924 when a Young Communist League and Young Pioneer cavalcade from Los Angeles rode to join an I.W.W. strike benefit party in San Pedro. We were going to perform labor skits and express our solidarity in song and speech.

As we rattled along, singing "Hold the Fort for we are coming, Union men be strong," our trucks were flagged down at the edge of town by a carful of strikers. We were told the I.W.W. hall at 12th and Center had been attacked by 100 vigilantes with axes, guns and blackjacks. The 300 men, women and children inside had been trapped, beaten, a giant cauldron of scalding coffee had been deliberately overturned and a number of children burned.

"We've been waiting for you, some of you come with us, help us stand guard for the night. The rest of you, please, get out of here fast, organize help, tell them back in L.A. what's happening here."

"After that," I told Gene, "I don't recall hearing much of San Pedro. The strike movement and the I.W.W. organizing drive was broken."

We turned towards home and Gene said quietly, "Now the continuity marches on. Now we'll try again, and some day the whole West Coast will be organized."

I did not respond. I had come by now to recognize this difference in us and, while I loved it in him, I could not adopt it as my own. He imbued each daily activity with the long view. Every detail was enhanced for its relationship to the bigger goal. Making revolution—in all its smallest and simplest routines—was part of the whole. I on the other hand pluggingly carried on my own Party work as a daily chore. Except for the rousing speeches I made on soapbox or speaker's platform, I bogged down often in frustration at the insignificance of the maze about me. While Gene's daily tasks on the waterfront were imbued with the grandeur of labor's drive for organization around the country, I was concerned only with the immediate problem of organizing the small group of sympathizers who would support the maintenance of the newly opened Marine Workers Industrial League on Fourth Street.

In September we were sent up north. Gene was assigned to the Pan Pacific Monthly, a magazine which had been published in Shanghai by the Pan Pacific Trade Union Secretariat of the Red International of Labor Unions, with Earl Browder as its editor. Now it was to be published in San Francisco with Harrison George as editor and Gene as his assistant.

Mama was worried, angry. She said, "You don't go off to a strange city to have a baby alone." But I was determined to show this baby—and Mama—that neither it nor she were going to interfere with my freedom.

Work on the magazine deepened Gene's interest in the national and race aspects of the exploitation of Mexican, Black and Asian workers in California. With the magazine geared for distribution to the revolutionary movements in the Far Eastern countries, now Gene studied the national liberation struggles in China, the Philippines, Korea, India, and Southeast Asia.

After blackmailing my brother-in-law into getting him a job driving a truck (using my advanced stage of pregnancy as the lever), Gene then ignored irate shopowners clamoring for their deliveries. His truck stood parked on the street much of the time while we spent hours at the public library researching data for articles for the magazine.

We rented a very small studio room. With a bed that swung out of the wall and a small table that was actually a wide shelf, we lived in luxury without furniture. Golden Gate Park was our private front yard and the foghorns performed for us alone. Although Mini and Al lived nearby we saw them infrequently. Bill lived with them and that, combined with Al's animosity toward Gene, palled the few efforts Mini and I made to maintain family relations. Instead, she and I saw each other alone during the day. Gene and I were fascinated with our work and we loved the city, yet by late November we decided to go home to Los Angeles.

The contrast between the two cities was too much for us. San Francisco, a cosmopolitan commercial port, was a liberal, strong labor town with a trade union leadership integrated into the political life of the city. To us our party comrades appeared stodgy and comfortably routine in their concentration upon being a somewhat maverick but benign rank and file within that movement. Their main activity appeared to be that of offering good resolutions and progressive election slates inside the staid, craft unions over at Labor Temple.

Back home, Los Angeles was the open shop citadel of the country, blatantly and cruelly anti-labor, racist, unorganized. Dominated by agri-business, the oil monopolies and the Hearst dynasty, the mailed fist of government was not gloved. Now confrontations were becoming sharp and bloody again as the new unions Gene had helped organize, the unemployed movement he had helped build, the party he had helped lead, were fighting for their right to exist. We had to be there.

IV

Tim was born on November 30, and the nineteen Black, Mexican, white and Asian mothers on the charity ward at the Los Angeles County Hospital clucked over the little girl who obviously had no husband, no wedding ring, only a mama and papa to visit her. Gene did not get to the hospital for a week. He was in the San Pedro jail, arrested during one of his street meetings in front of the Marine Service Bureau on Seventh Street. Arrests, raids on the union hall, confiscation of bundles of leaflets and literature was now a regular occurrence. Just as regularly, Gene and the others came out of jail, re-opened the union hall, ordered new literature, mimeographed fresh leaflets, held more meetings on the docks.

Earlier that month he had been arrested with others in San Bernardino, a small town east of Los Angeles. Our children's summer camp, operated by the Young Communist League, had been raided by a posse of American Legionaires led by local sheriffs. Fifty children were forcibly removed to Juvenile Court. The adult counsellors and maintenance staff were charged with "conspiracy to teach the tenets of communism." They got six months to five year sentences in October and in mid-November a local hall rented for a protest rally was denied at the last minute. Eight comrades arrived from Los Angeles and, according to a local news account, they entered a crowded restaurant and occupied a table. "Frank Waldron and then Lawrence Emery mounted the table" and began to explain the issues of the "Red Camp Case." They were forcibly evicted and proceeded "to speak on the street without a permit." "A tumultuous assembly" resulted in their arrest.

Eventually Gene got to the hospital and proudly carried his first-born home to our bedroom in the small cottage Mama and Papa had rented for the five of us. Despite her disapproval, Mama lost her heart to the baby the moment Gene put him in her arms saying, "Here, grandma, he's yours too."

Gene and I saw little of each other. Behind the fragrance of orange and lemon groves there grew the loud cry for "Jobs or Relief," and angry shouts for "Bread or Wages." Politicians talked about prosperity around the corner, but meanwhile there was no social security, no unemployment insurance, no welfare departments, no government responsibility to feed, clothe or house the millions thrown on the scrap heap of capitalism.

The demand for immediate emergency appropriations and for a permanent system of social security was viewed by employers and government as the harbinger of social revolution. They declared open war. The very right to protest had to be fought for in Los Angeles. Meeting halls were raided nightly, militants and Communists were arrested, held without arraignment for "investigation," released and then re-arrested.

Meanwhile, I was chafing, restlessly. I nursed our infant, scrubbed his diapers and carefully observed the rigid schedules prescribed in those days by government pamphlets on infant training. But no great surge of mother love enveloped me. Mama adored the baby, but carefully left me in sole charge. Papa sat at the crib crooning Jewish and Russian lullabies resurrected from my own childhood. Gene came home from his meetings or jail absences to stand gazing at his sleeping son. Only I was an unfeeling monster; except in the silence of the 2 a.m. feeding. With the child pulling at my breast and the exciting world outside stilled, the small body in my arms and I did communicate. But with the morning came the beat of struggle that passed me by.

I was under strict orders from everyone—Y.C.L., Party, Gene, Mama—"You can't get arrested; you're a nursing mother; the baby is only a few weeks old." Mama was explicit in her determination to make me take sole responsibility for the consequences of having the baby. I came to realize what she had meant when she had said that I, not Gene, would be trapped. Ours was the first baby among the young activists, and everyone—aunts, uncles, comrades—watched my adjustments.

Ours was practically a test case. Could a woman's independence and revolutionary activity be combined with motherhood? But the faulty premise was that we were all watching *me*, not Gene. The issue was whether *I* could juggle it all; and I couldn't.

Not getting arrested meant staying out of street actions or public meetings. I taught classes, wrote leaflets, served on committees that planned actions for others who would get arrested. I felt guilty. Our small group of Young Communists at the university were arrested distributing anti-ROTC leaflets. Our high school youngsters became dropouts on the eve of graduation in face of a school board decision that members of the Y.C.L. "will not be entitled to a high school diploma."

Fulltime organizers were on non-existent payrolls. Mama and Papa paid the rent for the cottage we shared, supplied the food we ate and gave us carfare to go to our meetings. Papa still worked irregularly in the needle trades downtown.

While scrubbing diapers on the back porch and trying to think up a good headline for our latest leaflet, I overheard Papa and a visiting uncle talking as they sat in the sun near Tim's carriage. My uncle asked: "So, has he found work yet?"

Papa pulled at the white netting over the carriage hood. "What do you mean, has he found work yet? Who says he is looking for work?"

"Not even *looking?*"

"Why should he look? He's busy."

"Busy, I know, But he has a wife and now a child. Surely, a man needs money when he has a family."

"Why?" Papa's customary gentleness had a testy edge. "They live here, we manage."

"Yes, I know," my puzzled uncle pressed, "but it's not right they should live this way, off of you."

Papa turned angrily, "What do you mean, not right? Right for whom? They work for the Party, for The Cause. What greater work is there? And since when does one have to get paid for such work?" he paused and added realistically, "when there is no money anyway?"

V

It was mid-January, 1930. Gene had been away since New Year's Day, after our family dinner celebrating my 21st birthday and Tim's first month.

I lay in the dark, unsure why I had suddenly wakened. The baby's breathing in the crib along the wall rustled the air faintly. The bedroom door opening onto the kitchen clicked shut as a narrow sliver of light appeared at its base. Gene was home. Blinking in the light as I closed the bedroom door behind me, I saw him at the sinkboard. He turned slowly, still gulping at the milk bottle in his hand. I gasped. Black and blue discoloration, turning yellow at the edges, capped his swollen eye. A long, dark scab cut diagonally across the upper and lower lip. His thick hair lay matted, flattened to his skull, his shirt sleeve hung in a loose tear, brown stains dotted his shirt-front.

I embraced him cautiously, but he reassured me as he enveloped me in a bear-hug. "I'm all right. I think I look worse than I am. Anyway, it happened a few days ago, so I'm better than I was."

Mama appeared at the dining room door, Papa peering over her shoulder. Their anxious eyes belied their calm. Mama said casually, "We just wanted to know you are all right." Then, "Why don't you get out of those stinking things, better throw them in the garbage pail," and, pushing Papa ahead of her, they retreated to their bedroom.

Only at the word "stinking" did I associate the awful stench with Gene. I drew a hot tub while he slowly shed his clothes, dropping each piece on the kitchen floor. Yellowing black and blue marks discolored his rib cage and the small of his back. He moved quietly through our dark bedroom to the bathroom, noiselessly closing the adjoining door that led to Mama and Papa's room. I gingerly picked up the foul-smelling clothes, carried them out the back door and dropped them into the garbage can, replacing the lid carefully so it wouldn't clatter in the dawn's silence. I smiled a little grimly as the thought struck me that the garbage man might suspect Gene of having committed a murder. The brown stains on the clothes were dried blood, the awful smell was obviously a combination of congealed blood and sour sweat fermenting in some filthy hideout. The final incriminating evidence would be my effort to dispose of the mess.

Back in the house I rolled the crib out into the kitchen, listened for a moment to the infant's light snore, adjusted his blankets and shut the bedroom door on him. When Little Ole Reliable in the kitchen started to wail on schedule at six o'clock, I was still awake. Gene had fallen asleep, spent and relaxed with his arm flung across me as he lay on his side. I snaked out from under, closed the door behind me, content and at peace. Gene was home.

He had gone into Imperial Valley in mid-December in response to a minor news item about a pending strike among 23,000 Mexican and Filipino lettuce workers.

La Union de Trabajadores del Valle Imperial had led a strike there two years earlier and then disintegrated. The Associacion Mutual del Valle Imperial was organized, with Mexican consulate and U.S. Immigration sanction, to watchdog the work agreements between U.S. labor contractors, the workers, and the Mexican government.

Gene returned from his exploratory trip badly shaken by the inhuman living and working conditions of the field laborers, the prevalence of child labor, and the bitter divisions fostered by the growers between Mexican, Filipino, Japanese, Black and white workers. He reported to the Party and T.U.U.L. committees in Los Angeles that a spontaneous walkout was imminent and he urged our active support.

Some were wary of getting involved in a premature strike that in all probability would end in defeat. Gene argued, "We can't sit here and talk our blueprints for struggle. The strike is going to take place, these minority workers are pitted against a Goliath combination of the growers' association, the police and county government. And you are afraid of our contamination with possible defeat!"

Although the old character of the Party and Y.C.L. leadership had changed, oldtime comrades still clung to the familiar insulation in the Boyle Heights Jewish quarter. But they were outvoted, and Gene went back to Imperial Valley on the second day of the New Year. This time three comrades accompanied him—a Japanese, a Mexican, and a Filipino.

VI

On January 6, ten thousand workers walked out of the lettuce fields. With more than 77,000 in the Valley, the massive operations did not close down, but they were badly crippled. Newspaper reports admitted that "California's most valuable single crop dropped to 50 [freight] cars a day as against 100 cars a day earlier this week."

Growers and private guards were deputized. Police enforced

a curfew in Brawley and El Centro and warned that white "strangers" seen talking to local farm laborers would be arrested. A migrant camp of Filipino strikers was bombed. Striking families were evicted from company shacks, and when Ida Rothstein of the Workers' International Relief and Leo Gallagher of the American Civil Liberties Union arrived from Los Angeles to set up a tent colony and food station, they were arrested and the supplies were confiscated.

Gene and his small group worked clandestinely with militant contacts among the strikers. They issued leaflets in the various languages, including many Filipino dialects. They helped establish the first united committee in which the many races worked together for the first time. They concentrated on organizing permanent field and shed committees that would outlast the strike itself. They involved women and child laborers in activities.

We learned from the newspapers that 25 Mexican strikers had been arrested, including Gene. A smuggled message told us that the Mexican prisoners had been forcibly deported, and that Gene had been beaten in his cell by deputy sheriffs. The Reverend Clinton Taft, aristocratic-looking chairman of the American Civil Liberties Union, went to the Brawley jail to investigate. He later filed charges of physical assault against Imperial Valley County Sheriff Charles L. Gillette. At the trial in February, Taft told the court:

". . . when we entred and simply announced ourselves as being down from Los Angeles, interested in the civil rights of three of his prisoners, Sheriff Gillette flew into a rage, using profane and vile language, assaulted us with kicks, attempted to strangle me and violently forced me out of the door."

Gillette testified on his own behalf, saying: "Taft became abusive, I told him to leave and when he persisted, I put him out; if he got hurt it was because the door was too narrow; I did not strike him."

However, within hours of Taft's visit, Gene and the others were released and told:

"Get the hell out of town. We find you here again, you won't walk out of here a second time."

Now in the early morning, as my fingertips lightly traced the hard scabs on his face, Gene whispered, "I'm going back. I have to. They live there. They can't run away to L.A. I've got to go back."

And he did, again and again, secretly slipping in and out of the Valley towns; meeting with strikers in the dark, shades tightly drawn.

The strike was broken through the collusion of the U.S. Immigration Service and the Mexican Consulate. Mexican strikers were rounded-up by the truckload and dumped across the border a few miles away. The Filipino strikers became isolated and could not continue alone. Gene and the local activists concentrated on strengthening the permanent committees which became the Agricultural Workers Industrial League.

A few weeks later the lettuce sheds at Brawley and Calexico were struck solid and R. P. Moore, secretary of the Western Growers' Protective Association, admitted that only 50% of the packers were working in Holtsville and El Centro. This time it was no spontaneous, unorganized walkout, but an action taken by strike vote and one that held firm in face of the grower-shippers' refusal to negotiate. After eight days and during the height of the season, the strike was won and a uniform, Valley-wide wage increase was enforced.

VII

As local organization and leadership became stronger, Gene travelled less frequently into the Valley. He concentrated again on organizing unemployed councils throughout the southland and building the longshore and marine workers' union in San Pedro. Recognition of the union's new strength came from a local town newspaper that noted:

"Harbor and shipping interests warned today that the Marine Workers Industrial League, led by two Communists, Frank Waldron [Gene] and Lawrence Emery now holds the forward position in San Pedro and has begun to make itself felt in labor circles."

When the first nationally synchronized Unemployment Day of Struggle scheduled for February 26 was suddenly postponed to March 6 according to word from New York, our local movement was too broad to be manipulated and it was decided to go ahead with the original date and then to participate in the new date as well. Fierce police action was expected since daily neighborhood demonstrations for jobs or cash relief were being regularly smashed with police clubs.

On the evening of the 25th Papa and I sat at the kitchen table rolling newspapers into tight wads, giving each a sharp twist and stacking them in front of Mama and Gene. Gene stuffed these into a large, visored cap he kept putting on his head, thumping his fist on top, taking if off and packing in more newspaper wads.

Mama lined the back and shoulders of the heavy peacoat that lay stretched out on the table, and sewed a cloth lining over this inner packing. She handed the coat to Gene, saying, "Try it on, I think it needs more packing."

Gene grinned, slipped into the coat pulling up the collar. He brought the bulging cap over his eyes, stuck a drooping cigarette into the corner of his mouth and with exaggerated motions he slouched about the room in Hollywood gangster style. Papa and I laughed while Mama followed Gene about, patting the back of his coat, testing its makeshift padding. Behind the laughter, there was unexpressed tension. I wondered how effectively our paper paddings would shield Gene from the inevitable policeman's club.

I had angrily reconciled myself to the instruction that I was to stay away from the demonstration. Instead I was a member of the Reserve Committee that would pick up the leadership baton after the expected arrests.

A carefully planned organization of defense squads went into action for the first time on February 26, in response to the Mayor's warning that the demonstration would be prevented "at all costs." We borrowed too, from the 1924 San Pedro experience. Our speakers chained themselves to tree trunks and street posts. Each time one speaker was clubbed down, like a string of exploding firecrackers others popped up around the circular City Plaza. Gene's arrest got a descriptive paragraph in one of the newspapers:

"... a striking figure in a seaman's peacoat, chained to a lamp post at the Mission Church of Our Lady, Queen of the Angels, on the west side of the Plaza ... a half dozen police cut his chains and dragged him through the protesting crowds to a black maria to jail."

The period between the February 26 and March 6 demonstrations was tense. Lieutenant William Hynes of the Red Squad and the Mayor's Office boasted that their raids and arrests had broken the back of the movement and were "decimating the riot leaders." The new unions in Imperial Valley and San Pedro, the Unemployed Councils, the T.U.U.L., and the Party were each forced underground organizationally even as they continued their activity and struggles.

The day before March 6 the newspapers reported that "secret precautions" were being taken throughout the city. "Law abiding persons" were warned "to stay away from City Hall tomorrow to prevent being caught in the mob or in handicapping officers in suppressing possible disorders."

The next morning ten thousand men, women, and children tried to march to City Hall, their banners demanding bread or jobs. Machine guns were targeted on them from roof tops. One thousand police on foot, horseback and in patrol cars clubbed, tear-gassed and horse-bumped them into sidestreets. Falling, fighting, marching, singing, shouting, the demonstrators inched their way through side streets and over barricades towards their elected city official, Mayor John C. Porter. All they wanted was to present their needs. City Hall was guarded like a medieval fortress. Inside the frightened Mayor hid from his hungry, jobless, constituency. Like many others, Gene and his defense unit had been beaten into unconsciousness and dragged by their feet to a patrol car and to jail.

We counted our injured by the hundreds. We checked the jails hourly for those arrested. We tracked down two children arrested for the crime of having stuck their tongues out at officers.

We pored over news accounts of March 6 demonstrations in other cities. With envy we read of San Francisco where the Mayor had given the demonstrators police escort and from a rostrum erected for the occasion he had publicly accepted the written demands of the unemployed. But this was the exception. Thousands were in jails and hospitals around the country. One hundred ten thousand had marched in New York; 100,000 in Detroit; 30,000 in Charlotte, North Carolina.

Eleven days later the Reverend Clinton Taft appeared before the Los Angeles Police Commission to charge brutality and illegal arrests at the March 6 action.

Police Commissioner Mark Pierce shouted, "I won't listen to any arguments on behalf of Communists. The more the police beat them up and wreck their headquarters, the better. Communists have no constitutional rights, and I won't listen to anybody who defends them."

Lieutenant Hynes defended his Red Squad, "My men have never beaten up anybody, unless they are justified."

Gene's scalp wound, badly festered when he was refused medical care in jail, required surgery. Two weeks later, his head still bandaged, he was arrested when, according to the newspapers, he was "in the midst of an assertedly inflammatory address to longshoremen at the harbor and was booked on suspicion of criminal syndicalism."

VIII

Of the many arrested March 6, seventeen went on trial in April and for eleven days Judge Bogue, in a state of bewilderment, kept muttering from his bench, "Incredible! Absolutely astonishing!"

American Civil Liberties Union attorney Leo Gallagher, a deceptively mild-looking, grey-haired, wiry fighter, exploded the first shock for the startled Judge when he challenged the entire jury panel. Gallagher charged the defendants would have a fairer trial if the Commissioner would "stop passers-by on the street and take them into court for jury service."

The Judge spluttered at Gene and Party organizer Carl Sklar who were acting as their own attorneys:

"You can't make Communist speeches to prospective jurors. You can't tell them there are different standards of law for the rich and the poor."

On any given day now some fifty people were either in jail, in court, or beaten by police on the outside. Physical and legal self defense became simultaneous weapons of the local unionization and unemployed struggles. A delegated conference of local organizations set up a "general self defense organization" whose purpose was "the physical protection and defense of all militant struggles, organizations and demonstrations of the working class, to protect them from the reactionary attacks of the fascists and the state apparatus."

On the legal front the International Labor Defense conducted orientation sessions throughout the city enabling arrested workers to defend themselves in court. Frank Spector, Southern California head of that organization, and one of the seventeen before Judge Bogue, told the court:

"When the laws are against the interests of the working class and the courts are essentially an instrument in the hands of the employer class, we advise workers that the laws be violated and the court decisions be ignored."

In its summation, the prosecution intimidated the jury: "If you will not convict them, then you will show that you too are against our government."

Gene told them:

"A verdict of guilty will mean you approve the exploitation of the working class by the capitalist government. It will mean you approve police brutality and that you agree with Police Commissioner Thorpe that we ought to be deported. But even if you put us in jail now, you can't break our Movement. Hundreds, thousands of others will take our place and carry on the struggle until this system will be abolished and the dictatorship of the proletariat, as in the Soviet Union, will be established."

Our comrades in the courtroom were no less startled than was Judge Bogue and the reporters to hear Gene tell the jury:

"It is because I love my country and the American people from which I spring that I fight today and will always fight in the interest of the people. It is our country, it is our Bill of Rights, it is our American way of life that you would betray here today."

This view of Americanism espoused by a revolutionary militant was a new concept when 24-year-old Gene advocated it in early 1930; although I had first heard it in Gene's class up in Woodland less than two years before.

On the eleventh and last day of the trial we sat scattered around the courtroom, reading newspapers, talking quietly, awaiting the jury's verdict.

Gene sat down beside me and asked, "You heard the news?"

I nodded and he went on, his words half muffled behind his cupped hand:

"We don't know yet how wide the net has been cast, until we do we're all sitting ducks. If we get out on bail here, I won't come home tonight. We've got to find out how extensive the new arrest-warrants are and what our response to them should be."

With the familiar light touch of his forefinger to his lips and then to mine, he walked away. It was six weeks before I saw him again.

From newspapers brought to us in the courtroom we had learned that one hundred shed and field workers in Imperial Valley had been arrested the night before at union meetings where they had been preparing for a Valley-wide conference to discuss wage demands for the coming cantaloupe season. There were hints at more arrests to come. District Attorney Elmer Heald had told newsmen in Brawley that morning:

"For two months following the lettuce strike of last February my office secured the assistance of secret service investigators of the J.H. Boling Detective Agency to gather evidence concerning the operation of the Communist Party in the Imperial County and of affiliated organizations.... much valuable information was obtained relative to the intention of the Communist Party and other radical organizations to perfect and put into operation a militant strike in Imperial County...."

During the next weeks scores of Mexican union activists in the Valley were deported. The headquarters of the Agricultural Workers Industrial league on J Street in Brawley was wrecked. Under the guise of serving numerous "John Doe" warrants, police raided homes and offices all over Southern California. People were herded to jail, held 72 hours and released without being booked. A day or two later they were again arrested, held, not charged, and released. Over and over again. Organizationally, every group went deeper underground. Our system of liaisons became complex.

The grand jury indicted seventeen T.U.U.L. and Party activists on "conspiracy to foment revolution during the cantaloupe season." This was later changed to the more stylized charge, "suspicion of criminal syndicalism" involving charges to overthrow the government on a number of separate counts that could total 42 years in prison for each defendant. Of the seventeen, fourteen were arrested, but the police could not find Spector, Sklar and Gene. They had disappeared from sight after leaving the courtroom that April 14.

IX

The Brooklyn Avenue street car rattled and swayed, almost empty on its past midnight eastward run. I sat with eyes closed, head flung back, the hard upper edge of the backrest cutting into my neck. I held the sleeping baby loosely in my arms.

On the bridge crossing the arid Los Angeles River bed, the pungent odor of the long-familiar gas works stung my nostrils. Without opening my eyes I knew we were passing along the edges of the old Mexican shanty town huddled in the dry dust. An essay I'd written describing this scene for a high school English class had once won high praise. Senior English and high school were five years behind me, but Mexican shanty town, the dust and the gas tanks' stink, were still there.

I was very late. It had been difficult to leave Gene and I had delayed long beyond the time I should have gotten Tim home.

It had been six weeks since that last day in Judge Bogue's courtroom. All this time Gene, Spector and Sklar had evaded the Imperial Valley warrants. They were hid in friendly strangers' homes, moving every few days to a new place. They stayed in contact with activity and decision-making processes through complicated courier systems. We were all waiting for a higher Party decision in New York as to whether they should or should not surrender to the Valley arrest warrants.

The trial of those originally arrested in the February 26 unemployed demonstration opened on May 6. By collective decision, with Gene voting against, Spector and Sklar appeared for this trial which meant, of course, voluntary surrender to the Imperial Valley warrants as well. Whether Gene should eventually surrender was still being debated. Now there were two bench warrants for his arrest—the Valley grand jury indictment, and his failure to show for trial on May 6. Various courts began to call in his bail on a number of pending cases around the county and Gene became a many-time fugitive bail-jumper while waiting for a Party decision on the big one—the Valley indictment carrying the possible 42 years' conviction.

Now, after six weeks, by roundabout route, I had joined Gene for one afternoon and evening. I had brought the baby at his request. It was an unsatisfactory reunion. Much laughter and play on the floor with the baby, but between us the words came slowly. The tension into which we had been catapulted was too much for us. Gene paced the room, using me again and again as a sounding-board, exploding his frustrations one moment, gently apologizing the next.

Emotionally drained, swaying loosely on the streetcar, I was terribly tired. A deep, soul-tiredness. Tired with being pulled, pushed and pounded. Tired with trying to respond on so many levels for too many months. I wanted to be free of the many hands and emotions tugging at me. Free from home and Mama, whom I needed and resented. Free from Gene, tense and irritable in his hideaways and whom I was unable to help. Free from far-off committees arguing our personal fate with chilling objectivity. Free from our increasingly difficult underground activities.

Too many were in jail, too many were being arrested daily; yet our organizations miraculously struggled on. Lieut. Hynes had declared there would never again be a "Communist meeting" on the streets of Los Angeles. With the raids and arrests forcing us underground, he boasted, the back of the movement had been permanently broken.

We had to challenge this abrogation of the First Amendment. It was the young people, including the 14 and 15 year-olds in our children's organization, who planned the strategy and organized a gigantic May Day demonstration focusing on the historic American origins of that workers' day of struggle.

At the moment, however, as I walked from the car stop, I was preoccupied with what would happen to Gene and me. Would he stay and go to prison? Would he leave and become a political fugitive? Either way, we faced long separation.

To become or not to become a political refugee was a difficult decision. Although we knew that not we, but some committee somewhere, would make that decision for us, Gene had asked my opinion that afternoon. I had hedged, arguing both sides of the question. When the same issue arose 21 years later, I had strong opinions, but in late May 1930, I didn't know.

Such a decision demanded a realistic evaluation of the political scene and its direction. We recognized the need to utilize all constitutional and legal avenues in order to win people's understanding of the issues involved; but there was also the need to save movement people from being decimated by repression. We had also to consider the individual persons involved. Were they the type able to continue to serve the movement elsewhere, cut off from home base? There was the problem also of the risks of more severe reprisals against those left behind. There seemed to be no simple solution.

Gene was the only one left of the indicted who had eluded the warrants. The decision about whether he was to go or stay, being debated elsewhere, would come soon. We could only wait.

Three days before the Valley trial started in June, word

finally came. Gene was to leave for New York at once. Within a few hours, Mama, Papa, Tim and I were driven to a rendezvous with Gene miles out of town. We all transferred into a third car and rode another forty miles to where Gene was to board an eastbound train.

"Have you decided on the new name?" I asked. We had considered a number of possibilities during that afternoon together.

"What else but Tim?" he replied as the baby in his arms clutched his nose and pulled on his hair.

"You still prefer Ryan to O'Reilly, don't you?" he asked.

"Tim Ryan," I savored the sound slowly. "Yes, I like it, it fits you fine. O'Reilly is just too much."

"Okay, Mrs. Tim Ryan, I'll see you, some day, some place, I'm not sure when or where, but believe me, I'll see you. Hold on until then, will you?" The pleading grey-blue eyes betrayed the bantering voice. The others in the car tried to screen us in privacy by talking loudly among themselves.

"I'll hold on, but don't you forget I'm doing just that." My clutching hand contrasted with the lightness of my tone. And then he was gone. A tall, thin, long-legged silhouette in the sun. He jumped easily onto the moving train step. His ill-fitting suit jacket and hat, borrowed for the occasion because his peacoat and watch cap had become his trademark, made him a stranger even before he disappeared from sight.

The Imperial Valley case, after a two-week trial, ended with Carl Sklar, Frank Spector, Oscar Erickson, I. Horiuchi and Lawrence Emery being sentenced to one to fourteen years on each of three counts to be served consecutively at Folsom Prison. Young Danny Rojas was sent to San Quentin on an indeterminate one to fourteen years. One Mexican striker was turned over to immigration authorities, and two others were put on probation. Sheriff Gillette told newsmen that he would jail every union organizer in the Valley. A local editorial commented: "So ends, in all probability, the efforts of radically inclined groups to foment strikes among field laborers in the Valley."

X

The weeks passed, outwardly routine but inwardly I thrashed about. One moment I was confident I would leave soon to join Gene and so had merely to push through each day one at a time. The next moment I succumbed to a deep fear that I would not see him again, convinced I had to start a life of my own. Meanwhile I continued to live at home where Mama and Papa helped take care of Tim while I concentrated on Party and Y.C.L. activity.

When our leaflets called for a demonstration on August First—International Day of Protest Against Imperialist War—the mayor closed City Plaza to the public and declared that no demonstration would be allowed. At noon Lieut. Hynes' plainclothes Red Squad and hundreds of police fanned out in the area, forbidding passersby to stop. They patrolled the corners of the six streets running parallel or spokewise to the Plaza, and kept motor traffic moving briskly along Main Street.

A large truck moved slowly southward, its engine spluttering and coughing. It veered slowly into the left lane which brought it closer to the outer edge of the Plaza. As it reached the middle of the block, the motor hiccoughed loudly a few times and went dead. Before the startled eyes of the Red Squad, police and passersby some thirty young men, women and children jumped into sight in the truck bed holding aloft a banner the length of the truck: "Down with Imperialist War!" Picket signs waved, revolutionary song filled the air.

Red-faced and shouting, Hynes and his men rushed the truck. Arms waving, they demanded that the driver move on. Unruffled and laughing, the young man behind the wheel shrugged, "It's stalled, it won't go, and anyway . . ." He slowly threw the ignition key backward into the truck. Some of the police roughly pulled the driver out of the cab while Hynes and his men climbed the truck's sides. As their heads and shoulders appeared over the top, they were grabbed and pulled headfirst into the truck by the laughing, singing occupants. As traffic piled up on Main Street, hundreds of young demonstrators broke through police lines thinned by the truck diversion. They surged into the Plaza from side streets where they had been waiting in small shops, coffee houses and buildings.

The Trojan horse tactic had made a laughing stock of the Red Squad claim that "never again" would there be another "Communist" demonstration in Los Angeles.

XI

Seven months after he had left Los Angeles, I received

Gene's first letter. It was postmarked New York.

"Mi preciosa: by the time you get this I will with luck be gone again. In the months since leaving home I have been acquainting myself with T.U.U.L. and Party work in Detroit, Chicago and Pittsburgh, I would prefer to remain permanently in any one of these areas and have sent for you and our young 'un long before this, but our friends have decided otherwise. They advised against even writing you in all this time. Now I am leaving, reluctantly, for more distant places. This will be sent you after I get there. I do believe our separation will soon be over, so hold on a little longer.
                                        Adios,
                                        Irisher."

By the time official word came that I should proceed to New York, where arrangements would be made for my trip to join Gene, I was embroiled in a short-lived, but unexpected battle. On getting Gene's letter, I asked for my Y.C.L. Party transfer to "parts unknown," in preparation for the hopeful come-ahead word. My comrades smiled, despite the decorum of our committee meeting. We knew the "more distant places" Gene referred to could only be—Moscow! They were pleased for me that the months of separation might soon be over. Our party organizer, newly arrived from New York, sobered us abruptly.

"We cannot handle this request routinely. We would be guilty of rank male chauvinism if we agreed to transfer this leading young woman comrade merely so she may join her husband."

Confused, we agreed that he and I would discuss the matter further, that action on my transfer request would be postponed to the next meeting.

I had some heavy thinking to do. I was uncomfortable with my Party organizer's defense of me as a leading woman comrade. The more I hassled with the feeling that something was wrong the more I disliked the context in which the question had been placed. I felt I was being subjected, with praise, to a subtle male chauvinism which rejected the possibility that a woman can be wife *and* leading activist. Under the guise of upholding my rights, I was being told I had to choose between being a housewife at the beck and call of her man or becoming the classic version of an unencumbered male. For nearly two years I had juggled my Party activity and Tim's needs. No one, including me, had seen this as a collective responsibility. Now, again, I was being told that if I could not properly juggle my marriage and activity, I had to choose between them. I couldn't buy that. I had the right to my love for Gene, to Tim and my Party activity. One without the other wasn't good enough. Not for me. I did not know whether I would be able always to achieve this balance in my life. I damn well intended to try. I could only take one step at a time as the problem arose. It was true Gene had made his own choices, gone his own way. I need not follow him. My Party organizer said I must not follow him. Need not. Must not. All I knew was that I wanted to join him. The framework for my activity would have to be found within that context, always.

I told my Party organizer that I would appeal any decision he might make to keep me from leaving. I added, with a touch of sarcasm wasted on him, that I was sure there were enough more typical male chauvinists in our national leadership who would be shocked at the idea of keeping a wife from joining her husband. They would side with me, for the wrong reasons.

Although Mama and Papa staunchly supported me in my mini-fight, they were red-eyed and silent as they helped me pack for the journey that would take Tim from them, six thousand miles away across two continents and an ocean.

Three:
WORLD'S EYE VIEW

I

Our train slowly crossed the border onto Soviet soil. With face pressed against the window, heart pounding, I hugged Tim tightly in my arms and my eyes blurred with tears. High above, the wooden arch through which our car moved proclaimed: "Workers of the World Unite." I was in Mecca.

When the uniformed border control with the Red Star insignia on their fur hats came to collect passports, I barely resisted giving them the clenched fist salute. I wanted to hand them my Party identification—a more fitting entry permit into the Land of Socialism.

Reunion with Gene, awaited so eagerly, was almost eclipsed by my excitement at being in Moscow. I wandered the streets at every opportunity. Every detail had special significance: the broken, cobblestoned sidewalks and boarded-up empty stores—symbols of a painful past; Red Army platoons marching down the street, lustily singing revolutionary songs—symbol of a land where the people's army had triumphed. I smiled broadly at every beshawled peasant woman shuffling by in her knee-high, shapeless, stiff felt boots, the *valenki* I was soon to wear. I wanted to clasp the hand of each man and woman I passed. I wanted to shout "*tovarich*!" to all Moscow. Six thousand miles from home, I was Home. Here everything was truly "*nahsh*"—ours, everyone was "*nahsh braht*"—our brothers. After the last two years, the exhilaration at being one of the working class ruling majority was particularly gratifying.

Being an outsider, I sentimentalized the harsh realities of daily life. Life was tough and elemental that winter of 1931. Each day was a struggle to survive—personally, economically, politically. Stalin had declared: "We are fifty to one hundred years behind the advanced countries. We must cover this distance in ten years or we shall be crushed." The socialist countries which were to follow could afford a slower pace; the first socialist state could not.

The First Five Year Plan to rapidly industrialize a backward, underdeveloped giant was being compressed into four years. The rest of the world, floundering in economic crisis, scoffed at this mad dream. Even more unrealistic, they said, was Moscow's insistence that socialism would achieve this miracle of industrial growth without private foreign capital investment. There were no Italian Fiat plants in 1931, only the first Soviet AMO auto plant. There were no U.S. banks with branch offices in Moscow. Capital investment was squeezed out of a Soviet people who for many years were ill-housed, ill-clothed, and ill-fed—building for the future.

Yet even in those lean years there existed the concept of social benefits as an individual right. Free medical clinics, child care centers in factories, free education, rest homes, infinitesimally low rents—these were available to all. Back in the States twenty million were out of work, millions more were hungry and homeless, social security was a revolutionary demand being fought for in the streets.

Two blocks from the famed Pushkin Square on Tverskaya, then Moscow's main thoroughfare, the Luxe Hotel, home for all the foreigners and some of the Soviet comrades working at the Comintern, was our home too.

A conglomerate of nationalities, colors, races, and languages from all over the world, the Comintern and the Luxe put flesh and substance upon the concept of internationalism I had lectured about so often back in Los Angeles.

Official work was conducted through translators, while in social encounters we conversed in halting pidgin Russian, probing quickly for a common language—often a rudimentary German, French or English. At the very first introduction and firm handshake there was instant camaraderie, the fulsome acceptance of a fellow comrade. Legendary names of freedom fighters read about in Party newspapers back home became laughing wine- or vodka-drinking companions across the table in someone's room in the Luxe. Safe in Moscow, realxed moments were shared with comrades of whom one learned to ask no personal questions. Comrades disappeared, reappeared. We knew they had been on *commanderofka*—foreign mission. We asked no questions; instead we partook of the delicacies they brought back, mainly real coffee and good cigarettes. Others left not to return, gone home to countries where, in those years, having been in Moscow was cause for imprisonment.

I invested each unfamiliar personal hardship with an emotionalism about sharing the new, difficult Soviet construction. I took a puritanical pleasure in the very starkness of daily life: the communal kitchens and toilets down long, dark corridors; the cramped one-room with Tim ensconced behind a nook we created by pushing the large wooden wardrobe perpendicular to the wall at the far end of the room; spit-baths in a tin wash basin filled from a tea kettle heated in the communal kitchen; trips to the public bathhouse which became a social event; ration cards that produced little else than our daily allotment of bread. All these were sacrifices to the new society emerging slowly out of czarist poverty and the devastation wrought by civil war and imperialist intervention.

II

Gene was more pragmatic than I. Moscow was where he happened to be working—now he was leaving, and once again he was going alone.

The evening he broke the news, I sat wrapped in blanket and sweaters, legs curled under me. I could barely see his face as Gene paced slowly back and forth between the two beds on either side of the long walls. The dimly lit desk lamp shed a diffused glow through the towel we threw over it in deference to Tim, sleeping in his corner. As he paced, Gene told me of the weeks before my arrival.

Sent by the American Party to Moscow, the general assumption had been that he would be either a student at the International Lenin School or a research worker— a *referent*—in the Anglo-American Section of the Comintern. He balked at both. He won the agreement of Dimitri Manuilsky, the all-decisive Soviet comrade within the top circle of Comintern leaders, that he work in the Far Eastern Section and prepare himself to go abroad.

Gene paused, looked at me somewhat quizzically and waited

for my reaction as he told me he was leaving soon for the Philippines, saying, "It is a U.S. colony and we have a special responsibility." He was going to South Africa, "so closely related to the Negro Question at home." Then he was going to China—"the key to the whole Far East; the revolution there is creating a whole series of new concepts; we must understand them."

I shivered inside my blanket, but the chill came from within me, not only from the unheated room. Too much had been coming at me too fast. Los Angeles was only a few weeks back and now Gene's casual talk about going to these faraway places was beyond my comprehension. Yet all things seemed possible and normal to this young Tim Ryan who, upon leaving California, had shed his provincial Frank Waldron identity forever. I recalled the battle I had waged to join him, and I asked why, then, had he sent for us.

He sat on the edge of my bed, his hands cupping his pipe bowl, elbows resting on his knees.

"You have a right to be angry, I should have given you the choice. But I was told that you could come even if you decided to go back when I leave. I wanted these couple of months together. You can go back or stay, after I leave. It's up to you—but at least we're together now."

The admission of his love and need ordinarily would have satisifed me, but I pressed on.

"Why so soon? Wouldn't a couple years here at the Comintern be good, and we'd be together."

His words came slowly as he paced again. As always, now too he sought the precise words with which to convey his thoughts. He said a short stay in Moscow was beneficial. Exchanging ideas and experiences with comrades from other Parties was helpful. "But a long stay, the life of the expatriate, is not for me; it is not good for anyone."

Housed in a large, ugly, square building across from the Kremlin Wall, in its Moscow operations the Comintern was a form of think-tank, but a think-tank with organizational powers. It was divided into Sections—Italian, French, Anglo-American, East European, Middle East, Far East, etc.; the many comrades I had met were either representatives sent by their home Parties to head the Section or to do research work. Memoranda and position papers were prepared by the *referents* for their Section heads who, in meetings with top Comintern committees usually headed by leading Soviet comrades, hammered out policies and directives for each Party. While delegations from the countries visited Moscow frequently for such discussions, those staffing the Sections remained for years, working an eight to four o'clock desk job, living at the Luxe.

Gene said he wanted no part of this life. He felt these comrades became isolated from the problems of their home countries. They became abstract in their outlook, too influenced by the view from Moscow rather than by the realities in their own country. "If you are not in struggle, then what kind of a revolutionary are you?" he asked rhetorically.

I did not question Gene's need to move on in whatever direction his work took him. We were two component parts of a single whole committed, without reservations, to the movement and the Party and the dream for socialism. Now in Moscow I was miraculously part of the dream come true. If Gene was going abroad again, I was going to stay on alone for a while here in Moscow. I saw myself on the threshhold of new experiences and I knew, once again, that I had to keep taking one step at a time—with Gene if I possibly could, without him only if I had no choice.

III

The wife of the American representative to the Young Communist International had stopped by on my first evening. Pauline regaled me with humorous stories and confused me with cynical comment. She told me she had asked her Tamara to keep an eye out for a *nonya* for us. A *nonya* I was told, was a housemaid. The coalminer's daughter from Pittsburgh laughed at my shock. "You'll get used to it; they are indispensable." Never, I vowed. A maid! In Moscow?

The scramble for food was a constant preoccupation. The lack of it, the scrounging for it, the blocks-long queues at the mere rumor that something "is being given today." These were full-time chores and those who had *babashkas* (grandmothers) or *nonyas* were indeed fortunate. Washing laundry in communal kitchens and swinging heavy, gas-lit irons over shirts and dresses were other chores *nonyas* took over. They also aired the infants and toddlers for long hours on Arbat Boulevard and Sovietskaya Square. I was determined to manage on my own. As with workers at factories and employees in institutions, the one meal at the Luxe, available only to those who lived or worked there, was our mainstay; as was the open-faced sandwich of cheese or bologna we bought for breakfast each night before at the buffet in the basement. Although the food was badly prepared and reflected, too, the real shortage of meat, vegetables, fats, fruits, our meals at the Luxe were considered better than most, dispensed especially for us foreigners.

All infants received milk rations each morning at the neighborhood child care clinic. Those of us with older children rose early, or *nonyas* did, to buy a litre of milk and a few carrots on the street from peasant women squatting on the curbstone or in their horse-drawn wooden carts, ladling the raw milk from big cans. Most mornings these milk vendors would not accept the rubles I held out to them, but demanded payment in our bread or small sugar rations. The corner pharmacy dispensed free cod liver oil, Vitamin D source, to children under 12; our House Committee issued the certificate. There was no refrigeration, but since there was never food enough for the next day anyway, this created no problem. The search for food was a daily task.

One day I expressed concern for Tim's limited diet of kasha and carrots and Pauline suggested, "Why don't you ask Will Weinstone to let you use his ration book once in awhile? I do. You know that as American Party rep he has a book to the Foreign Specialists' store down the street. You can get almost everything there, and he doesn't use up all his rations, anyway."

I passed this fabulous store every day, a block from our hotel. Its giant glass windows were always discreetly canvas-covered. Well dressed foreigners and their *nonyas* moved in a constant stream in and out of its doors, laden with bulging shopping bags.

Engineers, technicians and skilled workers were being recruited by the thousands in Germany, France, England, the U.S. These foreigners were given preferential housing and good food sources. I understood the pragmatic need to satisfy these people in return for the technical and industrial know-how the new socialist state needed, but I could not understand why Communists, foreign and Soviet, received privileges not available to the ordinary Soviet citizen. Gene and I agreed we would not ask for the use of Will Weinstone's prized ration book. We would manage as everyone did. For special occasions, we sold a clothes item in the government commission store and then rushed to the open market on Arbat where, under government supervision, farmers brought their private produce to sell at high prices; but no ration coupons were necessary. Here we bought a few eggs for Tim, a pat of butter, a small chicken.

We were suddenly offered a new room and at first glance we negotiated the exchange with the couple who wanted to live on the first floor, free from the old, often out-of-order elevator. On the third floor we now had a very big, sunny room whose main attraction for us was a good-sized, walk-in closet with a big window and a door that closed it off from the main room. With Tim's crib in that space and the door closed we now could keep our light on, we could talk loudly, and we could entertain our growing circle of new friends.

To our room came also Gene's students at the Far Eastern University, young South Africans, Filipinos and Chinese who drank numerous glasses of hot tea as they debated the specific characteristics of the national liberation struggles back home and how the Comintern's resolution on this subject was to be applied.

Exhilarated at living in this international milieu, I was slow to realize that we were completely isolated from ordinary Soviet life. We did not even know any Soviet persons, except for Boris and Bob who lived in the Luxe and worked in the Comintern with Gene. All of the comrades living there and working at the Comintern were divorced from Soviet life. We were living in Moscow, but were not a part of it. No one could give me a plausible reason why this was so; no one I knew seemed to really care that it was so.

Boris was a China expert; Bob's specialization was India. Boris' wife Musa, a volatile, nervous chain-smoker, was on the faculty of the Soviet Institute of Red Professors. Bob's wife, Valerie, was studying in some high Party School. Bob had met Valerie in Detroit where he had been representative of the Young Communist International to the American Young Comminist League. He had brought her and her Russian-born family back to Moscow with him—her mother, father, two brothers and their American wives.

Boris and Musa had recently returned from Comintern assignment in China and Bob and Valerie had been to India. The discussions in our room ranged from their experiences abroad to our asking them questions about Soviet life. But they were not typical Soviet citizens and our isolation was not lessened by them.

Upon our return to Moscow in 1937, we could find no trace of them. No one would or could tell us anything. During my third return trip in 1941, I saw Valerie walking towards me on Gorky Street. I started to greet her warmly, but she passed me with a slight flicker of recognition. Insisting upon answers from comrades, I was told that Bob had been executed and Valerie, only recently released from prison, carefully stayed away from all foreign comrades. I was told for her sake to leave her alone. We never heard anything at all about Boris and Musa. In the purges of the Comintern in 1937 and 1938, the very international activity and foreign travel demanded by the Comintern became the basis of charges of "foreign agent" that sent hundreds of Soviet and European Comintern workers to labor camps and firing squads.

Impatient to get into work, irritable at being tied to Tim day and night, overwhelmed at the time-consuming household chores, I finally admitted defeat and succumbed to that which I said I never would. We got a *nonya*. Fresh from the village, Olya moved in, sharing Tim's closet room. Providing bed space, even a corner in a communal room, was a must. Recent arrivals from the countryside, these women had no permit to remain in the city unless they had not only a job but a place to live. Although Olya and I were both only 22, she radiated a strength and practicality and know-how I badly needed, and I leaned heavily upon her for the next two years. Under her friendly care Tim thrived and rapidly became bi-lingual. While I developed a workable, pidgin Russian to communicate simple, badly constructed sentences with Olya, on the street and in the shops my two-year-old translator amused the Russians who stood by watching Tim transmit my needs to store clerks.

Gene was leaving soon and I decided not to get embroiled in the tensions of a new job until he left. Instead, with Olya to care for Tim, we went often to the theater and the opera and the open concerts in the park. Then it was September and Gene left—Comintern representative to the Communist Parties in South Africa and then to the Philippines.

IV

A few days later Weinstone phoned and asked me to come to his room to discuss some work possibility. There I met two Americans, Grace and Eva. Grace I had known in Berkeley. I had heard she and her German-born husband were in Moscow where he was working at the AMO auto plant, and I had planned to look her up. Eva was introduced as "a comrade from Chicago." We grinned and said we knew each other. She was married to one of

Valerie's brothers who worked as a printer at the English language *Moscow Daily News*.

The job being offered was that of social studies teacher at the newly organized Anglo-American school for children of foreign workers. I had read of the project, but was not interested. Also, I told Weinstone I had no college degree; I had never taught school.

Under prodding I admitted, yes, of course, I had led Young Pioneer groups and taught Young Communist League classes, "but that's not the same as teaching academic subjects in school."

Weinstone insisted, "We need you there." I was not clear who the "we" were nor why Weinstone, representative to the Comintern, was involved. Grace was to teach geography and math; Eva, English. Together the three of us were to be the Party core in a motley group of American and English staff and parents. Working with foreigners in Moscow was not quite my idea of integration into Soviet or international Party life, but the persistent "We want you to do it" settled the matter.

Grace, Eva and I swung into hectic pre-school opening preparations, making subject outlines, meeting with staff and parents. Three weeks later the House Committee at the Luxe asked me to come to the office where they took my ration card and Tim's and handed me a new thick booklet. To my question in pidgin Russian, they explained that this was our new ration assignment to The Foreign Specialists' Store.

"*Ya ne xachoo*," I said slowly. "I don't want it." The rapid fire response was too much even for Tim. An English comrade waiting nearby to pay his rent, came to our rescue. Apparently my new job category put me into the Foreign Specialist classification; this was the ration book that went with that status. I could get no other classification unless I gave up that particular job. So, despite my protest, I acquired access to the Foreigners' Store—much to Olya's delight, as she had no qualms about it like I did. I felt somehow insulted, an Outsider who had to be bribed and placated like other foreigners.

Within a month after its November opening, our school had sixty children, divided into three age groups. First at School Number 23 on Pokrofski and then at the newer four-story building of School Number 24 in the same district, we shared facilities with the neighborhood Soviet school. However, at the behest of both the Soviet authorities and our parents, we maintained a completely independent stance. Fraternization between the Soviet, American, and English children was not encouraged. Grace, Eva and I could not ascertain why. Our seven-teacher staff and principal were both American and British; the Russian language teacher was sent to us from the Institute of Foreign Languages; and our music teacher was a member of the Bolshoi orchestra.

Life in California had ill prepared me for my first Moscow winter. I stood each morning at the tram stop weeping in frozen agony. Neither Olya's *valenki* nor my Russian *shapka*—that fur-lined leather cap with its large earflaps tied under my chin—nor a pair of Gene's longjohns cut down to size, relieved the pain. Later, however, I came to love the eight-foot snowbanks that lined the sidewalks and I learned to move freely and breathe deeply in the biting, dry, often 25-degrees-below-zero weather.

Minor crises exploded daily at school as American and British parents battled to transplant their native ideas into the Soviet system. Grace, Eva and I tried to pacify them while enforcing the regulations set us by the local school board. I was constantly angry with the parents because of their superior attitudes and contempt for all things Russian. When one child arrived with his silver fork and spoon from home because his mother objected to the coarse tin ones in the school dining room, I was ready to expel him and mama from our collective.

I confronted these attitudes by turning my social studies classes into sessions reminiscent of my Young Pioneer groups. We did a quick survey of the capitalist system and its economic crisis from which their fathers had fled to good paying jobs and special privilege in Moscow. I gave them a capsule view of Russian history, the reasons for the revolution, the goals of the First Five Year Plan, why these people were doing without today so as to build toward a new socialist society tomorrow.

Some of this had an impact and a number of the foreign specialists' wives complained to the principal that I was indoctrinating their children. They became upset, too, that I was not a member of their foreign colony but the wife of a Comintern worker. By late spring the school was functioning routinely and I was fed up with foreign specialists, their wives, and their children. When Weinstone mentioned an unfilled research position at the Profintern, I readily accepted.

V

Organized at a world congress in Moscow in 1921, the Red International of Labor Unions, known as the Profintern, was the center for Left labor unions breaking away from the Social Democratic International Federation of Trade Unions. In the U.S.A. the Trade Union Education League affiliated to the Profintern, as did the Trade Union Unity League when it evolved out of the T.U.E.L. in 1929.

In a sprawling, collonnaded white building on the banks of the Moscow river, the Profintern was to its affiliated, independent Left federations in 61 countries very much what the Comintern was to the Communist Parties abroad, with perhaps less disciplined, organizational clout than the Comintern. Its territorial Sections, like those of the Comintern, were staffed by representatives sent from the movements of each country.

Tim was enrolled in the nursery school operated by the Profintern for all its employees—political, administrative, technical, maintenance staffs. With some trepidation, I reported to the Anglo-American Section. There I met the British representative, the Communist trade union leader John McMahon, who was very tall, very thin and very friendly. His warmth helped dispel an earlier impression at the Luxe that the English comrades were very reserved and somewhat difficult to get to know. The American representative was Fur Union leader Irving Potash, short and slight, sandy-haired and affable. The Austrian Emmerich, a composite in gray both in coloring and personality, was, for some reason never explained to me, chairman of our Section. Twenty-year-old Molly was our secretary and mother hen. Jewish, and South African-born, she had come to Moscow with her mother in 1928. They became Soviet citizens and Molly mastered the Russian language. She was the pivot around which our Section functioned. In later years she was to work as translator in the Comintern and after the war she was sent abroad to work in Belgrade, Bucharest and Prague at the offices of the Comintern's international magazine. She returned to Moscow after the 1968 events in Prague.

In 1932 Molly and I became inseparable. Ideas flowed between us as an ever-running river. We examined and probed and argued all things personal, political, literary, historical, philosophical. Molly was thin and angular; her views were sharp and often acid-tipped; her satire dry and pointed; her laugh loud and infectious. Her personal and political loyalties and integrity were unassailable. Our instant friendship endured a lifetime. Despite the long years that were to lapse between our reunions, and with no letters exchanged between us, each time we met again Molly and I picked up a conversation and our friendship as though we had seen each other the previous day.

As the Section's research worker I followed the American and British newspapers and magazines. I built up an extensive clipping file and prepared data for Emmerich, Potash and McMahon. I gave reports to our weekly Sections meetings on labor trends and wrote articles for the Profintern's news bulletin and for Soviet newspapers and radio.

I soon realized that Gene's criticism of the type of work I was doing, which he had refused to do when he had arrived in Moscow, was valid. It was abstract research of newspapers and magazines that arrived infrequently. We unintentionally fed into the think-tank interpretations too often based more upon wishful thinking than on hard reality. Yet I enjoyed my work. I liked being part of this international movement. I liked being with these comrades from all parts of the world.

A bonus of my job was the privilege of attending night classes at the International Lenin School. These were organized for foreign Party comrades working in the Comintern, the Profintern and at the foreign languages publishing house. We met in our separate language sections with Soviet professors who often had translators at their elbow.

Gene had been gone a year. We had been told originally there could not be any correspondence, although later when I worked in the setup myself I learned that Gene and I had been naively acquiescent on this prohibition.

Some days I could hardly remember what he looked like and I panicked. Other times I vividly saw him pacing our room, felt his hard, gentle hand on my body. Mainly, however, I was happily immersed in living and working and feeling very self-reliant. Running our small household became more difficult for Olya since my Foreign Specialists' ration book was taken from me when I left the teaching job; but Tim was in school all day and she was free to scrounge for our food. I brought Tim home after work and rushed off to my classes. On rest days Molly and I and Tim explored the Park of Culture and Rest, picnicked on the Moscow river, and talked endlessly.

VI

In the Fall a Comintern commission selected from each evening school section one student to attend the full-time year-long school to which the Parties sent twenty to thirty comrades from the home country. Together with a Black comrade from New York, Helen Davies, I was selected from the American group.

A prestigious institute with high potential, the International Lenin School had inherent weaknesses which no one in the Comintern or the Parties sending the students recognized at the time. Separated from our home base, living in a foreign land whose language we did not speak and whose people we did not meet, insulated in a school compound where we were housed, fed, clothed, we studied the writings of Marx, Engels, Lenin and Stalin with professors who communicated through translators. Our academic point of reference was always the Russian Bolshevik Party and the Russian Revolution. Lenin's mercurial polemics over momentary tactics of a specific period, were taught us as irrevocable universal dogma. We eloquently echoed Stalin's published denunciations of Bukharinism and Trotskyism without even objecting to the fact that we were not allowed to read what Bukharin or Trotsky had said or written. On practical work tours to factories and villages, our glimpses of Soviet life were filtered through speeches made by Party and economic personnel, never by direct contact and conversation with ordinary Soviet citizens.

We lived in the center of the world's first successful socialist revolution, in the middle of exciting complexities of an historically new situation, but it was all pre-digested for us and reduced into Stalin's edict that the achievements were "to the glory of the Party," while "behind our difficulties are concealed our enemies."

It was in that year that Stalin proclaimed the rationalization which placed Party and State in conflict with the Soviet people. Vigilance in the early post-revolution years against saboteur remnants of the declassed former ruling class was an elementary precept.

However, Stalin now decreed that the class enemy was powerful, that it was in the factories, the government offices, the railway and water transport enterprises, the collective and State farms, inside the Party. He declared this enemy which had penetrated the whole fabric of Soviet society had "unlimited reserves in the population," that the Party leading the country to socialism was surrounded by a sea of hostility.

Neither in the Soviet Union nor in the Communist Parties abroad did leaders challenge this manifestation of Stalin's lack of faith in the attracting powers of socialism, his relegation of the Soviet population to the role of an unlimited reserve force for the class enemy. His concept was that this enemy, stripped of its former State and economic power, was becoming stronger, instead of weaker.

It was this wholly new view of the masses that became the basis for years of punitive repression and terror. Some twenty years later Krushchev admitted that these repressions—charges against "enemies of the people," framed trials, long imprisonments, executions—were used to cover up the economic and political mistakes of the leadership and to prevent discussions of those mistakes.

Those early years of unquestioning belief in a man who believed in no one, not even the cause he served, are difficult to understand, even more difficult to explain. We were conditioned by many factors. There was that damnable principle regarding the infallibility of whatever current leadership was in power, and Stalin, leader of us all, was the most infallible. The very monolithism which was our greatest weakness was portrayed as being our greatest strength. We were always soldiers in a revolutionary army at permanent war with a powerful class enemy whose tentacles encompassed the world. We lived and struggled in a turbulent sea of anti-Soviet, anti-socialist intrigue. Anyone who was not totally with us was against us. Spies, saboteurs, traitors were everywhere. Defending the Soviet Union, then a very young and new and single socialist state, was the primary need. Everything else was subordinated to its pragmatic, immediate needs to consolidate and grow. In permanent war, doubts or questions are treason.

For me personally, this world movement embracing millions took on face and form as I lived and worked and studied in Moscow and later travelled for the Comintern in Europe, Africa, and Asia.

Politically and organizationally, the Comintern's ability to organize and sustain and nurture the international cohesion of the Marxist movement was, at that time, practically the single factor which kept many of the very new and struggling Parties alive and enabled them to take root and grow. This internationalism and the existence of the first socialist state changed the course of history. They also shaped the lives of millions of revolutionaries everywhere who now had a powerful, living ideal that had a form and body they could relate to.

For me the bonds of internationalism never again were abstract slogans. They were bonds with living persons in every country in the world, and Moscow was the lifeline. Moscow was the realization of our struggle for socialism. Moscow was the only haven where revolutionaries from all over the world were safe and honored. Moscow was the center from which all revolutionary wisdom flowed. Moscow was not only a favorite city, a second home to me, it was an emotional state of mind.

VII

While I moved in Moscow from social studies teacher to research worker to fulltime student, Gene's experiences abroad were quite different. Arriving in Manila at the end of the summer rains in 1931, he disappeared into the illegal Communist Party. He travelled along its underground route for the good part of a year—from village to village, town to town, making contact with Party groups, peasant committees, with rubber, sugar and dock workers. He lived for weeks with Party chairman Crisanto Evangelista in a guarded hideaway. He met some of his former students at the university in Moscow who now, in their country, became his teachers.

He studied the armed peasant rebellions that had erupted months earlier in Bulcan, Mindanao, Bataan, Terbac, Tayug. He talked with strikers on the docks at Ibolo, at the Standard Oil operations in Manila, on the sugar plantations at Negroes, with unemployed demonstrators in Cabiao, Cabanatiao.

After months of travelling, listening, probing, questioning, Gene placed before the Filipino Party his belief that the greatest danger confronting this small, newly organized Communist organization was an accommodation to its illegal status. He outlined innovative security measures to protect the organization, but at the same time he said the crucial test was the establishment of working relations with the masses of people on the basis of struggle for specific issues. He urged that all Communists individually and collectively participate with existing people's organizations, with factory and trade union committees, with the rank and file in all reformist organizations;

student, peasant, cultural, intellectual groups.

The anti-imperialist national liberation revolution, he argued, must be taken out of the realm of abstract slogans and turned into a daily battle on "little issues" that determine the everyday lives of people, "such as reduction of rent and taxes, resistance to evictions, seizures of food and seed supplies, defense of every democratic right to organize, strike, free speech and assembly that is violated."

In South Africa, nearly a year later, the problems were different, but Gene's approach was basically the same. The Communist Party was emerging from a prolonged factional fight in which the all-white leadership and predominantly white membership had been charged with racism. In 1931 the Comintern had intervened from Moscow and the leadership, headed by Rebecca Bunting and her husband, were expelled. Their influence remained, however, and the issues were still being debated. The Buntings had rejected the primacy of the racial and national questions for South Africa. They opposed the Comintern's goal for an Independent Native Black Republic with "guarantees for the white minority." They had argued this would "favor a black race dictatorship that would turn the exploited whites into a subjected race." The Buntings claimed that not a national liberation struggle of the Native Black majority was the strategic goal, but the establishment of socialism by the proletariat—black and white.

As in the Philippines, Gene devoted the first months in South Africa to travelling, asking questions. He went from Capetown to Johannesburg to Pretoria, Nadelieni, Bloemfotstein, Potschefstroom, meeting Party and non-Party people, members in white and Black trade unions, leaders of nationalist organizations. Then he applied himself to the problems still tearing the Party apart. He helped initiate methods of collective work to strengthen the ability of the Black comrades newly placed into responsible positions of leadership. He helped establish the concept that the Party had to become, in the first place, the Party of Native Black workers, reflecting the Black Nation character of the country. At the same time, he called for an end to the practice of using "administrative, punitive expulsions" against those whites still influenced by the Buntings' ideas. He urged "the need to win over vacillators." He exploded the bombast of those white comrades who refused to work inside the white workers' trade unions under the guise that they were militantly opposing white chauvinism. "White chauvinism is fought where it exists, not in words from the outside," Gene countered. He argued, too, against those comrades who refused to work in the reformist organizations, white or Black, under the guise they were protecting the independence and purity of the Party. At the same time, he combated tendencies to subordinate the Party's policies to accommodation with the reformist leaders, "in the interest of unity."

Earlier the Party had issued the revolutionary sounding call for all native Blacks to burn their compulsory Passes, to violate all apartheid regulations. Gene helped the new leadership rescind this policy. He called it a racist provocation because the predominantly white Communist organization had demanded acts of heroism and economic suicide from the Blacks which no white person was called upon to equal. Without the hated Pass a Black worker could not leave the segregated compound to work in the city. To call for individual violations of apartheid rules by Blacks alone, without a high level of mass movement support and involvement, was to pit the Blacks against the White state apparatus in adventurist isolation.

Gene noted, "We must not throw out slogans wildly . . . [we need to] think through which forms of mass struggle had matured for action, which forms of struggle must be prepared for, which can be called for immediate realization."

VIII

Late in January, 1933, I was sent to Berlin to renew my expired passport. There was neither U.S. embassy nor consulate in Moscow at the time. President Roosevelt officially recognized the Soviet Union's existence only in November that year, sixteen years after the Russian Revolution. The comrades at the Comintern did not explain their urgency to have my passport renewed at that particular moment, and I did not ask why. I was intrigued at the idea of travelling. I was given my passport, a modest per diem expense account in foreign currency, and the address of a small shop where I was to present myself. I memorized my identifying words well.

A week later I sat in a coffee house on fashionable Kurfurstendamm with the person who had been summoned after my appearance at that shop. Now we conversed in a potpourri of his German, my childhood Yiddish, his few words of halting English.

Short, stocky, very blonde and young, Gr. had a delightful sense of humor which put me at ease the very first morning I met him. As often happens on such telescoped occasions, and with the immediate warm acceptance I had learned at the Luxe and at school, in these few days we had established a camaraderie that knew no past or future, only the present.

But Gr. was worried. "What a time to send you, to send anyone to Berlin," he grumbled. "Don't they know what is going on here?"

I had been apprehensive but too stoic to express my own fears. Now I wanted him to put into words what I had avoided. I asked what was wrong. Hunched over the small, round, lamplit table like a couple absorbed in low-toned love-words (we hoped), slowly stirring his cup of hot chocolate as I toyed with the cream torte, Gr. retorted harshly, "Don't tell me you are as dense as they are. Look around, don't you have eyes?"

It was the tea hour, and the restaurant was crowded. At the tables sat well-dressed women and their escorts, the majority of them smartly uniformed, leather-belted, Nazi Brown Shirts. On the streets where I had wandered about alone, I had been jostled by loud-speaking, laughing, arrogant Nazis in uniform. They roamed in packs, forcing others off the sidewalks as they passed. I was frightened by this menacing world in brown. I wanted to seek reassurance in the outlying working class districts, at Party and trade union centers where I hoped to feel the pulse of the anti-fascist opposition. But, Gr. initiated me at our very first meeting, that was one thing I was not to do. I was to act at all times like a disinterested tourist. "Go shopping, go sightseeing, go to movies," he said.

Now his uneasiness fed mine. "In less than a week," he continued, "will be the elections. Hitler's gangs are confident, they have reason to be; they become more arrogant each day."

As we parted for the day, he warned, "*Gottes Himmel*, don't use your Yiddish on anybody, you hear? Speak only English. And don't forget, you are a holidaying tourist, not interested in politics around you." He promised to try to get me out of Berlin before election day, and he did.

Actually, Gr.'s unease and my own disquiet were somewhat unusual. The tragedy of the time was that neither the Social Democrats nor the Communists in Germany believed fascism was a specific threat.

The Social Democratic Party and its powerful labor movement had become an appendage to the bourgeois Hindenburg government, settling comfortably for big crumbs of reformist concessions. Strongly tainted with avid anti-communism, they were blind to the need for working class unity and blind too to the rising tide of Hitlerism.

The Communist Party, like the Comintern, throughout the early 1930's believed that the social democrats were the sole obstacle to the imminent victory of the dictatorship of the proletariat around the world, and in Germany particularly. The Party proclaimed again and again that as a result of its activity "fascism in Germany in the Hitler form [is] on the downgrade," that "delivering the main blow against the Social Democratic Party is the core of Communist policy in Germany."

Meanwhile power was being handed over to Hitler by the Hindenburg government, step by step. The Nazi leader was appointed Chancellor on January 30, 1933. Twenty days later the Nazis burned the Reichstag building, claiming the arson was a Communist signal for the start of the revolution. Together with two other Communists, George Dimitroff, who worked in Berlin with the expatriate committee of his Bulgarian Communist Party, was framed for the fire. Its real purpose was achieved, however, when the German parliament voted 441 to 84 to turn over all its constitutional authority to Chancellor Hitler. With this act, fascism came to power legally in Germany, even while it still could not muster a majority of the popular vote in the last pre-Third Reich elections held March 5, 1933.

The Brown Shirt Terror was unleashed. The divided and still-sparring Communist and Social Democratic Parties, together with the trade union and mass movement organizations, were all smashed. Genocide of the Jewish people escalated the political executions into the many millions.

In Moscow the winter of 1933 passed uneventfully. We studied, we attended meetings; I rushed between school and the Luxe. In October, Gene came home. Of the five years since I had arrived in Seattle, we had been separated for three. In the last two years we had each experienced new levels and areas of maturity, as well as an independence from one another. We needed time to readjust to the kind of person each had become. But there was to be no time. He was leaving for Shanghai in three weeks. We hid pleading, questioning eyes behind too-polite words, each waiting for the other to bridge the self-conscious gap.

Tentatively I brought my new achievements to him. I needed his approbation. I needed to impress him. He brushed aside my somewhat bragging accounts with the same contempt he had expressed earlier for these areas of activity when they had been offered to him. He cut through my words with the cryptic question, "How many nights with whom did all this cost you?"

Horrified and furious, I fled our room and retreated into school. There I immersed myself in study and sought ego solace in a personal relationship I had until then resisted. To me Gene's question reflected his low opinion of me, his belief that I was not capable of achieving these positions on merit. In the more personal sense, the implication of that question destroyed what I chose to regard as the unique commitment of our relationship. I did not realize at the time that Gene's put-down reflected his cynical awareness of the most elemental, and usually only, way in which women could move upward, in our movement as elsewhere.

I knew this to be true, but only abstractly. I had lectured in Los Angeles on The Woman Question under Capitalism. I had listened to the incessant political gossip from New York to Moscow regarding who had slept with whom and, most importantly, why. None of this had touched me personally, until now. I could not forgive Gene, nor he me. We each were handling badly our first serious rift. We needed time, and there was none.

The night before he left for Shanghai Gene told me he had been urged to take me along. It appeared that on this particular mission abroad a wife was considered desirable.

"With matters unresolved between us, I could not ask you," he said. "Would you have come?"

Angrily, I retorted, "You'll never know now, will you?"

"I want you to know that when I said I couldn't take you, the comrades insisted on assigning an 'official wife', and I refused. I am going alone."

He left the next morning with a parting shot. "If you go back to the States before I return, leave Tim here for me."

"Like hell I will," I shouted at his disappearing back.

X

School ended, students left for home and I was called before a commission in the Comintern. Across the table three comrades pored over an open file—my political dossier. They passed papers back and forth, read in silence, then began to question me through a translator.

"We see by your party record that you have worked under illegal conditions in your home party." I nodded.

"Tell us the circumstances, describe the methods of security used, your estimate of those experiences." Another world. Another time. I tried.

"Of course, your conditions were not comparable to those of comrades and parties working under fascist and colonial oppression." I readily agreed.

"But for an American comrade to have had those experiences is somewhat unusual, yes?" I didn't know. They were forced on us by circumstances and we had improvised as best we could.

"In Germany and Italy, in Poland, in the Mideast, Africa, Asia, the people's movements and our Parties struggle under severe illegal circumstances, the lives of millions are endangered." I nodded.

"We would like you to serve these movements—" I gasped audibly, tried to cover it with an enforced cough. "—actually, it is most routine work, but helpful and needed."

I realized as I listened that my earlier Berlin trip and another two months later to Paris had been preliminary tests. Apparently, whatever the qualifications, I had passed.

Four-year-old Tim was placed in the Comintern's International Children's Home at Ivanovo, 140 miles northeast of Moscow. Olya and I embraced and went our separate ways. Only Molly remained to welcome me home each time I returned to Moscow.

For the next year I back-tracked my way across Europe again and again. From Stockholm to Athens, London to Warsaw, anti-fascist committees and national liberation front centers worked in enforced exile. Some functioned just across the border of their homeland. The Africans and Asians were far from the movements they helped nurture. The struggles to restore democracy in the fascist countries and to win national independence in the colonies of Britain, Germany, France, Holland and Italy were forced into illegality by the ruling classes. Hounded by police and infiltrated by the various national equivalents of the FBI and the CIA, these committees-in-exile and the movements in the home countries worked under hazardous conditions.

Only the Comintern placed its international resources of organization, finances, personnel and know-how at the disposal of these democratic and independence struggles. Whatever its own internal weaknesses and rigidities, this support was the Comintern's greatest achievement. Less than ten years later, the war alliance of Britain, the U.S. and the Soviet Union leaned heavily upon these organized resistance movements in Europe, Africa, and Asia.

In the early 1930s, however, the situation was quite different. The levels of illegality were complex. Like many others, Gene was a political representative of the Comintern, working with the movements and organizations in the countries he went to. Unlike Gene, I and others were not part of this often large contingent active in various parts of the world. Instead, we serviced the needs of all these committees, movements, and individuals, helping them to maintain contact with each other, enabling them to exchange opinions and analyses, bringing them financial sustenance. All of these were simple acts which could be performed by the postal service, if the people's struggles we aided had not been outlawed.

I travelled for a year, a liaison for persons and movements and organizations I never met. I saw only one contact in each city where I stopped and, as on my first trip to Berlin, I was under instruction to enjoy the tourist life until I was sent on to the next city. Periodically, I was sent home to Moscow for a week or more, and then went abroad again. For days on end I talked only to train porters, hotel clerks, travel agents, restaurant waiters. The highlight of each day was the brief coffeehouse or park bench meeting with my contact. But these, too, remained anonymous faces. Only with Gr. in Berlin did I develop a personal friendship. Whenever possible I would route myself through his city, establish independent contact with him according to a method he gave me, and for a few hours, a day, a night, I was a human being again.

In late spring I returned to Moscow determined to win release from my assignment. Gr. had told me that no one had lasted this long in the grueling routine of isolation; a couple of months was the most anyone had been able to take. I knew that it was time for me to pick up Tim and go home to the States. My international experience, all of it, from the moment I had arrived in Moscow, had been sensational. Now I knew I should go home, back to my own country.

In Moscow, before I could tell my chief of my decision, he informed me that I was to leave for Shanghai in four days. Such an assignment was irresistible, and I voiced no objection. I was told, too, "Your husband is in Shanghai, and although you may be there for a time, you are to be guided always by our security rules, not his."

I fled the narrow, dark corridors, walked blindly toward Red Square, turned in at the foot of Tverskaya, walked its length to the Luxe. Shanghai. Gene. Was it possible I could be there—and for some time—and not see him?

XI

I arrived in Shanghai in the middle of the damp, humid summer and found the city fascinating, repelling, and strangely frightening. A city of contrasts. A citadel of foreign white supremacy and extra-territorial rule. Modern skyscrapers lined the Bund, a broad promenade along the Whang-poo river. From their leather and chrome offices, the bankers and mercantile corporate managers siphoned off China's wealth to the home country. Foreigners lived in modern homes surrounded by parks behind bamboo stake fences, exempt in their personal, business and political activities from the jurisdiction of the Chinese government. There existed within China an independent exploiting world where foreign nations maintained their own courts, police force and exclusive control over their own nationals.

To the north and northeast, the city finally belonged to the Chinese. In narrow alleys, in the stink of open sewer drains, they crowded by the hundreds of thousands; the homeless living on teeming streets, huddled around tiny fires over which they cooked a spoonful of rice; sleeping in rags, mothers hugged children to their breasts in doorways and on curbstones.

Shanghai was a city in which it was too easy to conform to the life of the arrogant American tourist. My work demanded I do just that, yet I shrivelled at the prospect of playing at being a part of the Western white society in China.

Somewhere in that noisy, garish city there was a powerful, illegal Communist Party. In rural provinces to the north and east there were Soviet governments established by the victories of the peasant Red armies. However, as in Europe, I was not to see or feel or know these revolutionary movements. After making contact, I was to do nothing, only wait.

Horrified at my first sight of whites being carried in rickshas pulled by bent, sweating "coolies" along The Bund, down Bubbling Road, Nanking Road, and through the narrow alleys in the Chinese quarter, I remonstrated to my contact, "How can they! I'll walk or not go out at all; I won't ride in one of those."

He sternly instructed me, "You will do as all whites do here. You will not walk, you will take rickshas and you will do so at your hotel door."

He smiled approvingly only when I mentioned that for a few days I would be squired about town by the French ship's officer I had known on the month-long trip from Marseilles.

I lay on my mosquito-netted bed, uneasy, more lonely than usual, trying to rest before dressing for dinner. Above, the wooden paddle fan droned ineffectually. The closed balcony and window shutters seemed to hold the sultry air in and muffled only slightly the street noises.

There was a light tap at the door. Probably the maid with fresh towels I thought, as I opened it. I saw first an outstretched hand offering a single, long-stemmed rose, then the broad, towering shoulders in well-tailored summer grey, the lean, tanned face, the blue eyes that crinkled as he said:

"Welcome to Shanghai, may I come in?"

My spluttering "How did you know? We shouldn't. . . ." was muffled against his shoulder as he caught me up in a bearhug and slammed the door with his foot. I joined his infectious laughter with gratitude at the answer to my loneliness—and what an answer!—but finally I managed, "Seriously, you shouldn't be here. I'm not supposed to see you."

Gene laughed, "Nonsense, how do you think I knew you were at the Palace Hotel? Relax, I'm pulling rank on you and your boss, okay?"

I was confused, but too happy to argue. The estrangement in Moscow suddenly dissolved.

"Come on," he urged, "get dressed. I'll take you to dinner." I hesitated, wondering how he would take my reply.

"I can't. I have a dinner date with a friend from my ship, he'll be here in an hour, and . . . ."

"I know," he interrupted lightly, "you are to be seen with him as much as you can." I could hear the quotation marks around his words.

"Okay," he said, "see your friend while he's in town; we have time. I understand you're staying awhile."

"I don't know. I'm not sure of anything right now."

"Well, you are." Turning to go he used the gesture of so long ago, putting his forefinger to his lips and then to mine, he said: "I'm glad you're here," and left.

My heart soared, but my mind nagged: Why now and not in Moscow? Am I going to be that easy, without demanding explanations? Is this for real or a game he's playing? I didn't care. If it was a transitory game, I'd play it. If it was for real, I wanted that too. My hurt id, my silent defenses of my individuality and dignity—all so vital in Moscow—evaporated. Shanghai, I love you.

XII

The next few days passed quickly. My ship's officer, impressive in his summer whites, came daily, sometimes alone, sometimes with his French friends. We went to the race track built by the British in the center of the city; we dropped in for drinks at the exclusive Shanghai Club; we did the night spots. I was caught up in the social whirl so highly approved of by my contact. I even learned to hide my distaste at using rickshas.

My ship's officer finally sailed and, although my contact insisted I accept invitations from his French friends who continued to call, I began to spend more and more time with Gene. My contact obviously knew this but neither of us mentioned it. Evidently, Gene was in an official position to make his own decisions on that matter.

Unlike the past, Gene did not talk of his specific work. When he said, "I have to go out," I remained at his apartment. When he said, "I'll be away for a few days, I'll call when I get back," I stayed at my hotel and went through the tourist motions.

I did not know how he shed his outward life as the privileged foreigner living in his tastefully furnished, servanted apartment in the French Quarter of the International Settlement, nor how he disappeared into the life of the central committee of the Chinese Communist Party working illegally in Shanghai. I did not tell him of my contact meetings nor did I discuss with him my puzzlement at the indeterminate status of my unusually prolonged stay.

Gene did expound at length, but in general terms, his views

on the Chinese revolution, the country's history, traditions and experiences which molded the unique revolutionary situation. He detailed the long lunches he had with Madame Sun Yat-sen and expressed admiration of her vision for the New China. He described his visits into the Soviet provinces and he referred approvingly to decisions being taken there which made the Chinese road to socialism somewhat different than the one taken in the Soviet Union. At that time in the early 1930s this difference was not very obvious to the other Communist Parties abroad. Gene did not take sides, he merely emphasized the logic of different circumstances in each country.

Of his work with the Comintern group and its relations to the Chinese central committee in Shanghai, he voiced impatience with "advisers who come here with blueprints made elsewhere."

I teased, "But that's what you are, an outside adviser, aren't you?"

He grinned, "Yes, like the others." Then, "But at least I'm trying to understand what's happening here. We've got to know the country, we have to listen to the people here, we have to learn their experience. Comintern resolutions are guidelines, not instructions."

Gene had arrived in Shanghai at a critical moment. He became involved in sharp recriminations among the Chinese leadership and the Comintern group regarding a real threat to the Soviet provinces and the Red armies. Gene knew well the history of the party's different stages and changing tactics in the anti-imperialist, national liberation struggle. I generally was familiar with the early 1920s stages of united front cooperation with all anti-imperialist elements. The Communists broke with the Kuomintang in 1927 after the workers' uprisings in Shanghai and Canton had been crushed by Chiang Kai-shek who had suddenly moved from a national front with the Communists to become commander-in-chief of an army financed and equipped by the U.S. and Britain.

Sharp differences regarding the new course erupted after 1927. Those in the Chinese Party leadership in Shanghai continued to depend upon the classic view that the city proletariat and the trade union movement were the key to the revolution. They were supported by the majority of the Commtern group who enunciated the generally accepted view in the international Communist movement at a time when the Russian Revolution was the blueprint for all.

Mao Tse-tung and the Red armies bypassed the cities where foreign imperialism ruled, instead leading successful armed peasant revolts and organizing Soviet provinces. After 1927, the Shanghai group, with the support of the majority of Comintern advisers, abandoned the united front and the concept of the broad anti-imperialist character of the struggle. They emphasized instead the task to win the city proletariat to the Communist Party.

In the Soviet territories where actual armed battles were fought, the new provincial governments and the Red armies sought and established military alliances with any local warlords who would place their armies in struggle against the Japanese invader and against Chiang's armies, which were fighting the Red armies instead of the Japanese. The central committee in Shanghai abrogated those alliances. Chiang Kai-shek launched a massive pincers offensive against the Soviet provinces which, shorn of their buffer allies, were now entrapped.

While the urgency of the military situation precluded a full assessment of responsibility, feelings ran high, and these were the issues Gene referred to obliquely. His veiled criticisms indicated his support of the views of the comrades in the Soviet provinces. These views were based upon the belief that the specific conditions in China merited different approaches to the movement in the strongly foreign-held cities as opposed to the vast peasant lands which made up most of China where the repressive state organs were splintered among local warlords fighting each other. As to the united front tactic, Gene believed that the very nature of these alliances with temporary allies inherently create shifts and change, that failure in one instance was no reason to abandon it in another set of circumstances.

The result of debate over how to break through Chiang's choking off of the Soviet provinces and isolating the Red armies, was the historic Long March, a year-long retreat of 100,000 men, women and children over 8,000 miles of mountains, rivers and plains, It was an offensive retreat that liberated areas, recruited troops, and reached the caves of Yenan to re-form the Soviet power, the Party and the army. It was a feat of herculean magnitude, but nonetheless a retreat forced on the Chinese comrades by the treachery of Chiang Kai Shek and the mistakes of the Communists.

Before this historic action began in late October, my own Shanghai dream-world burst. In September I was told I was leaving for Moscow in three days. Gene's "Damn!" pleased me, but it did not alter the tenuous status of our relationship. Neither of us would initiate serious talk about our futures, together or apart. The pleasant interlude was over.

The day before I left he asked me if I would carry back a confidential report to his chief at the Far Eastern Section. Reports and documents were relayed regularly through official channels; that was my job. But never had I transmitted anything not given me by my formal contact.

To my question, Gene cryptically replied that his report raised certain questions about the group's work here and it would not be accepted here for transmission.

"I want my views to get back there, but it's your decision to make. I'll understand."

By French liner to Osake and Kobi, on a Japanese cargo ship to Vladivostok, then ten days on the Trans-Siberian Railway across the breadth of the Soviet Union, I finally arrived in Moscow. After checking in with my own chief, I hurried downstairs to the Far Eastern Section where, with a sigh of nervous relief, I turned over Gene's document.

In preparation for writing this book, I tried to track down that report as well as others Gene had submitted during his work with the Comintern. My requests for access to the archives were buried in polite silences. With Party history too often officially re-written to suit pragmatic needs of the moment, the authenticity of that intriguing document written by an American Communist in China in 1934 could no longer be vouched for were it to be officially released now or at some later date.

XIII

My continual requests to be released to go home to the States were countered with "just one more trip." The weeks became months, each trip was followed by another, each sold to me on its importance, its necessity. Returning to Moscow in early January, 1935, after six weeks in Istanbul, Cairo, Haifa, Tel Aviv, I found Gene settled in our old room at the Luxe. He had just returned and was preparing to leave for the States. He grinned and asked, "You ready to come home with me?" So ended, without convoluted explanations, our strange hiatus. I cynically noted how quickly I won my release now that it was linked to his.

Dimitroff and Manuilsky, the decisive comrades in the

Comintern's political hierarchy, did not want Gene to leave. Although it was not generally known at the time, in six months there would be a bold shift in the Comintern's political perspectives. Gene's emphasis in South Afria, the Philippines and China on fluid broad coalitions and alliances which placed Communists in the mainstream of struggle for the everyday needs of people, was now the essence of what the Comintern would soon project. Gene was urged to remain in international work to help initiate this important shift. But he was adamant. If his experiences and work had been valid, he wanted to apply them in his own Party, in his own country.

We decided to gamble on the practical problems he faced, since we could not resolve them. There was the old Imperial Valley warrant, the many bail forfeitures on secondary arrests, and now the four-year fugitive status. Because these were all city and state cases Gene thought extradition would not be sought if he stayed out of California. The Imperial Valley prisoners had been released after serving two and a half years and he believed that his arrest on those same charges might not be actively pursued, especially in the present labor upsurge of the new Roosevelt era. Browder and Foster in New York were consulted and they upheld Gene's decision.

The bombshell was dropped quietly, after all other problems had been cleared away. Almost casually, Manuilsky informed us that we could not take Tim back, "not now with you. We will send him at some other time, under other circumstances."

Stunned, we listened in silence to the explanations. Our Comintern comrades placed us in the same category as the hundreds of illegal personnel constituting the active cadre of the international organization. They were particularly concerned that the recent recognition of the Soviet Union by the U.S. should not be jeopardized in any way by right-wing distortions of activities such as our four years abroad. Not only these activities but even our having been in Moscow was to remain a permanent secret. Technically this was possible because visas into and out of the Soviet Union were not stamped into one's passport but issued on a separate piece of paper. The whole aim was to return home as unobtrusively as possible and not ever refer to the past four years. For this purpose, a five-year-old child speaking only Russian during the five days of the ocean voyage, at passport control and in the first months of our return was a liability that could not be included.

Back in our room Gene paced grimly. With a drink in one hand and a chain-lit cigarette in the other, he sought to bring his emotions under control. For once, I remained silent. With back to the wall, I stood hugging my body with crossed arms, keeping it from falling apart. I could not accept this decision, yet the only alternative was to refuse to leave, to remain in Moscow with Tim; I knew the comrades would agree to that. But staying on here resolved nothing. Gene would not become an expatriate for me or for Tim; he couldn't. And the longer Tim and I stayed, the more reasons there would be against Tim's returning with me at all. I faced the fact that the only way to get Tim home was for us to go ahead and pave the way by assimilating ourselves quickly and fully into the home scene.

Many questions disturbed me. Living in Moscow was no crime; why did we have to conceal it? While the movements in the countries we had worked in were illegal and forced underground and had to be protected at all times, we individually were not. Foreign liberals and journalists swarmed about the fringes of the anti-fascist movements in Europe and the liberation fronts in Africa and Asia and spoke and wrote freely of their experiences. Why would the participation of Comintern activists be suspect?

These were the facts presented by responsible comrades. I was in no position to know how much was political paranoia and how much was reality. I did know that anti-communism at home was no less virile in its own way as it was abroad. Whether in Los Angeles in 1929-1930 or in Berlin in 1933 or Shanghai in 1934, the struggles for bread, democracy, independence were labelled an illegal Communist conspiracy. Everywhere we lived under the gun of repression. In choosing the life of the fulltime revolutionary, we were beyond the norms of ordinary persons. Only in Moscow were we and our comrades entirely safe. I thought of the few hundred children of all nationalities and races I had seen in my visits to Tim at the International Home. They were children of comrades working underground in Hitler's Germany, Mussolini's Italy, in Asia and Africa. They were the children of comrades who had been tortured, imprisoned or executed in their home countries for their revolutionary activity. Their children were growing up safe in the new socialist world. With them, Tim too would be safe, protected, given the best that socialism could offer. And it was only for a short time. They had promised.

Four:
SINKING HOME ROOTS AGAIN

I

Tired but exhilarated we walked briskly, our hands brushing lightly as they swung free at our sides. Stiff from sitting too long on small, hard, slatted, folding chairs in a room dimmed with clouds of stale smoke, we were at the same time pleased with the two-day Party conference out of which new policies and plans emerged. We walked along the lakefront savoring the moment. Gene broke the relaxed silence.

"That was a fine thing that happened this afternoon." I nodded.

"I envy you," he continued. "that is the way it should be, but rarely is. I know you were angry in New York, but look how it worked out. Me they accepted here because I had been sent, but you they now chose because they got to know you and respect your work."

We had travelled separately from Moscow, and, when I had arrived in February Gene had already been assigned as state secretary of the Party in Wisconsin. Shifting people around the country was standard procedure. While local organizations formally voted acceptance of the new leader, a thumbs-down vote was rare.

Returning from study and work abroad, I too was up for reassignment. I had been told there was no opening in Wisconsin. I could take over state education work in any one of a number of other state organizations. I was annoyed that neither Gene nor the comrades of the Organization Department had considered our assignments collectively. Gene had waited silently for my response. Irritated as I was, I did not hesitate. The estrangement abroad made me wary of separations. I knew some high principle was involved, but all I wanted was a Party assignment with Gene. I did not want to do battle for women's rights. In my perverse way I was still defending my right to be Gene's wife *and* a Party activist; it was still a single-handed skirmish.

So we had come to Wisconsin. Although I was without official assignment and Gene's Party wage was more promise than fact, it did not occur to either of us that I should look for a paying job. We hauled a discarded bed and table from a comrade's basement, we unpacked our single bag in the one room apartment we found off Wells Street near the lake, a few blocks from Party headquarters, and we reported for work; Gene officially, I unofficially.

Now at this Sunday conference, four months later, I had been elected to the state committee, to the state board, designated state education director and dubbed a fulltime functionary. This meant that the non-existent payroll doled out in pennies each morning was now divided five ways. In addition to Gene and myself there was our farm-raised trade union secretary—long-legged, nervous dynamo Elmer; also stocky, laconic Fred Blair, our organization secretary who knew every inch of the state and every oldtimer in Wisconsin, which his French-Canadian ancestors helped settle; and there was bouncy Sig, our youth organizer from New Jersey by way of a year around the university campus in Madison.

At first I had been inhibited about responding to friendly overtures. I was too burdened with the prohibitions placed upon us in Moscow and then repeated for emphasis in New York. They had created two young people without a past and I didn't know how to handle it. We could not refer casually, as one does to one's past, to California. The last four years were an unaccounted-for void. Talk of offspring left us silent, as Tim's existence in Moscow was to be forgotten. Only our new names of Eugene and Pegy Dennis created no problems. We had become accustomed to name changes and we liked the ones we had selected.

Gene adapted to the political scene in Wisconsin easily; I had some difficulties. For weeks he chided me about my public speeches. It appeared that I persisted in saying "we" when I spoke of the Soviet Union and China, and "you" when I referred to the American people. "You've got to get over this, Peg; it sounds awful, as though you were an outsider."

Under the pressure of activity I quickly rejoined the American people, in proper pronoun and in total identification. I had to move rapidly, though. I had a lot of catching up to do. We had missed four important years and we had come back on the eve of sweeping policy changes initiated by the seventh congress in Moscow, six months after we left.

George Dimitroff had emerged from a fascist prison to turn his Leipzig trial into a searing indictment of Nazism. He had proved that victories over Hitlerism could be won. Under his leadership and under the impact of world events, the Comintern reassessed its policies and tactics.

The shockingly easy take-over by Hitler in January, 1933 had shaken civil libertarians and Communists alike in all countries. The easy smashing of the two powerful working class parties and the labor movement, even as they squabbled among themselves calling each other the main enemy, had a sobering effect. Reassessment within the international Communist movement started before the Comintern congress sessions.

By late 1934, after the costly Long March retreat the Chinese Party readjusted its tactics and was now pursuing the anti-imperialist, all-people's front struggle against both Japan and Chiang Kai-shek. In France, a first-time official alliance of the Communist and Socialist parties, the confederations of labor and the liberal, democratic forces defeated a bold fascist electoral bid for power. In Spain popular front stirrings were emerging to block a reactionary challenge to the new conservative republic.

Now the Comintern shifted gears on two vital questions— its attitude toward bourgeois democracy and a broadened concept of the united front tactic into a people's front struggle against fascism. Dimitroff paid tribute to the heroism and sacrifice of our German comrades, but he added, "Heroism is not enough." He called for daily work among the people, including inside the fascist mass organizations on specific grievances which would bring the people directly into struggle with the fascist state.

In 1931 the Comintern and its affiliated parties had taken a dim view of bourgeois democracy. Its characterization of Social Democracy as the main enemy was in large part based upon its adherence to bourgeois democracy instead of proletarian revolution. The Comintern had charged:

"By drawing a contrast between the 'democratic' form of the dictatorship of the bourgeoisie and fascism, social democracy lulls the vigilance of the masses [and] conceals the counter-revolutionary character of bourgeois democracy as a form of dictatorship of the bourgeoisie, and thus itself serves as an active factor and channel for the fascization of the capitalist state."

In 1935, however, while still critical of Social Democracy's non-struggle adaptation to fascism's incursions, the Comintern congress declared:

"It is not a matter of indifference to us what kind of political regime exists in any given country, whether a bourgeois dictatorship in the form of bourgeois democracy, even with democratic rights and liberties greatly curtailed, or a bourgeois dictatorship in its open, fascist form."

It declared we Communists would "defend every inch of the democratic gains made by the working class." So was born the concept of the Communists' call for struggle against fascism as the main enemy of all peoples, in defense of democracy everywhere. It was a changed policy and concept that helped change the course of history for the next decade.

Under the impact of the costly experiences and with a new perspective that Communists everywhere would be moving into the broad mainstream, the congress enunciated for the first time the principle that the Comintern now "will avoid direct intervention in internal organizational matters of the Communist parties." It urged each Party to "avoid mechanical application of the experience of one country to another country and the substitution of stereotyped methods and general formulations for concrete analysis." Not until 1956, after Stalin's death, did some of the stronger Communist parties begin to examine these ideas.

II

We had been abroad during the worst years of the economic crisis. I had been in Moscow and Gene in the Philippines when Roosevelt became president in 1932 and his unprecedented measures to save U.S. capitalism created a furor. We were in China the summer our Party at its national convention branded the Roosevelt administration "a pro-fascist government," and warned that Section 7a of the National Recovery Act affirming labor's right to organize and bargain collectively through unions of its choice was a demagogic false promise. Events, however, proved less schematic than our Party saw them.

From its viewpoint and its needs, U.S. capitalism had two ways out of the crisis. It could take Germany's way to fascism or institute some government controls over the national economy while retaining bourgeois democratic processes. Because the country was not straitjacketed into fascism, despite specific fascist-like economic and financial measures, contradictory movements and big struggles erupted and the labor movement together with the Communists and the liberals reached an unprecedented level of activity, organization and achievement.

Returning in 1935 we had missed the initial stages of this totally new situation. We found new moods dividing the country. Some circles of Big Industry and Big Business, originally grateful for Roosevelt's drastic actions on their behalf, now turned against him. They demanded cutbacks in the social programs the Administration had conceded to the rising militancy of the unemployed and hungry. They demanded repressive action against the mushrooming mass movements. Vast government works projects—from road and hospital building to art and theater groups—had put millions to work. Workers in the unorganized Big Monopoly industries of steel, auto, rubber, communications and transport were running with Section 7a and unions were organized where none existed before.

In Wisconsin, as elsewhere, the pivot was the wide network of new organizations with which Gene and I had to familiarize ourselves: the Workers' Alliance of the unemployed and the project workers; the American Student Union and the American Youth Congress; the American League Against War and Fascism—a juncture point of labor and the middle class; the National Negro Congress—organized to counter the conservatism of the N.A.A.C.P.

Then there was the wave of industrial unions which put the stamp of militancy and independence on all the movements. On this labor front the battle was not only against the monopolies actively opposing the right to organize. The fight was equally sharp againt the dominantly white, craft union leaderships of the A.F.L. These new, militant industry-wide unions, based upon a new breed of formerly unorganized, young, Black and white workers, were a threat to their entrenched power—and they fought the new movement.

In Wisconsin the established labor movement had a unique local twist. The A.F.L. leaders were closely inter-connected with the Progressive Party state administration and the Socialist Party city administration of Milwaukee. In this governing third party dominance, a radical aura served as facade for a cynical, pragmatic conservatism. In the factories of Falk, Harnischfager and Allis Chalmers the new union activists contended with employers' Pinkerton labor spies. In the labor movement they battled oldtime, sophisticated Red scare tactics of the A.F.L.-Socialist leaderships.

But the industrial union drive did not abate. In Racine, Janesville, Kenosha, Milwaukee, the workers organized their new unions, ignoring orders that they disband and individually join the proper craft union. The Wisconsin Committee for Industrial Organization was formed inside the A.F.L. in November, 1935, with sixty-two union affiliations. The young leadership was closely allied to the political and anti-fascist coalitions being formed throughout the state.

Gene's manner of contact with all these diverse movements was individual, personal, casual and varied. Over a beer in a tavern with workers off a strike picketline he helped plan new, independent, rank and file action. In the kitchen of a C.I.O. organizer he helped committees map a two-prong campaign to organize the factory over employer resistance and to wrest a charter from the AFL. Lounging around the living room of Left Socialist Meta Berger, he discussed with young militants how to force debate within the Socialist Party for united action with the Communists. In hotel rooms with staid A.F.L., Progressive and Socialist Party leaders he argued, cajoled, smilingly threatened. He talked from the strength of a small but cohesive state Communist Party, which despite its 600 members, had more than one hundred union officials, nearly three hundred of its members active in the C.I.O. and A.F.L., and a popularity and influence far beyond its numerical status. And these leaders with whom he met knew that members of their organizations were joining our party at the rate of some sixty each month.

Gene's style of work was not too different than it had been at Woodland, in Los Angeles, with his students in our room at the Luxe in Moscow, in Africa or China. Only the specific circumstances were different. Of this style, native Wisconsinite Fred Blair, who had seen New York-sent organizers come and go, wrote years later:

"Objective circumstances during those years favored progress. But the forward strides taken by the people in Wisconsin did not come automatically. It required the kind of leadership and ability that Dennis furnished for the whole popular movement to leap so far ahead. It was the speed, decisiveness, boldness and imaginativeness that Dennis showed in putting the united front into effect that made a great difference.

"His power of convincing was equally effective with rank and file workers and with the most highly placed political and trade union leaders.... These people, even those who opposed him, developed a profound respect for Gene Dennis and his Party.... Gene left people on their own to solve problems for themselves, and often when they came to him for advice all they got was an encouraging smile or shrug, or a couple words after they had talked out their problems. But generally that proved sufficient. He always cultivated a feeling of confidence among those who worked with him, and those who did so never felt stifled or afraid to make decisions."

III

When the state A.F.L. leadership ordered the C.I.O. committee to disband or be suspended within eight months, Gene's office rang with fierce debate. In carloads the union activists, Party and non-Party militants, came from outlying towns. The mood was fighting mad and many urged a mass exodus from the A.F.L. "Screw the piecards, let's leave 'em cold," was the sentiment.

Absorbed in his slow-burning pipe, concentrating on packing fresh tobacco into its bowl, Gene listened. He asked questions—How many workers in the factory would leave the security of the established and national A.F.L.? Who had the work contract, the individual new union or the A.F.L. charter? The questions turned the anger towards discussion of hard facts, to reports on the specific situation in each factory, in each department.

Consensus began to form. "Gene's right; we gotta fight inside as long as we can;" "we gotta give the workers a chance to see who are the real splitters of the labor movement;" "we gotta consolidate C.I.O. nationally, not act alone;" "Gene's right." But Gene had given no "line." He had made no opening speeches or summary analysis. Those who had come to get The Word from The Leader had, instead, probed their own views and, given the opportunity to collectively examine the facts, had come up with the decisions Gene had known they would.

The decision to stay in the A.F.L. and fight for both unity and the right to industrial unions won the respect of the rank and file. So effective was this policy that the Federation of Labor's state convention at Beaver Dam that summer of 1936 was compelled to drop the September expulsion threat. The entire Wisconsin delegation to the A.F.L. national convention voted against the expulsion resolution. For the first time two C.I.O. leaders were elected to the state federation's executive board.

Six months later, however, in line with national policy, the Wisconsin state federation began to expel C.I.O. delegates from the Central Labor Councils. Physical force was used when the militants refused to relinquish their elected seats. The onus for splitting the labor movement was now squarely upon the AFL leadership.

Emil Costello, president of Federal Industrial Union No. 18456 in Kenosha, was also a newly elected member to the state legislature on the Farmer-Labor-Progressive Federation ticket. He was chairman of the C.I.O. committee and one of the two elected to the A.F.L.'s executive board at the Beaver Dam convention. That Board asked him to resign in compliance with the national A.F.L.'s actions to remove all C.I.O. people. Young Costello refused and was put on trial for "aligning himself with alleged Communists." He boycotted the trial, informing the Board that he was "too busy in union organization and helping to conduct the strikes at Bucyrus-Eric [one of the largest excavation machine building plants in the world] and at plants in steel and auto." As for the charge of following Communist Party dictates, his statement read:

"I take my instructions from the C.I.O. and Steel Workers Organizing Committee for whom I am active as field representative. Politically, I am anti-fascist. Among the wide circle of people in the labor movement whom I am proud to call my friends and associates there are Socialists, Communists, Progressives and Farmer-Laborites."

As a result of the expulsions, the C.I.O. formed a new, independent labor organization. In Wisconsin sixty-two local unions formed the independent C.I.O. state Council, affiliated to national C.I.O. Emil Costello became its chairman and Harold Christoffel, the young president of the new industrial union at the giant Allis Chalmers machine building complex, became its state secretary.

IV

The political realignments forming in other states appeared in characteristically different form in Wisconsin. Elsewhere around the country polarization was occurring inside both the Democratic and Republican parties. The single main issue was the social aspects of the Roosevelt New Deal programs. In Wisconsin the governing Progressive and Socialist third parties joined with the State Federation of Labor, the Workers' Alliance, Railway Brotherhoods, and the three state farm organizations to form the Farmer-Labor-Progressive Federation, an electoral alliance nominally to the left of and independent of the Democratic party.

To Governor LaFollette and his Progressive Party contingent, and to Milwaukee Mayor Dan Hoan and his Socialist old guard, the Federation was a horse-trade deal to deliver votes to each other. It was intended to meet the rising demand of their rank and file for militant, independent, united, political action.

We Communists were aware of the leaders' motivation. However, we welcomed the new formation as a possible embryo of a people's coalition. We urged broadening its base beyond the original founding organizations. Our comrades and other militants inside the new Federation, and inside its affiliated organizations, put substance into the form. Despite efforts of the Progressive and Socialist leaders to keep the Federation as an ad hoc electoral channel for themselves, our people organized active rank and file clubs in the neighborhoods.

The more the Hoan Socialists tied their party to the La-Follette kite, the more they claimed Socialist victory in getting into the Federation's preamble the socialist-tinged commitment to a future society based upon production-for-use. We Communists, however, saw the Federation as a broad, anti-fascist alliance committed to militant economic and social programs for immediate action, not a revolutionary substitute for the Socialist or Communist parties. We publicly urged Communist and Socialist working class unity outside the Federation while supporting the Federation for the broad coalition it should be. Rank and file Socialists supported our efforts, the officials turned us down cold every time.

We encouraged militant Left activists to become Federation candidates and we helped organize their campaigns. As a result, a core of young, first-time legislators, rooted in the new C.I.O. and anti-fascist mass organizations, were sent to the state capitol. At the same time, we were candidly critical of the specific weaknesses of the Socialist, Progressive and Federation leaders.

The 1936 electoral campaign throughout the country was a tightly-drawn, polarized battlefield. From Right field the cry was "Stop Roosevelt and Socialism." From Left field Socialist Party candidate Norman Thomas also claimed the issue was capitalism versus socialism. He accused the Communists of giving up the struggle and opting for reformist coalition politics.

In Wisconsin the Republicans and anti-New Deal Democrats denounced the Farmer-Labor-Progressive Federation as a "LaFollette-Socialist-Communist united front organized on orders from Moscow to destroy American democracy and its institutions." Inside the Federation the militants and Communists were red-baited by the LaFollette and Hoan people. Meanwhile the swastika-banded Friends of New Germany seig-heiled in the large German and Polish communities and the radio priest Father Coughlin spewed his fascist diatribes from nearby Detroit.

Our 1936 national convention declared the issue was the American derivative of fascism vs. defense of democracy and the people's social needs. We considered abstract calls for socialism, when neither the people nor the circumstances were ready for such fundamental social change, was not only illusionary but reactionary. Such unrealistic posturing, we charged, served to diffuse and weaken the struggle under the guise of revolutionary sloganeering. The convention resolution unequivocally stated, "Roosevelt stands for capitalism. He defends primarily the interests of Big Business and the Southern landowners." However, the social reality was such that we saw important differences between those forces in motion around Roosevelt and the New Deal and those around the decisive monopoly sector attempting to scuttle even the minimal social programs won in struggle, seeking a fascist-like stabilization of the country. The convention defined Roosevelt's vacillatory, unreliable stances, but saw his programs as a "middle course" which had caught the support and imagination of the masses of people. We urged the utilization of this "middle course." But, "under no circumstances," we warned, should the people's movements and working class organizations be subordinated to that limited course.

Our membership was deeply involved in massive

struggles—from the 1929-1930 beginnings of the unemployed movement to the first organization of independent industrial unions, a forerunner of the insurgent C.I.O. confrontations; we had helped win social security legislation, and forced, through mass struggle, the first-time acceptance of the principle of government responsibility for the social needs of the people, even under capitalism. Our activity as Communists had become decisive to the building of Left and Center forces which molded important changes in the fabric of our country. We shored-up and unified these diverse forces, no matter how confused and unstable one or another sector was at any given moment.

V

Before we swung fully into the 1936 campaign, I became, with some trepidation, the director of a three weeks— fulltime statewide Party school. "Director" as denoting head of a staff of teachers, administrators and service personnal, was a misnomer; I was all of these packaged into one. The idea started, as did most of our new projects, with Gene coming in one morning, leaning back in his old swivel chair, putting his feet on the desk, and throwing a couple of questions at us. This time it was, "What is the chief new characteristic of our Party membership today?"

Elmer fidgeted as usual. Fred stolidly sliced a piece of chew tobacco and passed the package to Gene who leaned down for the coffee can they used as spitoon, much to Elmer's and my protesting disgust. Sig, who loved a discussion, waited eagerly.

Slowly the consensus evolved that the membership had become individual leaders, each influencing a number of people with whom they worked in the shops and unions, in their community organizations. We also recognized that our recruits were a new breed—experienced activists, many from other organizations. We concluded that the greatest need was basic education in the Marxist relationship between our daily activity and our basic program and goals as Communists.

The idea of a fulltime school to train cadre for outlying towns and areas, and to refurbish those in the city, evolved slowly, although we soon realized this was what Gene had been leading up to. We had no money, no facilities, no trained teachers, but within a few weeks, as a result of enthusiastic money-raising and food collection around the state, our school materialized.

As director, organizer and the one full-time instructor, I drew heavily on my own Party school experiences. Unlike the Moscow school, Marxist theory in our classroom was linked to the American experience. Unlike the Woodland school, our students came from the picketlines and shops and mass organizations. We tested our theory against their experience, not the reverse. The stormy Case Tractor strike in Racine, the C.I.O. union drive at Nash Motors and Simmons Bed in Kenosha, in machine-building at Allis Chalmers, in Seaman Body Auto Parts in Milwaukee, the slowdown tactic on works projects in Oshkosh and Rhinelander, experiences working for unity with Socialists and Progressives—these were our points of reference.

As we had decided in that first planning meeting in Gene's office, the theme of our school was the United Front in its varied complexities. We examined the United Front, or coalition-building, as an expression of simply getting together with diverse persons and groups for a common immediate purpose.

The concept of the United Front as the crux of the Marxist-Leninist road to revolution itself startled our students. Our study of Marx, Engels, Lenin—and, in those days, of Stalin—emphasized a history of the revolutionary movement rich in struggle against distortions. We identified those who sought only immediate social reforms, forgetting they were revolutionaries. We analyzed those who disdained daily struggle in the name of devotion to revolution. We studied how unity with the mainstream was key to effective struggle. Without daily struggle, we instructed, there can be no revolution-making. Our students learned for the first time that "at the very moment of the October revolution," as Lenin wrote, the Bolsheviks made compromises to form blocs in order to win the support of the "petty bourgeois peasantry."

In our class on Party Organization we explored Lenin's precept that a revolutionary vanguard is always where the people are. In assessing our current practical activity in the state we tolerated no complacency. Gene took as a text Lenin's contention (in his booklet "What Is To Be Done"):

"It is not enough to call ourselves the 'vanguard,' the advanced contingent; we must act in such a way that all the other contingents recognize and are obliged to admit that we are marching in the vanguard."

Marching in the vanguard, Gene taught, was gauged not by how loudly we espoused socialism as an abstract slogan, but by the skill with which we brought Marxist-Leninist foresight and analysis into the immediate struggles; by our ability to correctly define the exact stages of the struggle and the specific relationship of class forces in each stage; by the effectiveness with which we project the road to socialism as an outgrowth of the experiences of that struggle; and most important, by our ability to organize people to act on issues and levels acceptable to them.

VI

I came to our school with a personal problem that at times overshadowed my enthusiasm for my work. I was almost two months pregnant. Irrationally, I had let it happen. Gene did not know. The problem was deeper than a merely on-again, off-again fantasy about creating a substitute child to the lost Tim.

There was an undefinable dichotomy in our lives. We worked exceptionally well together, although Gene was a hard taskmaster. He demanded more from me than the others. He showed less patience for my failings, while making allowances for those of others. However, we each found deep satisfactions in our separate and common activities. Aside from the short term, fulltime school project, I was responsible for the nightly classes we offered at the Workers' School, for our new members' classes, and for the monthly conference of Party club education directors. I rotated weekly to meet with our Party clubs in various factories, helping to put together their Party shop papers.

Gene avoided public speaking whenever possible, because of the permanent effects of his bout with tuberculosis that year in the desert. I, however, was blessed with a booming voice that needed no microphone and a fiery stance that swayed my listeners. I travelled the state speaking, debating, teaching. Then there were assignments stemming from my membership in the state committee, on the state board, and as chairwoman of the Milwaukee county committee.

Gene and I had strong, consuming, satisfying activity, but there was no separation between our official and personal lives. We were losing that unique intimacy we once valued so highly. We talked only of what we were each doing, no longer of what we were feeling. In Moscow we had nearly lost each other because of too much separation. Now I wondered whether we were losing each other because of too much of the wrong kind of togetherness. In classic fashion I sought the traditional solution to call Gene's attention to the personal me—I became pregnant. I knew I didn't really want this pregnancy, and I needed his supportive strength to go through with an illegal abortion. I would tell him when he came out to our school for that last weekend's graduation festivities.

The cabin we shared in the summer camp that housed our school was cold that night. I blurted out my news, immediately regretting that I had not told him, as I had told Mama in Los Angeles seven years ago, that it had been an "accident." As I expected, it was this that shocked him. He asked incredulously: "Since when is that how we decide important questions, alone?"

On the defensive, I flared: "And you'd give me a big political analysis of the world situation as a reason why we can't have a baby like ordinary people."

"Ordinary people," he repeated slowly, sitting on the hard edge of the narrow metal camp cot. "If we were ordinary people, Tim would be here, wouldn't he? If we were ordinary people, I'd be campaigning for more babies than you'd ever want."

"Like your Seattle pipe-dream," I mocked, wanting only to curl up in his arms.

"Yes, like my long ago Seattle pipe-dream." His resigned acquiescence to my sarcasm confused me and I wanted to comfort him, forgetting it was I who sought solace.

He looked at me curiously, "You aren't even sure you want this to happen, are you?" I wasn't, but I hit out angrily.

"And you are sure you don't, aren't you? Good objective, political control at all times, right? Just for once, just once, can't we react like human beings, not political automatons?"

The cot creaked, his hand touched mine, tentatively. "Yes, there's a lot of reasons I can't want this now, you know them. But it's done. Whatever you want is okay. We'll work it out."

I responded, "I'll get an abortion."

A week later I lay in bed, blood-soaked towels pressed ineffectually between my legs. I dozed fitfully. The abortionist had said there might be a little bleeding that would soon pass. He had warned he could not be called. There was no way he would respond. Now something was wrong. I was bleeding too much and I kept passing out. We had no phone; Gene had gone to the store down the street to a pay booth. I moved fuzzily in and out of consciousness.

Opening my eyes, I saw Gene at the foot of the bed. Old Doc, that friendly Party sympathizer who, without ever charging us, took care of Gene's winter pleurisy attacks and our minor coughs and colds, stood at my side. Lifting the blanket, he gasped.

"This is an abortion, isn't it? I can't touch her."

Gene reached across the small room, locked the door, put the key in his pocket. "You take care of her, Doc."

"She needs transfusions; she needs a hospital."

"Okay, let's go."

"I can't," Old Doc pleaded. "I can't be associated with this; it's an abortion!"

"I know what it is." Gripping the footboard, Gene's knuckles were white, his face grim. "You do what has to be done, Doc, and do it fast. I'm sorry, you're the only one who can help us."

The door was unlocked hours later after Old Doc nervously and silently packed me tight, administered various injections, wrote a couple of prescriptions, double-checked that the bleeding was lessening. He left with the instruction that I was to eat a lot of red meat, milk and eggs.

Although we subsequently saw Doc often, professionally and politically, none of us ever referred to that scene.

Meta Berger, a maverick Left Socialist, had taken us under her protective wing shortly after we came to Wisconsin. Now she insisted that I convalesce at her home outside the city. For a week I lived in a pampered cocoon. I was fed rare steak twice a day, handed rich eggnogs in-between meals. Lying on a chaise lounge, I read avidly from the large Berger library and sometimes, just daydreaming, I recalled a previous abortion experience.

In Moscow I was sent to a neighborhood clinic where a doctor confirmed my suspicion that I was pregnant. With an interpreter I appeared at the Luxe before a committee composed of three men and two women. It was not clear to me whom they represented; I had been told they were to pass on my request for an abortion. They asked only two questions. I have one child, yes? I intend to return to my capitalist country for Party work, yes? Request granted. Back at the clinic with my interpreter I got the document that would get me into the abortion hospital. There, with conveyor belt speed, but under controlled medical conditions, I was accommodated.

After two days, if blood counts and temperatures were normal, patients were released. Small fees on an escalating scale were charged since abortions were not considered dire medical necessities. Most of us paid nothing, while in beds next to mine women paid the top fee of fifty rubles.

Now luxuriating out at Meta's home, before returning to our reality of dingy one room apartments and one meal a day at the sleazy lunch counter down the street from Party headquarters, I faced the fact that while in Moscow it had been a faulty contraceptive, this time it had been a deliberate, confused cry for attention. While other women fought for work-recognition, I was still battling for my intimate relationship with Gene and our mutual, satisfying work; I needed both.

VII

With the fulltime school behind us and my abortion crisis resolved, we were again under the pressure of activity.

The strike of the newly organized Newspaper Guild against the Hearst-owned *Wisconsin News* and the *Milwaukee Sentinel* dramatically merged economic struggles with the anti-fascist movement. Union-busting Hearst was one of the nation's chief protagonists of U.S. fascism and an outspoken admirer of Adolf Hitler. The picketlines at the newspaper plants swelled to thousands—project workers from the Workers' Alliance and smartly dressed women of the American League Against War & Fascism marched together with strikers from Cudahy Packing and Harnischfager's Metal, and all mingled with Wisconsin's best-known columnists and reporters. National Guild president Heywood Broun declared the six months' long demonstration of solidarity "the most remarkable seen yet in any newspaper strike in the history of the country."

Four years earlier millions had starved before gratefully going to work on New Deal projects. Now they militantly closed those projects down. They went on strike for a living union wage and protested the firing of their Workers' Alliance organizers. They refused to work outdoors in zero weather without proper clothing provided by the state. When federal and state appropriations for works projects and relief were cut back, Communist and militant non-Communist caucuses organized confrontation with the liberal LaFollette administration.

From towns and rural areas across the state, project strikers and their families marched on the state capitol. They were joined by C.I.O. union members and led by the organization of the unemployed—the Workers' Alliance. They took over the state assembly chambers. While their children played tag in the domed rotunda and the aroma of stew simmering in giant cauldrons on the capitol lawns penetrated the halls, men in overalls and women in calico "legislated" appropriations for the hungry. Governor LaFollette refused to appear, but newly-elected Federation legislators joined their constituents.

On the second day of deliberations police, sheriffs and state militia stormed the sedate halls. They dragged us out of the leather chairs we had expropriated and overturned the field kitchen where we had fed many hundreds for two days. My mind flashed-back to the scalding coffee tank deliberately overturned on children in that raid upon I.W.W. headquarters in San Pedro some twelve years earlier in 1924, and I wondered, does nothing ever change? However, a few weeks later, the Wisconsin legislature voted a two million dollar emergency appropriation to increase wages on the projects and a 20% increase in cash relief payments to the totally unemployed.

Gene continued to stress the need for continued presure upon the large bloc of newly elected Progressive-Socialist-Labor Federation state legislators. He insisted the mass movements intensify, not diminish, the consolidation of electoral victories.

After the project workers' effective take-over of the capitol, a people's conference on farm problems and proposed legislation was held in early March, 1937, encompassing the upper Wisconsin farm areas. A short time later a statewide People's Legislative Conference was held in the state capitol.

Leaders of the Socialist and Progressive parties and the A.F.L. urged a boycott of the conference as a "Red take-over." Still, some 200 organizations from all over the state sent large delegations—local Workers' Alliance councils, farm groups, A.F.L. and C.I.O. unions, ethnic federations, Black churches, antifascist committees. Some fifty newly elected Federation legislators actively participated. Out of sharp debate, a tenuous unity was achieved around the main features of a number of social legislative measures they would fight for together.

Not before nor since has our Party successfully carried through such a complex and valid policy and activity as it did in the years 1935, 1936 and 1937. Amazingly enough, for persons who had never done this before, we developed, not in articles and reports but in action, the broadest, most flexible coalition relations within the mainstream. At the same time we delineated clearly our own independent Communist identification.

While we had a national presidential ticket, the energies of all Party members were concentrated upon the local and state levels where, intimately involved in grass root movements and organizations, we moved with people because we were of them.

Our effectiveness throughout the country was, of course, uneven. Our Wisconsin experiences became a "showcase" example at Party conferences and Gene was called upon to make lengthy analyses at national committee meetings. He was sent to meet with our comrades in Minnesota and New York where the Farmer-Labor Party and the newly-organized American Labor Party had complex relations with the Democratic Party and the Roosevelt New Deal similar to ours in Wisconsin with the Progressive, Socialist and Democratic parties and the Farmer-Labor-Progressive Federation.

Locally our comrades built the Federation clubs into centers of community struggle. They worked tirelessly for the election of those young militants who ran on the Federation tickets. They helped organize rank and file pressures upon the leaderships of the unions and other organizations to force them in a progressive direction.

Meanwhile, independently and as known Communists, we distributed a half million pieces of Party literature at factory gates. We issued weekly a special Wisconsin edition of the Party's national newspaper. At a time when that media was little used in electoral campaigns, except for President Roosevelt's fireside chats, we raised money for forty-four local Communist Party radio broadcasts around the state. We held few Party rallies. Instead, we officially participated in symposia around the state where I, among other comrades, debated spokesmen of other parties and organizations.

We were ruthless with the Republicans and conservative Democrats. We chided the vacillations of the Progressives and Socialists. We urged steps to strengthen the Federation. Appreciative laughter always greeted my quote of Browder's headline-getting charge that "Roosevelt roars like a lion and acts like a rabbit." Yet we emphasized, at all times, our tenacious activity in defense of all those positive aspects of the New Deal which the unholy alliance of the reactionary Republicans and Dixiecrat Democrats were out to scuttle.

Our national slogan at the time, "Communism is 20th Century Americanism," was not entirely precise in its theoretical concept. However, it became a popular form of introducing our belief that socialism was the ultimate solution to the people's needs. It also served to undercut the rabid anti-Communism introduced as a main issue by the reactionary coalition. It was an over-simplified but effective response to the flag-waving, law-and-order Liberty League clique's attempts to label us as foreign, un-American, subversive.

A novel feature that summer were the "schools on wheels" we sent into outlying towns and areas, particularly where our Party had no organization or a very small one. Trucks were equipped with loudspeakers and filled with Marxist literature. Brigades of comrades, many of them students from the University, toured different parts of the state. Stopping a weekend or a week in one area, forums were held, classes were organized, contacts were visited.

Gene continued to move with bold, innovative ideas, overcoming our hesitations with his sheer exuberance and belief that our Party could do anything it set its mind and energy to, just so long as we were in tune with the people. The rest of us could not accustom ourselves to his vigorous, almost defiant confidence in the new recruits and his delegating to them immediate leadership responsibilities. Elmer or Fred would caution, "They have not yet proven themselves as Party members."

Gene retorted, "What sacrosanct initiation do they have to pass? What are we, some kind of secret society?"

I argued that they were not well-versed in Marxism, and Gene impatiently challenged: "That's your department, isn't it? Get these comrades into your classes; help them integrate into the details of the organization. Damn it, they come to us with real struggle experience, we've got a lot to learn from them."

Most of these people grew into the responsibilities entrusted to them and we, "in the top," were kept from becoming a self perpetuating, closed bureaucracy.

It was an exciting, engrossing, satisfying time. Not all was perfection, by any means. Our policy of coalition and independence was not always well balanced. Some comrades worked tirelessly in the New Deal and Federation campaigns and in the new unions and Workers' Alliance branches, but not as Communists. Some interpreted coalition as working agreements with Progressive, Socialist and A.F.L. leaders instead of as struggle on issues which would sharpen rank and file pressures on these leaders. Oldtime Communists distrusted anyone not in the Party and could not adapt to the diversity of the movements we worked with. They were accustomed to having directives handed down among Party members and were inept at convincing non-Party people of the rightness of our views.

VIII

Coalition activity was based upon relationships of our comrades with individuals. One who became a very special catalyst was Meta Berger. Widow of the country's first Socialist congressman, she was a former school teacher, a member of the Teachers' Union and the State Board of Regents of the University of Wisconsin. She held a seat for twenty years on the Milwaukee School Board and the State Board of Education. Outspoken, militant, independent, she was now the prodding radical conscience of her Socialist Party leadership gone reformist. She was a thorny presence among her vast circle of friends, which included the upper echelon of state and local politicians.

When I met her, Meta Berger was sixty-three years old, a plump, white-haired, gentle-looking grandmother. I have seen her agitated, annoyed, impatient, and angry, but I never saw her lose her temper. Her finest weapon against political antagonists was a sharp wit administered with a derisive, yet disarming, smile.

Meta heartily approved of our Party's People's Front tactic. "Long overdue," she commented. She admired our bold, realistic work methods and she was won over personally and politically by Gene.

Our first introduction onto the local and state political scene was when Meta insisted, shortly after our arrival in Wisconsin, that we be her guests at the dinner opening the annual Socialist Party bazaar, a major event attended by all the bigwigs around the state. When we arrived we realized that as her guests we were to sit at the dias-table. Gene held back, urging that for her sake we lose ourselves on the main floor. But she took each of us by the arm, circled that long table, and stopped at each chair, saying to the surprised occupant, "This is Eugene and Peggy Dennis, the new Communist Party leaders in Wisconsin. You may as well meet these two young people now; you're going to have to work with them whether you like it or not."

At large parties in the living room of her home at Thiensville, and at small luncheons in her city apartment, Meta brought together Progressives, Socialists, labor leaders and a sprinkling of college presidents and professors to meet Gene. Her admiration of his lucid and innovative political views propelled her to expose others to his influence. For us these gatherings were invaluable.

The house on the bluff overlooking the lake became, too, a personal retreat. We came alone for a quiet weekend, a brief vacation, for acceptance into a family circle. Meta would ask us many questions about the international movements, but on state and local affairs her knowledge and experience gave new dimensions to our own work.

She was invited to visit the Soviet Union as a member of an American trade union delegation. When she hesitated, Gene urged, "Go see for yourself." Friends and family warned that she would antagonize her anti-Soviet Socialist leaders, but she decided to go.

Anything Meta Berger did or said or wrote was news in Wisconsin and was picked up by the wire services as well. Upon her return her article, "I Saw Russia," created much interest. Her Socialist Party leaders were furious, and Mayor Hoan removed her from his prestigious campaign committee for re-election.

She wrote that she had come away with "respect and admiration for the Russian system." She candidly admitted that there were many things she did not know about the Soviet Union, including the question of "political prisoners." She knew only what she had seen.

"There are no rich and no poor, no owners and no beggars . . . socialism in Russia is not the finished and perfected product, and no one is more insistent on this fact than those who wrought the new order against all odds."

In a secret meeting in her absence the Socialist leadership censured her for these views and for her united front cooperation with the Communists. She appeared before her party's state committee and made an impassioned speech, later published under the title, "I Take My Stand." Meta turned the charges against her into an accusation. They charged her public admiration of the Soviet Union embarrassed the Socialist candidates; her outspoken attacks on the Nazi German government alienated the large German vote; her advocacy of united action with the Communists violated party policy. Meta told the state committee:

"Comrades, I am guilty on all three counts of this indictment. I am proud to be guilty and I do not ask to be excused. I ask your support."

Presenting militant counter-charges of her own, she emotionally made reference to the Hitler concentration camps where German Socialists and Communists alike were interned. She called upon the membership to reject the Red-baiting of their leadership. She concluded with the appeal:

"Almost a century ago, in a little document which rang around the world, a man who has been proved a prophet exhorted us, 'Workers of the world, unite.' I remind you, comrades, while there is yet time."

In the hours spent in her home as she worked on her statement, and again when I read it in print, I was deeply moved by her action. I admired the courage of this woman who, now late in her life, could have basked in the comfortable position of being The Grand Old Lady of the Socialist Party to which she had devoted her life. Instead, with her "I Take My Stand" speech Meta Berger deliberately forfeited that honorary, elitist role her leadership would gladly have assigned her in exchange for her silence. She had to expose what she believed was wrong with her party.

She resigned from the Socialist Party in 1939, at a time when anti-Communism was at a peak in the mass movements, after the Hitler-Stalin Pact. She said at that time:

"I cannot run with a pack that howls for the blood of Red witches when the very hunt is a violation of the liberties by which we Socialists will survive."

Meta Berger died in 1944 at the age of seventy-one.

IX

Late in the spring of 1937 Gene and I decided to try to get to Spain. In the first days of the fascist revolt against the two-year-old democratic government we read avidly and with grim satisfaction the headlines:

"Fascist Rebellion Losing Ground." "Fascist Line Crumbling." "Spain Arms Labor to Crush Fascists." "Workers' Revolutionary Committees Distribute Arms." "Fascists Losing on All Fronts."

Then the headlines began to change and we read with concern:

"Nazi Planes Rushed to Spain;" "Mussolini Aids Spaish Fascists;" "British Government Accepts French Proposal for Neutrality Agreement;" "FDR Drives Neutality Measure Through Congress."

Two weeks after the Franco revolt erupted, our Spanish Aid Committee in Milwaukee got embroiled in a fight for the right to use the City Auditorium for our first public meeting. A permit was refused and, symbolically, our aid to the Spanish war for democracy merged from the start with a struggle against our own local anti-democracy forces.

The Spanish Aid committee became the medium through which, for the first time in local history, the Progressive, Socialist and Communist parties officially participated together. This unity was formalized in the leadership executive positions held on the Committee by Meta Berger of the Socialist Party, Katherine Duncan, wife of Governor LaFollette's political secretary, and myself as representative of the Communist Party.

News of East and West European anti-fascist volunteers fighting in Spain began to appear in the newspapers in early November, 1936. American recruitment started slowly and surreptitiously. The State Department declared it a prison offense for any American to violate the government's neutrality embargo against Loyalist Spain. The French government patrolled its borders with Spain; volunteers caught trying to cross were interned in prison camps.

By the end of March, eighty Wisconsinites were fighting with the Abraham Lincoln Brigade. Gene and I knew them all, most of them personally. Each had come for an interview bearing recommendations from people we knew in their local area or organization. Political orientation was done in New York but we spent time talking, getting acquainted, weeding out the obviously emotionally unstable or wrongly motivated. There were few of those.

Parents and young wives shared with us the cherished, infrequent letters received from volunteers. Young Fred Palmer, electrical worker from Madison, wrote: "I have met comrades here of seventeen different languages; every nation and every religion is represented in this proletarian army." Milwaukee Vocational School stuent Clyde Lenway was the first local fatality.

The gnawing need to be there grew. Speaking night after night at meetings rallying solidarity and financial and medical aid was not enough. Helping to pass resolutions in organizations demanding that President Roosevelt lift the neutrality embargo was not enough. Sending others to join the 35,000 from fifty-three countries now fighting in the International Brigade was not enough. We had to put our own bodies on the line. Our persistent requests to be allowed to go to Spain were finally granted by the Party's national leadership in New York. In June Gene and I sailed for Paris.

Five:
MOSCOW AGAIN, NOT MADRID

I

Despite our impatience, the days of waiting in Paris passed pleasantly. We were told to do the tourist bit, to stay away from the committee arranging our underground passage to Spain. There were too many French police and British and American "neutrality" agents sniffing about.

Although restless and eager to be on his way, Gene fell into the routine and we enjoyed a relaxed, intimate interlude between the concentrated activity we had left behind and the uncertainty of the immediate future.

Returning from one of our many visits to the World's Fair, we found a message directing us to a dinner date in a family-style restaurant down a narrow, cobblestoned alley in Montmartre. There an American comrade Gene knew introduced us to two others—one French, the other German. Over dinner and bottles of wine, we listened avidly to the latest military and political news from Spain.

In turn, we answered questions about the Spanish aid campaigns back home. We speculated about the possibility of Roosevelt's lifting the neutrality sanctions. The French and German comrades felt that if he did, London and Paris would have to follow.

We sat talking, relaxed, smoking the American cigarettes Gene passed around. Then the French comrade abruptly said:

"You are to go to Moscow at once, comrades. The messages came this morning."

Gene looked at the others, waiting for them to laugh at the joke. The German comrade sat silent. The American shrugged,

"That's right, Gene. We got two cables, one from New York, the other from Moscow."

"But why?" Gene demanded.

"The Moscow cable doesn't say. Browder's says something about 'reporting,' probably just a brief side trip."

Still puzzled, Gene turned to me, "You will wait here? Or will you go on ahead if your turn comes up while I'm away?"

Before I could answer, the French comrade shook his head. "No, comrade, the messages are explicit. You are both to go to Moscow. Until you return to proceed to Spain, neither of you are any longer under our jurisdiction."

After a hectic shopping expedition to buy gifts for Tim and Molly and tins of American cigarettes and coffee for friends at the Luxe, we boarded the train the next day.

II

We spent a restless first night in Moscow, housed in a modern two-story addition to the third floor of the Luxe. Phone calls to Boris and Musa, to Bob and Valerie, brought only strange voices saying, *"Ne sdez,"*—not here. Molly was somewhere in the city; we didn't know where.

The small room with its low-slung, undersized Swedish-style furniture irritated us. Gene swore angrily each time he bumped his shins on one of the two couch-beds lining the short walls. The following morning when the car came to take him to the Comintern, he carried with him my repeated instructions—"Find out how we get in touch with Molly; make arrangements for us to see Tim right away."

I spent the day prowling the city, renewing acquaintance with familiar streets and squares, gaping at all that was new and strange. Narrow, cobblestoned Tverskaya had become widened, asphalted Gorki Street. New buildings overshadowed old shabby ones. Slow-plying, horse-drawn carriages were losing their trade to small taxis that darted around pedestrians who still sauntered in the middle of the street as they had when there were only a few official big black cars to avoid. However, it was the old landmarks that welcomed me home. The international bookstore on Kuznetsky Most; the fur shops in Petrofka; the old Metropole Hotel which had formerly been off-limits for us because it was where foreign journalists and dignitaries stayed and where "certain types" of Russians furtively sought foreigners' favors. The Bolshoi Theater; the glass-domed galleries and balconies of the always crowded GUMM department store; and, of course, Red Square, the Lenin Tomb, the Kremlin Wall, the Basle Cathedral. I walked all day, not touristing as in Paris, but caressing with eye and heart the old awareness that I was Home; that unlike anywhere else in the world, here was the embodiment of all we were working towards.

Gene returned late that evening and by his mere stalking into the room it shrank further in size. He bumped into a small blonde-wood chair; it fell on its side like a piece of doll's furniture and he kicked it angrily. The lines at his mouth were drawn, his lips thinly pressed, his face grim. It was an expression I knew well—an attempt to control anger, to prevent words and emotions from exploding.

I curled up on the bed, my legs drawn under me to leave free the narrow space in which he was already pacing. I waited and waited. Then finally I asked what had happened.

In a flat, distracted tone, he said: "Molly now works at the Comintern, in the Press Department. She still lives way out somewhere with her mother and has no phone; she'll call you tomorrow."

"Tomorrow?" I shouted. How could Molly and I be in the same city after two and a half years and casually wait until tomorrow?

Silence. Gene paced. I tried again. "What's wrong?"

Again, ignoring my question, he said: "We don't have to go to Ivanovo; they'll bring Tim here."

More silence, more pacing. Finally I screamed, "Goddamn it! Talk, will you?" He looked at me, surprised. He sprawled across the opposite couch and began.

Manuilsky and Dimitroff had greeted him warmly, asked many questions about the political situation in the States, and then told him our trip to Spain was cancelled. Casualties were running high. Too many leading comrades had been killed. The decision that no more were to go into combat had reached New York after we had sailed.

"What did you say?" I prompted.

"What the hell do you think I said?" his frustration turned on me. "I argued. I pleaded. I charged unacceptable elitism. I got nowhere."

"So when do we go home?" Rejecting the disappointment, I latched on to practical matters. "We should visit Tim before you get into discussions here."

"Relax, we're not going anywhere. New York and Moscow have already agreed, while we were waiting in Paris. I'm to be Party representative to the Comintern here for the next couple of years."

My response was inane. "You're kidding!" I was intrigued; yet I knew Gene would not like the Luxe-Comintern way of life any more now than he had in 1931. But the decision was already made and he was angry.

"By the way," he broke into my thoughts, "they offered us a consolation prize." His voice was heavy with sarcasm. "We can take a fast few days behind-the-lines, a V.I.P. jaunt into Spain before I take over here —"

"And?" I prompted.

"I turned it down, of course. How arrogant can one get? Too damn precious to fight, but allowd to bring good cheer to those fighting and dying; a handshake and a pep talk and a 'carry on, boys' and out? No, thanks."

III

Our immediate concern in settling-down for the long stay was to get a room large enough to include Tim, preferably one in the old section of the Luxe. When Gene called from his office at the Anglo-American Section to tell me I should go look at Room 28, I hurried down the familiar long, dark, first floor corridor. Heavy webbing crisscrossed over the doors, knobs and keyholes of numbers 28 and 29. In three separate places on each door were heavy wax seals that gleamed red in the dim light from the small communal kitchen directly across the narrow hall.

The wife of an English comrade whom I had previously known slightly came out of room 30.

"Hello," she stopped, tea kettle in hand. "You're the new neighbor, are you?"

I explained I had been told to look at Room 28, but obviously I couldn't get in.

"Well, you had better not touch those trappings, against the law, you know."

I asked did she know what infectious disease had been quarantined here, and how long had the fumigation seals been on. She gave a mirthless cackle.

"You *are* a new one, aren't you? Those were Mingulin's

rooms; did you know him? They came for him during the night, they did, and his family got put out a couple of weeks later. Those are security police seals, they are, and you mustn't touch them."

I fled the corridor, not waiting for the slow elevator, climbed the five flights, locked the door and collapsed breathless on the bed.

Mingulin. A round-faced, mild mannered instructor at the Lenin School, later assigned to the Anglo-American Section of the Comintern. One of the few Russian teachers who had spoken English. Dull. Unassuming. I recalled only one incident involving Mingulin. He had been expounding some Marxist-Leninist theory in class. In a burst of creative thinking, I had volunteered some simple American analogies and sat back waiting for the approval I expected at my ability to reduce profound political theory based on German and Russian Party history to everyday Americanese. Instead Mingulin responded coolly.

"Comrade Ryan, you are here to learn what Marx and Lenin said, not to improve or improvise on them; you will please remain with the text." Everyone laughed. I reddened, chastised. And now orthodox Mingulin had been taken by the security police.

Gene came home pleased. "I understand it is actually an apartment, two rooms—28 and 29—and there's a small balcony, too. Sounds fine; did you like it?"

I told him about the sealed doors and what the English neighbor had said. I ended flatly, "We can't take it."

"The room is unimportant," he replied slowly. "We can take it; it's just a room. As for the other, something is happening. I don't know what."

So many comrades were gone from the Comintern, he told me. At his old, Far Eastern section—Safarev, Bob, Boris, others—all were gone. From the East European sections, the Italian, German sections, too. "When I asked about them or assumed they were abroad, people shook their heads and whispered, 'Don't ask questions; they're just gone, that's all.'

Curled on the bed, I watched him warily. Gene paced and we each avoided the questions that hung silently in the air between us.

We moved into Rooms 28-29, laying the ghost of Mingulin to rest in a thick layer of silence in which we also buried our confusion at the contradictions in Soviet life we could only glimpse superficially in our Comintern-Luxe isolation.

Socialist construction was booming. So much was still needed, but so much had been accomplished. Food and bread rationing was gone. Gone, too, were the peasant women and their curbstone barter of milk for our store-bought bread. The Foreigners' Store was now open to the general public. While fresh produce, meats and some dairy products were still available mainly at the old Arbat farmers' market for high prices, the shops once so empty a few years ago, now were stocked with assorted cheeses, sausages, hams, canned fishes and jams. Although shopping was still a laborious, time-consuming chore, the search for food was no longer the desperate, unsuccessful mission it had been in 1931.

The Second Five Year Plan had been completed ahead of schedule and *Pravda, Izvestia* and the English *Moscow News* daily featured stories of the prowess of worker-heroes. Yet beneath the buoyancy of confidence there lurked an uneasy mistrust engendered by Stalin's warnings that no one should be trusted. "Good workers can be wreckers, Stakhonovites (honored production pacesetters) can be wreckers." Suspicion of neighbor, fear of neighbor, spying on neighbor, that was the essence of this latest of The Leader's warnings.

The new Soviet Constitution was lauded around the radical world; giant industrial projects across the vast land were completed; consumer prices were cut; life was better and promised much the Soviet people had not dreamed possible.

And yet, as in 1933, Stalin once again portrayed the socialist society and the Party under seige, threatened by old revolutionaries and socialist cadre, all of whom, he claimed, were foreign agents, some of them "from the very first days of the October revolution."

We did not know at that time that the few public show trials of Old Bolsheviks were but the tip of the iceberg. We did not know that hundreds of thousands of Party and non-party socialist cadre were being imprisoned and executed as political deviationists, spies, saboteurs. We did not know the extent of those purges, but we cannot claim we did not know what was happening. We knew that the Comintern had been decimated. We read of the public trials. True, we read in silence, puzzled and uncomprehending, but we read the accounts and we accepted them. We saw it as part of the brutal realities of making revolution, of building an oasis of socialism in a sea of enemies. We accepted the belief of infallibility of our leaders, the wisdom of our Party. Facts and claims to the contrary were rejected as the very proof of that anti-Sovietism that demanded the vigilance Stalin urged.

Only nineteen years later, when the Soviet leadership admitted the terrible hoax and the needless murder and imprisonment of millions, only then did we allow ourselves to see. Only then, for a short time, was the concept of infallibility of leadership challenged.

In 1961 and again in 1965 when for a short time Soviet people talked to me freely of those years, I found that our reactions in the Luxe had been not too different than those of the Soviet citizens. Many told me the same story. When the security police came for one's neighbor, one shrugged uneasily. "The evidence must be there, the Party would not act otherwise." When the police came for you or your wife or husband or brother or sister or mother or father or uncle or aunt or close friend, "you knew it was a horrible mistake; you believed it would be rectified in a few days." And they waited in silence for almost twenty years for the Party to correct its "mistake."

At the Luxe in 1937 the English-speaking comrades became an insulated group. To our rooms came a stream of English, Australians, Canadians, Irish, Welsh, Africans, Indians and Filipinos. The one subject no one mentioned was the trials, the arrests, the disappearance of comrades from the Comintern and the Luxe. It was as though we each knew we could not trust ourselves to open the lid of that Pandora's box. Our talk was social and banal. Our laughter became too brittle. Our political talk was limited to events back home. There the issues and struggles were clearcut. With bottles of wine, tinned fish, cheeses, loaves of bread on the table, we laughed and drank and ate and danced to the plaintive songs of Edith Piaf played on the highly-prized small victrola we had brought from Paris for Molly.

IV

Tim came to us, a quiet, watchful eight year old, overwhelmed at first by his new family, his new freedoms and the big city, after more than three years in the children's home. He spoke no English, Gene spoke no Russian, and I used a pidgin Russian limited to names of simple objects and a few action verbs. Hands and facial expressions were our chief means of communication. While Tim and I jabbered in my unique brand of the language, with Gene it was total hand-touch. He held the boy at his side in casual embrace while he read at his desk. He walked hand in hand with him down Gorki Street, stopping at bookstores for Tim to pick his choice for the week. He taught the child open-hand boxing in evening jousting, played chess with him by the hour, and when the snows came they skied out at Kuntsevo, the Comintern's weekend resthome. For minor crises, like laying down ground rules and resolving disciplinary questions, Molly was our interpreter.

He became the spoiled darling of our Luxe community. He loved our parties and would wait expectantly for one of us to waltz with him. Off in a corner he would carefully imitate his father's intricate tango, flamenco or Irish jig. Now they were the inseparable Tims—*Bolshoi* (big) and *Malenke* (small).

Gene's old friend Crisanto Evangalista, recuperating from a long illness, came often to our rooms. With Tim's arm around his neck he sat quietly telling the boy, in quite good Russian, of his life as a Filipino freedom fighter.

Many Americans came to our rooms that summer and fall, seeking Gene's aid as Party plenipotentiary. Some wanted to go home although they had become Soviet citizens when they had come with their families in the early years of foreign worker recruitment. Others wanted American Party recommendations as they faced grueling political cleansings in their factories and institutions.

Anna Louise Strong came, agitated and impatient. She was having difficulty getting clearance for a trip into Far East Siberia. She wanted Gene to vouch for her political reliability. I was puzzled why this internationally-known author and long-time friend and resident of the Soviet Union needed Gene as reference. Her no-nonsense aggressiveness seemed more than adequate to carry her through most situations, as her many books on the Soviet Union indicated.

Later Anna Louise Strong was declared a foreign spy in one of Stalin's periodic purges. The American Communist Party remained silent, and exonerated her only after the Soviet comrades did. When she moved to China, I received personal notes and her newsletter for a few years. She died there in 1970.

Eslanda Robeson came one evening with two problems— her husband's decision in London to return to the States after many years abroad as a successful expatriate actor, opera and concert singer; and his decision to send young Pauli to live in

Moscow, "in the only country free of racism." Strongly affected by what he had seen on his first visit to the Soviet Union, powerfully moved by the Spanish civil war and the growing showdown with fascism around the world, and developing from a cultural nationalist into seeing the Negro national struggle as part of the international socialist struggle, Paul had decided to go home, more activist than artist.

Eslanda agreed, but she had some doubts too. Gene listened quietly. He gave no actual advice, but he did comment on Paul's greatness as an artist which, Gene said, flowed from his deep involvement with his people, with all struggling humanity. "There are no walls between artist and the class struggle for Paul. He will find his own way to fulfill himself in both."

Regarding plans to send Pauli to Moscow, again Gene was non-committal, saying only, "If you do, I urge that you make it publicly well-known, and be sure the practical arrangements are such that you can take him home whenever you wish."

Through the open connecting door, I saw Tim's close-cropped head bent low over his writing book as he sat huddled at the large square dining table, his stubby fingers gripping the pen as he concentrated on his lessons for tomorrow's school day.

V

Earl Browder and William Z. Foster arrived in Moscow after New Year's. For ten days all Moscow had been a festival town. It was the first celebration of *Dada Moroze* (Father Frost) and the *Yolka* (Christmas tree) in Moscow I could recall. Buried in deep, shimmering snow, the city glittered with giant lit-up trees in all the squares and parks. We swooped down on shops suddenly bursting with food and gift items, and our festivities for our friends around our own brightly baubled *yolka* were adapted to the days and nights filled with children's theater, children's concerts, children's folk festivals, and skiing at Kuntsevo.

Then it was over and our household lapsed into an uneasy tension. Browder and Foster arrived for Comintern mediation of their differences regarding American Party policies and tactics.

Just before the holidays there had been a critical examination of the work of the British Communist Party, with Harry Pollitt and other leading comrades coming from London. At those deliberations Gene had surprised and miffed the English comrades with his analysis of what he termed the British Party's inadequate policy towards the national liberation movements in the British colonies. He charged the Party with paternalism in its political views and chauvinism in its lack of active support to the colonial struggles.

Now the American Party was under scrutiny and Gene had invited Foster and Browder to our rooms for dinner the day after they arrived. I knew them only slightly and was overwhelmed at having these personages together at my table. In 1928 Gene and I had sat with Foster in a skidrow coffee-house in Seattle while Bill encouraged Gene to return to Los Angeles. Then, as now, I was in awe of this veteran labor hero who, together with Eugene Debs and Big Bill Haywood, were to me of legendary proportion.

Browder I had met briefly in Milwaukee during his 1936 presidential tour. Gene of course knew both of them from the seven months he had worked in the east after leaving Los Angeles in 1930 and from his frequent trips to national committee meetings from Wisconsin.

Now Bill Foster walked into our rooms, without greeting either Tim or me, complaining about his own noisy room. He peered out our windows, punched the mattresses on our beds, asked about the noise levels from street and neighbors. I had the impression that if our rooms pleased him, this tall, spare, querulous man would not hesitate to commandeer them for himself.

Shorter, stockier and colorless, Earl Browder came in silently with a nod to me, a head pat for Tim. He retained throughout the evening that distant, withdrawn air I had noted in Milwaukee. Over the years to come I was unable to figure out whether it masked a self-conscious shyness or a cold disdain.

Despite Gene's efforts, the evening was a dismal, constrained failure. Knowledgeable of the political animosities and policy differences that had surfaced between these two leaders of our Party, Gene had hoped to ease tensions before the official discussions started. Their political differences were real, but Gene felt they were not insurmountable.

In our Party's view a qualitative change had taken place in the U.S. as a result of the 1936 elections. The labor movement, particulary through the C.I.O., and the Black people's struggle had achieved a new level of political maturity and independence. Labor's economic programs had been incorporated into the progressive electoral coalitions; for the first time since Reconstruction the demands of the Black people were consciously, if still inadequately, being raised in these electoral alliances.

With the New Deal social programs under attack from the Right Wing, they became the rally point of defense for the entire left-of-center spectrum. Inside the Democratic Party left-center coalitions took on organized form and became decisive in California, Washington state, Michigan and Pennsylvania. In other states some twenty-eight coalition electoral tickets crossed party lines to bring together progressives from both major parties and independents. In addition, Minnesota, New York and Wisconsin had strong third parties. Throughout the country the forms were fluid, the issues and unity were paramount.

Because these new independent forms, whether inside or outside the two major parties, assured the 1936 victories on the basis of struggle actions, the New Deal as a vehicle for this diverse movement changed its character, in the opinion of our Party. From being the program of the liberal wing of the Domocratic Party the New Deal became a political umbrella embracing a conglomerate of progressive independent action. President Roosevelt, a facile and astute politician, responded to this leftward trend and also to the political debt he owed this massive constituency.

Internationally, fascism was on the offensive. Loyalist Spain was losing its war. Peking, Shanghai and Canton had fallen to the Japanese. Mussolini's troops occupied Ethiopia. Hitler had annexed the demilitarized Rhineland zone and was threatening to march into Austria, Poland and Czechoslovakia. London and Paris was talking compromise and appeasement. In this world scene, Roosevelt electrified the anti-fascist forces with his speech in October, 1937 in which he called for a "quarantine of the aggressors." Peace and anti-fascist advocates, together with the Communists, worked to implement this verbal commitment and win even broader involvement in the struggle based upon the President's call.

As might be expected, the post-election situation and our changed analysis of the home and world scene aggravated divergent opinion inside the Party. Browder too often and too uncritically attributed to Roosevelt and the top labor leadership the leading role in the people's coalitions. He tended to accept the words and programs of liberal New Dealers as accomplished deeds. He appeared to relegate to the coalitions a role subsidiary to the President's liberal posturing.

Foster swung in the opposite direction. He underestimated

the character, diversity, breadth and fragility of the new movements. He complained that we Communists allowed "official leadership of the day to day struggle to rest mostly in other hands than those of the Communist Party." He measured our vanguard role only in the narrow sense of what we did and said publicly in our own name. He shrugged off as inconsequential the new kind of vanguard role we were exercising inside the mainstream.

Foster's characterization of the massive C.I.O. and democratic movements as "this great spontaneous movement" puzzled those Communists deeply involved in organizing, influencing and strengthening the activities and directions of those movements. "Spontaneous" was hardly the word for what they were helping make happen. Foster demanded that this "great spontaneous movement" be channeled into a national farmer labor party at a moment when the coalitions had opted to use the New Deal for their own purposes, and simultaneously to organize other independent state and local forms.

Without mentioning either Browder or Foster by name, the national committee steered a third course. Bypassing Browder's euphoric reliance on Roosevelt, the committee's post-elections analyses emphasized "the growing independent power and political consciousness" of the working class which influenced "the Democratic Party in a progressive and democratic direction." Opposition to the formation of a national farmer labor party at the time was expressed emphatically: "The Party will resist any [such] attempt," the documents stated, and would "support all those measures of the Democratic Party and the Roosevelt administration which have a progressive character."

Now in January, 1938 Browder and Foster came to Moscow to debate their positions. At these Comintern discussions, as well as in subsequent articles and reports, Gene developed further the views of the majority of the national committee which he had helped shape before leaving for Europe in June of the previous year.

Gene argued that a common policy and tactic had to be based upon agreement on three major questions: First, acceptance of the fact that the people's united front against reaction and fascism was the central strategy of this period; second, a realistic and bold estimation had to be made of the exact forces, trends, groups, organizations and individuals that could be won to these coalition movements; third, there had to be clarification of the new ways in which our Party as vanguard works in these specific circumstances.

He warned against relinquishing to Roosevelt and the liberal Democrats leadership of the coalitions in which the needs and the role of labor and Black people were paramount within the unity of the anti-fascist, progressive directions of the liberal, progressive spectrum. He urged that the Communists must at all times, and independently of the coalitions, "candidly and honestly examine the limitations and shortcomings of New Deal legislation" and should "help overcome the slowness with which many of these [social] policies [of the New Deal] are realized in governmental action." These should be done, however, "in such a way as to improve, not exacerbate" our coalition relationships. As for the formation of a national farmer labor party at this time, he called such a move "hasty," "provocative," and warned that it would "narrow down the progressive alignments."

Out of the Moscow discussions that January came the decision that Gene return home at once, despite having served less than one year of the usual minimum two years and often five-year stint as representative to the Comintern. He was to become part of the national leadership in New York, at the "Center."

Manuilsky and Dimitroff defined Gene's new responsibility as that of "balance" between what they saw as Browder's reformist tendencies and Foster's sectarian leanings. The "balance" between these opposites, in political terms, is not simply centrism. It is a complex effort and difficult need to effect a practical, working relationship between the revolutionary goals of the ideologically advance guard and the fulsome participation of that vanguard in the immediate struggles of the broadest strata of the people.

The Comintern had urged upon Browder and Foster a big responsibility for Gene and he was understandably pleased. At thirty-two he had been tapped to work closely in national leadership with our two top Party leaders, fifteen and twenty years older than he, and on the basis of *his* political views, not theirs.

He was startled when I burst into tears and pleaded that we not go to New York. "Any other state or city," I begged, "but not New York, and not into a national position." I had always been uncomfortable with and somewhat derisive of national Party leaders who had breezed into Los Angeles and Milwaukee, made big speeches, knew nothing of our local and state problems, were not interested in helping us with them in any practical way, and breezed back to Party headquarters in New York. Was Gene to become one of them now? And where would I fit into his new life?

Of course I did not affect the decision nor Gene's enthusiastic acceptance of it, and we prepared to return. For the same reasons as given three years earlier, Tim went back to the International Children's Home. Leaving him a second time was less traumatic but no easier. Before Browder had left Moscow he had mumbled something about the possibility of getting Tim home in about a year, due to "an improving political climate." I paid little attention. I no longer believed promises. My only choice remained the original one, that of remaining in Moscow with Tim or going home without him.

Six:
VIEW FROM THE TOP

I

We thoroughly disliked New York from the day we arrived, and we did not overcome that dislike in the twenty-three years we lived there. We were stifled by the strident, crowded, ugly bigness of the city, shocked by the ghettos, and repelled by the dim, dirty subways in which humanity sweated, pushed, rushed. A half block from our East 19th Street railroad flat the Third Avenue "El" clattered day and night. The inferno of that first summer left us gasping for breath in the sooty, heavy humidity.

Gene was now our Party's secretary for politics and legislative affairs. More important, he had become Mr. United Front, doing on a national scale what he had initiated in Wisconsin—coordinating, organizing, encouraging coalition movements and struggles; working with non-Communist individual leaders, militant rank and file groups, and Communist Party organizations in state and local situations.

The current circumstances were different than they had been in 1935-1937. Before, the people's organizations were on the offensive, winning skirmishes and battles on the economic and social front. Now they were in defensive disarray. Bankers and industrialists were on a sitdown strike, withholding needed expansion investment funds, and their representatives in the legislative chambers were cutting back on social appropriations. A newly formed Un-American Activities Committee served as a divisive weapon against the labor and people's organizations. Capitol Hill and the White House became the target of both the grass roots movements around the country and the reactionary offensive of Big Business. Gene and I now spent part of each week in Washington.

Ten millions were still unemployed. The new Federal Social Security Act, victory of the unemployed struggles, provided only minimal benefits to a limited number. Less than three millions were working on government projects at $50 a month. Black workers comprised 14.4% of the totally unemployed and received less than half in benefits than white workers on projects in the south.

"That Man" in the White House, with charm and flair, encouraged the militancy of his Left flank, pragmatically placated his right flank, and cunningly used one against the other. He met sympathetically with leaders of the American Youth Congress, but supported a minimal youth aid appropriation. He empathized with an angry Black leadership, but accepted as expedient a Southern wage differential in the Wages and Hours Act, and did not support the anti-lynch bill. He did not oppose the formation of the first Un-American Activities Committee, headed by Martin Dies of Texas, even as he continued liaison with the Left. He talked a stirring anti-fascist foreign policy, but did nothing to prevent a fascist victory in Spain and the peace-by-piece sellout of Western Europe to Hitler.

Giving the President a greater liberal aura than he deserved was a First Lady who concerned herself with the controversial social issues. Eleanor Roosevelt urged patience upon those in the coalition movements with whom she worked, while she needled the President to listen to them.

On Capitol Hill a solid bloc of Northern Republicans and Southern Democrats carried the legislative ball to scuttle the New Deal. A large but nebulous bloc of New Deal Democrats, militant independents, Farmer-Laborites and liberal Republicans battled, in varying degrees, to plug the cracking dikes.

Within these divisions, the Communists moved with realistic and practical know-how. The main tasks were to safeguard the high stage of labor and peoples' organization achieved during 1936; to keep the coalitions intact despite attack from the outside and growing divisiveness inside; to shore-up the vacillatory Roosevelt "Center" forces; to channel all energies of the movements towards defeat of each specific thrust of the Right wing.

Convinced that "millions of Americans," as Gene wrote, while not yet convinced that socialism was the only permanent solution, were seeking an immediate way out of their pressing problems, the Party's emphasis was on organized mass actions to break the sit-down strike of finance capital and its legislative representatives. The Party's strategy was sloganized by Gene in a report to the national committee—"Resistance, Reform, Recovery" as the immediate goal; a "progressive, anti-fascist government" with the participation of the majority of the people as the intermediary goal; "socialism, the ultimate solution."

Of the Roosevelt Democrats as allies in the struggle, Gene wrote: they "blow hot and cold; they advance elements of a good program and then retreat; they nibble at ideas for controlling monopolies then stop short of enacting them." He insisted that "peoples' organization is the only assurance for progressive action."

II

Gene and I moved about Washington unobtrusively. A few congressmen like Vito Marcantonio of East Harlem, John Bernard of Minnesota, and a couple of mavericks from Wisconsin and Washington state, saw us openly in their offices, often took us to lunch and, as Meta Berger had done in Milwaukee, pointedly introduced us to colleagues along the way. But most of the New Deal legislators, labor leaders and government agency people met Gene cautiously in borrowed apartments under security precautions reminiscent of our years abroad. Through them many of Gene's and Browder's memos were relayed to the President's attention.

I was Gene's Girl Friday. I spent hours at the Library of Congress. I made rounds of various committee hearings. I saw those people who foolishly or chauvinistically believed it safer to meet with me than directly with Gene. I digested and summarized long reports and wrote memos. I clung tenaciously, however, to the one activity I could call my own, that of managing editor and feature writer of the new magazine the Party had initiated with Gene as editor.

This little journal with the long title, *National Issues: A Survey of Politics and Legislation; A Practical Guide to Action*," attracted a small working collective of capable young economists and political analysts in New York and Washington. Although widely read in legislative circles, it was short-lived. It became a casualty when our coalition relationships were scuttled in 1939.

The Un-American Committee witchhunts began to take their toll. Many in the coalition movements believed they could buy immunity by giving the committee what it claimed it wanted—Communist headrolling.

Factionalism and charges of "Communist control" against militants now eroded the once-unified C.I.O. In an effort to alleviate the situation, Communist Party caucuses in the unions were liquidated, Party shop newspapers and factory clubs in C.I.O.-organized industries were disbanded. The entire Party leadership approved this action, including Party chairman Foster who explained that these moves reflected the new role of the Communists within the labor movement. We were "no longer an opposition force," he wrote, we now held "many official posts" in both the A.F.L. and C.I.O. and we now "shared the official responsibility of carrying on the movement."

Our Party caucuses also had been the source of friction with the left and progressives inside the unions who resented our procedure of meeting separately to determine the attitudes we would take at union meetings before even hearing the members' discussions or views.

From its positions of strong participatory and leadership strength the Party gave up those independent organizational forms within the trade unions that had become an obstacle to the unity it believed decisive to the struggle. This unity was being battered by the Un-American Committee outside the labor movement and by redbaiting cliques inside.

These dissolutions did create other problems which were not dealt with and therefore weakened our work. Freed from these rank and file caucus and Party club controls, leading Communists in the unions became elitists who consulted only with individual Party leaders and practical union considerations increasingly dominated the Party's political decisions.

In this intricate new period the three divergent trends within the Party continued to surface sharply. Browder continued to delegate the democratic front movement to a subordinate, supportive role to the Roosevelt-labor leadership. Foster continued to demand Party control over the broad, diverse coalition movements. Gene continued, with the majority of the leadership, to argue that leadership would be determined by "correct policies, actions and positive contributions" in order to strengthen "an all-embracing front of all democratic forces."

III

In Washington and on his trips around the country, Gene

moved in his old style of relaxed ease, wry humor, and person-to-person contact. In New York he moved in a coiled tension, enmeshed in daily buffering between Browder and Foster, juggling ego-trip personality clashes of various comrades. We had no truly personal friends. Internalized political considerations dominated relationships.

He came home each night tired and somewhat grim. With highball in one hand, a chain-lit cigarette in the other, he would pace, often taking two hours to unwind. He talked out the day's events, tomorrow's problems. He related whom he had seen, re-evaluated the decisions he had been called upon to make, commented wryly on the various comrades he had contended with. I came to know more about each of them, what had transpired at closed meetings, and his personal opinions of them, than these comrades could possibly imagine. My sounding-board role was, I soon realized, his only opportunity to be his unguarded self. I was the only person he completely trusted not to use these self-revelations and personal opinions against him at some other time in formal, official situations.

When we were not in Washington, I worked on the legislative magazine in New York. I kept our voluminous clipping files. I wrote up the notes acquired in our last trip to Washington. I played my sounding-board role at home as patiently as I could. Sometimes I travelled with Gene, serving as his contact behind scenes at various united front conferences—the second World Youth Congress at Vassar College where I met Eleanor Roosevelt; the national pilgrimage of the Workers' Alliance; legislative conferences in the South, Northeast, Midwest.

I had been assigned to work with Gene when we had returned from Moscow. Also I was told I was not to be assigned to a Party club or committee, because of the contacts I maintained in Washington. I accepted both decisions without comment.

I was unsure of myself in this new, sophisticated circle at the top. I was self-consciously uncomfortable with these national comrades whose every casual opinion I still tended to accept as thought-out wisdom. I was aware, too, that in his new Party responsibilities Gene needed the kind of personal support only I could give him. I was in no pioneering mood to place any "me" needs first.

So began what became a lifetime pattern, that of being Gene's unofficial assistant; although he carefully called me "my co-worker." The work was always fascinating and we worked well together, arguing and battling all the way, but in the end one of us influencing the other. As the years passed, I sometimes lamented my lost individual public identity. But by then I no longer seemed able or willing to muster the stamina to rebuild a different relationship with Gene, with the Party, or to restructure my own priorities. Gene and his work and his needs became sublimated into being my special political contribution. This pattern became even more frozen quite early when I learned that at the top in New York, unlike in Wisconsin, every political opinion I expressed was assumed to be Gene's views and they were quoted to grind axes I knew nothing about. I became circumspect in the presence of Gene's co-workers. I owed Gene and our work that much.

After a year in New York we had not yet gotten accustomed to Gene's $30 a week salary. To us it was a fabulous sum whose regularity never ceased to amaze us.

Living off Mama and Papa in Los Angeles while Gene worked for the Trade Union Unity League and the Party, sharing bare essentials with the Russians building socialism in the years of severe shortages, dividing pennies five ways each morning in Milwaukee before we knew whether we could have breakfast—this was for us the normal life of the fulltime revolutionary.

Now in New York I puzzled at the burgher-like stability in the homes of those very few of Gene's national co-workers whom we visited on rare occasions. The household possessions, the comfortable flats in Yonkers and Upper Bronx, the homes at Croton-on-Hudson, the summer cottages, the staidness of nine-to-five routines, the absence of the lean and hungry look—all these added up to a security and stability alien to me.

After ten years, Gene and I owned nothing except our clothes that fit into one suitcase. We were still nomads living with the feeling that anything might happen at any moment to send us on our way again, by Party assignment.

Suddenly all this changed and we began to take on some of that staidness that had puzzled me. Gene came home with some extra dollars in his pay envelope and we talked about moving away from that clattering "El." We wondered whether our new wealth could provide an apartment uptown, maybe even near the river, "where we can breathe and walk," Gene said. At one point he added, "Better look for a little extra bedroom space; no sense in moving again later." To my puzzled question, he drawled with deliberate casualness, "Well, Browder told me today that Tim could probably be brought over by the end of the year."

I looked at him dumbly. No joy or disbelief. No excitement nor doubt. Just flatly, "Why now?"

Gene was not surprised at my lack of response. He understood my having blocked out all vulnerability on the subject of Tim. He replied quietly:

"I'm not sure why. Frankly, I don't want to know the details. Browder inferred something about Washington atmosphere, a way of doing it now without publicity."

We had all been intrigued many months earlier when Browder had suddenly brought over his Russian wife, Raissa, and their Moscow-born sons. I caustically wondered now, could a pricking conscience suddenly have made Tim's return possible? I didn't understand what our friendly contacts in Washington had to do with it, either. But all these were in the realm of what we termed "technical" questions that one did not probe, even when they affected you personally.

We found our new apartment on the sixth floor of a small walk-up building, west of Broadway, off 171st Street. It was immediately dubbed "our blue heaven," because it was on Haven Street; because we were high up; because from the back windows of our bedroom-study there was an unobstructed sky stretching westward across the Hudson River below us; because off the entry was a small hall bedroom—waiting for Tim; because we loved the place. We became the possessors of cheap, imitation maple furniture which we handled like priceless antiques, bought on the $10-a-month-for-two-years installment plan at Ludwig Bauman's on West 34th Street. We began slowly to rebuild our Marxist-Americana library to replace the ones we had twice abruptly left behind—in Los Angeles and Milwaukee. The phrase, "When Tim comes . . . ," crept often into our conversation. The city suddenly became tolerable and I began to occasionally beg off from making the weekly trips to Washington.

In August we made plans for the vacation we would take after the three-day national Party conference in Chicago September first. We were going to Meta Berger's place on the lake in Wisconsin.

On August 22 came news of the Hitler-Stalin Pact. The bottom fell out of the small dream-world Gene and I had foolishly lapsed into for a brief, unguarded moment.

IV

Hatred of fascism was the marrow of the coalition movements. The enemy of the working class was the American pro-fascist who would ape Hitler's way of dealing with labor. The enemy of the Black people was the American racist who embraced Hitler's genocide. The enemy of the artist and writer, the actor and teacher, the lawyer and middle class businessman was the American fascist who, like Hitler, would destroy hard-won democratic rights.

Everything we Communists did and advocated was rooted in the conviction that it makes a decisive difference to the majority of the people and to the revolutionary movement whether a bourgeois-democratic or a fascist form of capitalist government is in power.

Internationally, the Soviet Union had won the admiration of millions for its consistently principled efforts to achieve cooperation with the capitalist democracies to jointly block fascist aggression.

Now came the pact between the Soviet Union and the arch-enemy of all humanity.

I sat on the floor and growled like a cornered bear. In utter shock, I wailed and pleaded: Say it isn't true! Gene paced in silence. Then he exploded:

"For Chris' sake, shut up. Why the hell don't you think before you shout!"

He stalked into the bedroom and at the desk thumbed through the large pile of manila folders which contained the newspaper clippings I worked on daily. He returned and thrust a folder at me. "Here, read these, since you apparently have a short memory. Read them." He began pacing again, and I opened the folder. Over the months I had clipped, dated, read, filed and forgotten the news stories. Gene had not.

Like a well-written plot the clues had been there, loud and clear, heralding a predictable outcome that climaxed on August 22.

In early March Stalin told the world in his report to the Soviet Party's 18th congress:

"It is already the second year that a new imperialist war has been going on ... from Shanghai to Gibraltar, involving over 500 millions of population. ... The war is waged by aggressor states which are infringing in every way upon the interests of the non-aggressor states, primarily England, France and the United States, while the latter are retreating, making concession after concession to the aggressors. ∴. Without the least attempt to resistance and even with a certain amount of connivance by the latter. Incredible, but it is a fact."

There followed day by day, week after week, month into month, the record.

In late *March*—U.S. Senator William Borah charged that Britain had encouraged Hitler's occupation of Czechoslovakia and Austria. The Soviet Union proposed a nine power conference to consider mutual assistance pacts against aggression. Beginning *April*—U.S. recognized the Franco fascist regime in Spain. Albania falls to Mussolini. U.S.S.R. urged an Anglo-French-Soviet pact against Italy, Germany, Japan. Early *May*—Britain rejected the Soviet call for alliance; instead Prime Minister Chamberlain proposes a non-aggression pact with Hitler. The Soviet Union informs the Western democracies she will act alone, if necessary, to protect her borders. The Baltic states sign pacts with Hitler. *Mid-May*—Moscow rejects London plan; Western newspapers admit that plan would leave Russia fighting Germany alone in defense of the Baltic states. Stalin is quoted: "Warmongers are accustomed to have others pull chestnuts out of the fire for them;" Moscow reaffirms it will accept only full military alliance of reciprocity. *June*—Latvia, Estonia sign pacts with Hitler. The Pope in the Vatican says he will do everything in his power to prevent a Western alliance with the Soviet Union. *July*—Nazi troops occupy Danzig. British Secretary for Overseas Trade discusses trade agreements and division of world markets with Germany. Finland, Baltic states declare they will honor their pacts with Hitler, will resist any Russian or Western attempts to protect them from Nazi designs. Beginning *August*—Germany threatens Poland. Soviet Union expresses fear of a second Munich, this time at her very borders. *August 22*—Germany and the Soviet Union sign non-aggression pact. Soviet officials emphasize this is not a pact of mutual assistance or military assistance, and reaffirm Soviet readiness to conclude mutual assistance pacts with Britain and France.

I sat crosslegged on the floor, the clippings strewn about me. The record was there. I had forgotten. Gene paused, "Well?"

I bargained. "All right, but this doesn't mean that overnight fascism is acceptable."

"No one says it does. The Soviet Union has outwitted the bourgeois democracies in their attempts to get Germany and the Soviet Union to fight each other while they stand by, then pick up the pieces. That's all. Nothing else has changed."

V

We left for Chicago as planned, looking forward to our vacation that would follow. News of Hitler's invasion of Poland reached us on the first day of the national conference of 650 Party activists in Chicago. Declaration of war by Britain and France came the next day.

In response to the President's immediate pledge to keep America out of the war, the Party meeting in a public letter declared its support of Roosevelt's position "against American involvement in the war or in the rivalries and antagonisms which have led much of Europe into chaos." The statement called for U.S. cooperation "with the Soviet Union on behalf of a peace policy which would prevent the realization of new Munich betrayals."

Two weeks later the Party leadership sharpened its characterization of the war; it had become "an imperialist war for which the bourgeoisie of all belligerent powers are equally guilty." On October 13 the small Political Committee scrapped the policy which had determined the Party's every action for five years. In a major statement it declared:

"The present war between two imperialist groups . . . has at one blow wiped out the former division of the world between the camps of democracy and fascism. . . . Therefore the slogans of anti-fascism can no longer give the main direction to the struggle of the working class and its allies, as they formerly did in the period of the struggle for the anti-fascist peace front and people's front . . . not only the old division between Republican and Democratic parties, but also that between the New Deal and anti-New Deal camps, is losing its former significance."

What had happened between August 22 and October 13? I didn't know. What had happened to Gene's assurance that nothing could change our opposition to fascism? I wasn't sure. We had returned home directly from Chicago, our Wisconsin vacation cancelled, and I saw little of Gene. He was in continual sessions downtown. He came home tense, preoccupied, silent, refusing to be drawn into discussion. He appeared deeply troubled. As I read the typed drafts of documents he brought home and the daily newspapers I continued to clip, I began to surmise some of the reasons.

After the announcement of the pact came startling statements by Soviet Foreign Minister Molotov. He now claimed that Hitler fascism was "just another ideology;" that "one may accept or reject the ideology of Hitlerism as well as any other ideological system;" that it had become "not only senseless but criminal to wage a war camouflaged as a fight for 'democracy'." He chided "short-sighted people" who had gotten "carried away by oversimplified anti-fascist propaganda." He said that the very existence of the Soviet-German pact attested to a change in German foreign policy.

The record of facts leading up to the pact had reassured me. Now Molotov's defense of the pact shocked me. I could understand the pragmatic, tactical character of the pact, but this reversal of analysis of fascism and rejection of the years-long commitment to fight fascism which dominated our international movement was reprehensible. And if Molotov's statements were necessary diplomatic gobbledegook, then why did our own Party have to reverse its policies and analyses? Couldn't we understand and explain Moscow's need without making a complete about-face here, deliberately severing our lifeline to the millions in the anti-fascist coalition movements we had helped to build?

I demanded plausible answers, but Gene did not respond. He was in conflict. It was inconceivable to him that there could be a dichotomy between any Communist party and the Soviet Union. For Gene, there had to be good reason for the Soviet reversal, even if it were not clearly visible yet. The October 13 statement was an act of faith in the infallibility of the Soviet leadership. It had nothing to do with the simplistic charge levelled at us of "taking orders from Moscow." It was the underlying belief that the needs of the Soviet Union are paramount in the class struggle, that its leaders are always wiser than we.

So it was not the German-Soviet Pact that destroyed the anti-fascist alignments and our relations with them from September, 1939 to June 22, 1941. It was the inability or unwillingness of the American Party leadership, including Gene, to analyze the American scene independently from Moscow. It was the ingrained habit of the membership to say, even when it had doubts, "Our leaders know best."

I was incapable of dealing with the implications of these questions. Then, as always, immediate events crowded in. These doubts and questions were buried in silence, a silence similar to that in which we had in Moscow buried the ghosts of Mingulin, Boris and Musa, Bob and Valerie.

A few days after the October 13 statement reversing Party policy, Gene suggested that we walk along the river. I knew this was no relaxing interlude in our tension-filled, silent days. Walking-along-Riverside Drive in such circumstances meant to talk of things best not said in the apartment where we always assumed electronic bugs had us under constant FBI surveillance.

As we walked, Gene told me what I already surmised, that our policy shift created a new situation. "We are now in sharp opposition to the Roosevelt administration. We may come under severe attack; how soon or how drastically, we don't know."

I listened quietly. I sensed what was coming. I had lived this scene and this conversation before. Los Angeles. Judge Bogue's courtroom. News of the Imperial Valley indictments. Gene sitting down next to me in that courtroom, telling me then, as he was telling me now, "trouble ahead." Gene's voice broke into my trance and I realized I had missed part of what he was saying.

"So I'll leave in the morning as usual. I'll take nothing with me." He smiled. "Well, I'll wear a couple of extra shirts, put some extra pairs of socks in my pockets. You stay in the apartment, go out often, make a point of talking to neighbors and the building manager. If you hear nothing to the contrary from any messenger, then three weeks from today lock up the apartment, take nothing with you, spend a few hours losing yourself in Macy's or somewhere; I don't have to tell you the routine. Then take the train to Poughkeepsie, be in the public library there at four o'clock sharp. Either I or someone else you'll know will meet you. Okay?"

I nodded, and he answered my unasked question. "I don't know where all this will lead. We may be back home soon. We may not. It depends on the war and the political climate. For the time being, only two or three of us are going to be 'unavailable.' Let's just look towards Poughkeepsie for now, three weeks from today. Right?"

Right.

Seven:
WORLD AT WAR

I

That early November rendezvous at the Poughkeepsie public library began seventeen months of so-called "underground" living in various backwoods cottages on either side of the Hudson River. Ours was a waiting-stance, and I enjoyed every minute of it.

We absorbed ourselves in simple things. Gene hauled and split logs for our woodpile, repaired broken roof shingles, built a rough-hewn chess board, transplanted and tenderly nursed roots and bulbs collected on the long walks and picnics we took with our newly acquired German shepherd, Smokey. We daily studied a self-prepared course in Marxist readings; evenings we sat before the fire or on the summer screen porch, lazily talking about the state of the world. Gene rarely paced, and even the political articles we worked on created none of the old tensions or debates between us. We saw no one for weeks at a time. In our isolation we drew closer, attuned in long silences and occupied in pleasant routines, sensitively aware of every nuance of each other's thoughts and moods. The days passed gently, yet we knew the hiatus had to end. What we didn't know was how.

Every six weeks I went into the city where, by prearranged contact, I picked up Party documents, newspapers, magazines, and delivered Gene's messages, opinions, articles, Periodically he drove into New Jersey or Connecticut or Pennsylvania for two or three days for a meeting of the top leadership including the "unavailables."

On the edges of our tranquil life, the world lumbered on towards war. Between them, Hitler and Mussolini eventually occupied all of Europe from Norway to Greece. The French surrendered Paris without a battle. Kings and queens fled to London where they comfortably declared themselves to be governments-in-exile while in the occupied countries resistance movements fought back heroically. In Asia and Africa the Japanese, German and Italian armies moved onward while the British and the French feared the national liberation struggles as much as they did the Nazi-Mikado-Italian take-over of their empires.

At home the year 1940 was a year of confusion and realignment, with the Roosevelt Administration changing its course, but in an ambivalent manner. Throughout that year Gene wrote in his articles that U.S. imperialism could go either way in the war it had not yet officially joined. He warned against tendencies within our Party "to oversimplify problems." He chided comrades who "over-emphasized" the antagonisms between the imperialist powers and therefore negated from their thinking the possibility of an American and British *rapprochment* with Nazi Germany against the Soviet Union and a course of domestic reactionary policies that would flow from such an alliance. At the same time, he criticized *Daily Worker* editorials that tended to underestimate contradictions which render more acute the imperialist war. Contradictions which could compel, he said, the decisive section of American finance capital "for its own immediate interests, to improve its relations with the Soviet Union, nothwithstanding its firm and unchangeable hostility and enmity towards the Land of Socialism." These contradictions, at home and abroad, must be utilized, he urged, "by the working class and its proletarian state in its own interests in the cause of peace and socialism."

Gene helped formualte our Party's official characterization of 1940 as the year of the "phony war" and our opposition to the Roosevelt steps to embroil the country in all-out aid to Britain. However, he warned against a schematic, simplified view of rapidly changing developments and he sought to prepare our Party for various possible directions.

"The Yanks Are Not Coming" became the cry of millions. The national conventions of both the A.F.L. and C.I.O. and the national Farmers Union, the Railway unions, all passed anti-war resolutions.

So strong was this anti-war sentiment that the President, deeply committed to aid Britain, won an unprecedented third term largely on his campaign promise, "Your boys are not going to be sent into any foreign wars."

Although in tune with the anti-war moods in the country, our Party steadily lost ground in the movements it had once exercised decisive influence. We were unable to successfully explain at that time, except to ourselves, the valid reasons for the Hitler-Stalin pact, the Red Army occupation of eastern Poland and the six months' Soviet war with Finland. Especially difficult for our former allies to understand was the abrupt end to our anti-fascist activities. Rightly, we were seen reacting to Moscow's changed course, not our own. Our criticisms of Roosevelt and the New Deal and our opposition to his third term campaign were too similar to those of the pro-Hitler, "America First" reactionaries whose fascist sympathies placed them in opposition to the President's course in foreign affairs.

If our Party's relations with its former coalition partners were changing, so were those of the Roosevelt New Deal. With each step-up to tie U.S. production to British war needs, the Administration nibbled away at its own New Deal social programs. Labor welcomed the opening up of jobs in war industries after two years of economic recession, but it resented the new conservative positions of a government it had come to feel was on its side.

The influx of Black workers into industry and into the armed forces exposed the deep-rooted racial discrimination and segregation within what they had come to see as a progressive administration. Volatile charges were levelled at both Roosevelt and the liberals and Black leaders threatened to withdraw their support from the New Deal.

With his former coalition alliance in disarray, the President relied now on the Southern Democrats and conservative Republicans to put through his cutbacks in social legislation and appropriations, and he gave free rein to a counter-offensive. The Dies Committee went on a witchhunt rampage in Boston, Pittsburgh, Baltimore, Philadelphia. Browder was arrested on an old passport violation charge which had lain dormant and served one year of a four-year sentence. Communist and union organizers were arrested in West Virginia, Oklahoma and Iowa. In California, Party state chairman William Schneiderman had his naturalized citizenship revoked, although the Supreme Court later restored it. Anti-war organizations were raided by super-patriotic vigilantes and FBI agents in Chicago, Detroit, Milwaukee, New York, Washington state, Colorado, Texas and Tennessee.

In the face of a rash of anti-democratic laws passed that year, the Party extricated itself from the "foreign agent" Voorhis Act by disaffiliating from the Comintern, and it responded to the Alien Registration McCarran-Walters Act by dropping 4,000 non-citizens from its membership rolls, although a select few in top leadership remained.

This accommodation reflected a tendency to capitulate to legalism as a substitute for struggle, but it also reflected a need to keep the Party functioning despite these "legal" attmepts to legislate it out of existence.

Our opposition to a Roosevelt third term further isolated the Party from our former coalition friends and the labor movement, although we were, in this, on the same side as John L. Lewis, who staked and lost his C.I.O. presidency on a Roosevelt defeat.

II

In the numerous articles he wrote throughout 1940 from our Hudson riverside hideaways, Gene analyzed why in 1933-1940 the needs of the liberal wing of American capitalism had, in part, coincided with some of the immediate needs of labor and the majority of the people, and how that coincidence had now changed. He argued against the "lesser evil" theory that permeated the labor and democratic movements in the 1940 campaign. He also analyzed the ways in which he believed the New Deal had changed, showing that the people's organizations no longer held the independent, often decisive, role within the coalition that they had in the earlier years.

I was not entirely convinced and therefore was relieved to read in his articles continuous warnings against narrow, go-it-alone tendencies that grew under the impact of our Party's break with the New Deal coalitions. Despite his analyses in support of our changed policy, Gene urged Communists and progressives to colaborate with New Deal activists on the basis of struggle for partial issues of agreement. He advocated support to individual candidates of both major parties, "depending on their records and their positions," while always guarding "against opportunist deals and agreements." He offered "non-parliamentary campaigns" around social programs that would "strengthen independent political action of labor and the people."

He teased me about my "lesser evil tendencies," and then

added seriously, "Be patient, things will be clearer soon. Either this war will become more blatantly imperialist as far as the Administration is concerned, or it will become clearly anti-fascist and you may yet be able to cheer wholeheartedly for your side. Our tactics will change with any change in the situation. That's what tactics are for, and we've got to remain fluid, not boxed-in either way."

No matter how valid our abrupt changes may have been, our most active comrades were caught in a bind. They were deeply within the mainstream movements they had helped to organize. Our policies were now counter to those movements and counter to the very basis on which we had originally helped build them.

We got a personal glimpse of this problem when my sister came to New York that summer for the national convention of her union. After a grueling week as one of the leaders in an official minority opposition, Mini came to the Newburgh ferry upstate where we met her and drove to our cottage at New Paltz. We had not seen each other for ten years, since that day I boarded a New York-bound train with 16-months-old Tim to start the slow voyage to join Gene in Moscow. Now as we embraced the years fell away, the old liking for each other was still there.

Playing the charming host, Gene quipped and teased affectionately all day, but by nightfall he was plying her with questions. Mini was president of her San Francisco local of the International Ladies' Garment Workers, a member of that union's Northern California Joint Board, and a member of the Party's state committee. She worked an eight hour day as a presser in a dress factory.

In response to Gene's questions, Mini's hazel eyes lost their lack-luster tiredness and the volatile, dramatic style—which I had always envied and like everyone else always succumbed to—came to the fore.

"It was pretty rough," she told us. "We're going against a powerful mainstream of feeling. I know," she hurried to concede as Gene gave indication of interrupting, "going with the mainstream is not always right. But," she added, with deliberate, exaggerated rolling of her words, "believe me, being right but alone isn't easy and I'm not sure what that accomplishes. I wonder, Gene," her voice became serious, "do you comrades here think that with a resolution or an article projecting a correct policy, we out in the field can overnight shift gears?"

Gene did not reply. He was not interested in expounding his

views; he wanted to get all he could from this young woman who was both local union leader and Party activist, deeply involved in practical work.

"Yes, I carried through our new views at the convention," she continued. She had been selected by the radical caucus to serve on the convention's political action committee. It was her job to oppose the expected endorsement of President Roosevelt's third-term candidacy.

"We did good battle. But you should know, if you don't, that my local membership back home does not support me in our opposition to the third term. I am their president; whose policy do I carry through, theirs or that of our Party?"

"What happened around the third term question?" I asked.

"Well," Mini said, "I admit I was scared when I had to give the minority report on the convention floor. You know, I've done a lot of public speaking, I've been in strikes in the canneries and through the 1934 general strike, but I was more frightened at having to take on the hostility in my own union than fighting the bosses back home."

The endorsement recommendation touched off a prepared "spontaneous" floor demonstration of thirty minutes of shouts, applause, snake-marching with Roosevelt banners. Carnegie Hall was packed, delegates on the main floor, visitors and invited guests filling the boxes and tiers.

When the demonstration wore itself down, union head Dubinsky announced, "Sister Carson of San Francisco has the floor for a minority report opposing endorsement of our great President" — "or words to that effect," Mini added, tensely. "Bedlam broke out. The Roosevelt banners came up again and there were boos and catcalls and Dubinsky stood there smiling, allowing the demonstration to start all over again."

"What were you doing?" I asked.

"Standing at the mike, shouting 'Mr. Chairman!' I was getting angry and forgot my fear. Our people say my speech was good. But what use was it? No one listened. Minds were closed. I know, opposition had to be voiced, of course. Our people were pleased. But now I go home and face my membership."

After only three days, we reluctantly drove her to the Newburgh ferry, and I was restless and moody for some time after her brief visit. I envied Mini her stable roots in San Francisco. We served the same movement and the same Party, but in such different ways. As the ferry pulled away from its slip that morning I wished I, too, were going home to Wisconsin or California where we could take political and personal root.

III

In the spring of 1941, Gene returned from one of his three-day meetings and, changing his clothes, suggested we walk, despite the rain and darkness. The back road was muddy and roughly ridged. The rain, while heavy, fell gently, and Gene's voice seemed disembodied in the darkness. He said abruptly:

"We're going to Moscow, in two weeks."

My breath escaped with a faint hissing sound. The other shoe had finally dropped. The waiting was over.

"Do you want to go?" I asked too casually.

"What difference does it make? We're going—" a pause, and then, "for a long time."

We walked in silence. I stumbled, he took my hand. I pulled my hood lower, but the rain kept blurring my vision.

"You'll be glad to go back, won't you?" His words broke into my confusion of thoughts. An excited, warm feeling at the prospect of returning once again to the Moscow I loved. Tim. Molly. The invigorating feeling of being in the center of our great world-wide movement. Yet there was also a reluctant feeling that, no matter how attractive, this was not what we should be doing. So when Gene said, almost pleading, "There's Tim and Molly—," I retorted curtly, "Don't dangle them as consolation prizes. We've got to stop uprooting ourselves every couple years." Suddenly remembering, I asked, "What do you mean, 'for a long time'?"

Official opinion was that world-wide war was going to erupt, whatever the eventual line-up of the countries would be. Routine communications between the Parties and the Comintern would be disrupted for many years. The request had come that each Party send a responsible leading comrade capable of independent opinion to work at the Comintern for the war's duration. At the meeting he had just attended, Gene had been selected, despite his opposition.

After a slow, month-long Pacific crossing on a small Soviet freighter and ten days on the train from Vladivostok, we arrived in the Soviet capital in early June. Despite our mixed feelings, arriving in Moscow aroused the excited pleasure and the deep feeling of home-coming it always did.

Bringing our bags into the room the comrade who had met our train said, "Your son will come tomorrow. Comrade Dimitroff asked that I tell you. He and comrade Manuilsky will see you at midnight," he said to Gene, "the car will come for you." I was told Molly and her mother now lived in the Luxe and in minutes we sat over glasses of strong tea, picking up our talk as though it were only yesterday, instead of three years, since we'd been together.

Gene returned to our room at close to four in the morning. Loosening his tie and hanging up his coat, he asked, "What does *chort-viz-mi,* or something like that, mean?"

I hesitated. "I think it means 'What the devil.' Why?"

He laughed. "That's the first thing Manuilsky said when he embraced me."

Puzzled, I pressed, "Why?"

"Well," he drawled, grinning. "You won't believe it, but they don't want me here. They were annoyed as hell that it was me that came. Dimitroff said they got the message when we were already on the high seas, or they would have vetoed it."

"Some kind of re-run of Spain?" I offered.

"So it seems," Gene agreed. "You know what Manuilsky asked?" I waited.

"He asked 'Who back there always wants you out of active leadership? Is it Foster or is it Browder?'"

"What's he talking about?" I was startled.

Gene shrugged. "What's important is we're going home. Dimitroff said, 'We can do with someone who can be better spared than you.' S-o-o-o, a couple weeks of discussions here, and we go home." Quizzically appraising my silence, he asked, "You disappointed?"

Rubbing my forehead slowly, I replied flatly, "No, I guess not. Just tired. These constant changes get a little too much, I'm afraid. Right now I think I'll just concentrate on Tim's coming tomorrow."

IV

The early June days passed uneventfully. Tim had arrived, an eleven-year-old with memories of his earlier stay with us, so the adjustment was easier. School was out for the summer and he was excited with the sudden changes in his life.

Gene was deeply involved in the Comintern discussions, and since we were to leave soon I did not seek work but gladly accepted requests for articles from Soviet Radio and various magazines.

On June 22, while Tim and I were at lunch, the radio loudspeaker began to splutter. I paid no attention. I could not understand what was being said anyway. Tim suddenly dropped his fork and shouted, "It's war! We're at war!"

I gaped foolishly, "You sure? With whom?"

"The Germans! he shouted. "They attacked us this morning."

I rushed to the telephone, Tim headed for the door. I shouted for him to wait, "We'll go together as soon as I talk to Papa."

Gene's voice came across the wire, tersely. "Yes, I know. I'll put someone on to give you a translation of what Molotov just said on the radio. I don't know when I'll be home, as soon as I can. Don't let Tim roam alone today. There may be air bombings."

Molotov's announcement, as it was read to me, had been brief: "Today at three o'clock in the morning, without any claim having been presented to the Soviet Union, without any declaration of war, German troops attacked our country, attacked our borders at many points and bombed from their airplanes our cities. . . ."

In the street Tim and I gravitated to the groups of men, women and children gathered at corner loud-speakers which, however, were now silent. Many decided to jump a streetcar to their factory, saying, "There will be a meeting, some discussion, a mobilization."

Our first air-raid came that night, although next day talk in the bread shop claimed it was a rehearsal, not the real thing. All we had heard was the roar of planes overhead—theirs or ours we didn't know—as we were rushed downstairs to the basement.

On the third day, Gene came home with news that, for the moment, at least, drove the war out of my mind. He was leaving for home in twenty-four hours, and he was going alone. It was impossible, he had been told, to send us out together. "They promised you would come soon, if it will be at all possible."

Everything was happening too fast. The world was bursting into flames, tomorrow was non-existent. Gene was going home, I was remaining behind. There had been so many partings in our past. There was little left to say. Instead, Gene clowned and laughed with Tim who had a very simple view of it all. There was a war on. The socialist land was under attack. Papa was going home to fight in the way the Party had chosen for him. Mama and he would stay together, for how long the Party would decide too. After their last bear hug, Gene and I embraced silently. With a light touch of his forefinger to his lips and then to mine he strode quickly out of the room, and Tim called, "Keep well, Papa."

V

A week later we were informed that all children should report to their schools for evacuation. Teachers were to move out with their classes to pre-assigned safe-zones hundreds of miles into the interior.

Although not compulsory, the response was prompt. Everywhere on the street one saw children, small suitcases in hand, walking toward their school buildings, tearful silent mothers and fathers walking beside them. Some parents preferred to send their children to relatives, but most felt there was greater safety in having them under organized, official protection. Only "individualistic" and "irresponsible" parents, I was told, would not heed the urgent request that the children be sent to safety.

Tim said he would rather go back to Ivanovo, to the children's home which was the only real home he knew, instead of attach himself to a Moscow school group of strangers. At the Comintern the comrades agreed.

The night Tim left I lay in bed scolding myself for crying. I told myself I am not alone. In hundreds of villages and towns and throughout Moscow, wives and husbands, mothers and fathers and children are separated by a war only ten days old, maybe never to meet again. I am not alone. Yet the emptiness and fear each felt had to be borne alone. However, after that first night I experienced little loneliness, and no aloneness. Living and working in Moscow at war was a fulltime job.

On July third, Stalin spoke over the radio and the seriousness of the military situation was revealed to us. Hitler's one hundred and seventy divisions were on the offensive. We had been caught unawares. From Murmansk to Sebastopol, all along the Western border, cities and towns were bombed, villages occupied. Lithuania, Latvia, Western Bylorussia, Western Ukraine—all in Nazi hands. The Red Army was in retreat. War refugees were moving eastward.

Stalin said the very existence of the Soviet Union was threatened. He proclaimed the "scorched earth" policy that was to astound the world and confound the invaders. In retreat, every village and town was to evacuate all rolling stock. "Not a single engine, railroad car, single pound of grain or gallon of fuel is to be left behind for the enemy." What could not be withdrawn, "must be destroyed."

"Our war for the freedom of our country will merge with the struggle of the peoples of Europe and America for their independence, for democratic liberties. . . . In this war of liberation, we shall not be alone."

The issue was once again joined. I could now, as Gene had said a year earlier, cheer wholeheartedly for my side. The Soviet-British agreement for joint action in the war was signed July 14. President Roosevelt declared U.S. aid would go to Moscow as well as London.

For the next three months our Moscow days and nights were governed by air alerts. For weeks in late July and throughout August they came almost around the clock. Molly and I walked during our lunch break in the park of the Economic Achievements Exhibition out in Rostokino where the Comintern was now housed in a large, very modern white building. In low voices we expressed only to each other our uneasiness at each morning's communique announcing the continued "retreats according to Plan." From Minsk in the northwest to Kiev in the southwest all Soviet land was occupied by the Nazis.

Odessa was under seige. The German juggernaut was inching towards Moscow. Ours was not so much a personal fear, although who could deny that that, too, was present. Ours was the unspoken fear of "Why? How could it happen?"

However, we were too busy to indulge these moods for long. While all citizens from sixteen to sixty gave one night or day a week at home or at work to civil defense assignments, Molly and I volunteered for nightly duty, either at home or at the Comintern. Of the four categories—blackout control, firespotter, house guard, shelter aide—we chose the first two.

It was not claustrophobia alone that drove us restlessly from the air raid shelter with its tiers of wooden bunks where packed humanity slept, read and talked in the dim light, waiting for the all-clear to release them to climb sleepily upstairs to bed. Molly and I agreed it was the inaction, the indignity of passively "allowing" the bombers to control our lives. Outside, at least, we actively fought back.

The planes roared overhead, the anti-aircraft guns popped in the distance, the giant searchlights pierced the black sky. We hunched for moments in doorways as shrapnel from AA guns dropped around us, then we continued our solitary rounds patrolling the streets, the inner courtyards. On the roof, we worked as a team, carrying pails of sand and water as we darted between the small incendiary bombs that dropped like flashing flares. On street and roof there was no fear, only energetic anger.

I learned, however, to appreciate the value of the air raid shelter as a different kind of morale-builder. One night we had been sent home unexpectedly early from work where we had signed up for duty, so Molly and I joined the regulars in the shelter. The large, low, sub-cellar was unusually crowded, and that night there was an unusually heavy air attack. Both planes and AA guns seemed directly overhead. The five-story structure above us trembled and creaked again and again. The shrieking whines coming from the unseen skies appeared to be heading directly at us. The shelter became strangely silent. No one talked, no one slept, no one read. We listened and we waited. Suddenly an elongated whine, an eruptive roar, the building shuddered and swayed, the lights went out. A muffled cry, a collective low sigh. A momentary silence. Then, with one voice, we began to sing. Softly, then louder. In the many different languages of the Comintern, our voices rose.

Marching songs of the Soviet Red Army. Songs of the Spanish loyalist fighters. Songs of the German and Italian revolutionary movements. The Internationale. Without pause, we sang. We knew we were not hit. We weren't sure whether or not we were buried in our deep cellar. Shelter aides moved quietly. Inadequate emergency lamps were lit, drinking water was passed to the very old; whimpering babies were cuddled. At the all-clear, I climbed the stairs, unafraid, grateful to my shelter mates.

We were a very tired people that summer and fall. Despite disturbed, sleepless nights, everyone went about their regular jobs by day and in after-work free hours and on rest days we travelled in trucks to the outskirts of the city to fill sandbags used to pile higher and higher around each building, or we dug new trenches in the spreading maze that surrounded the approaches to Moscow.

News of air raid casualties were muted in the press, but we knew that nearly five thousand had been killed or wounded, that factories and a hospital had been hit, that fires on the outer edges of the city were frequent. By the end of September, tensions grew. Food supplies were scarce. This did not bother me personally, because for three months now I could eat nothing but hard-dried bread-toast and weak tea—a nervous stomach was the only outward sign of my own tensions and fears.

Although Moscow had become a city noticeably void of children, a few schools did open even as parents were again urged to send all children and old people out of the city, eastward. The theater season opened with curtailed repertoires because a core of each group had been evacuated or depleted by military call-up. Curtain time for all public events was now six o'clock or earlier so that people could get home before the heavier night raids started. The Conservatory of Music now gave most of its concerts in the afternoon.

VI

Two weeks before Moscow was officially declared under siege, I received a telephone call informing me that comrade Dimitroff wanted to see me that night. The car would come for me, I was told, after the night's all-clear signal. It was early dawn when I was ushered into a very large, sparsely-furnished office not in the Comintern building out at Rostokino but inside the Kremlin, in the center of the city. Dimitroff rose from behind a massive desk at the far end of the room and walked toward me. His broad face lit up in a smile, his outstretched hands took mine in a firm grip. He led me, not to the long, narrow, conference table standing right angle to his desk—an institution in every Soviet official's office—but to a small round table surrounded by arm chairs. Waving me into one, he sat opposite while his translator, an older, grey woman, sat next to him.

His big head, framed halo-like by his long hair, was familiar to me. I had caught a glimpse of him in 1934 when I had stood with thousands in Red Square shouting our welcome to his triumphal return from the death jaws of Hitler's prison. Now I wondered if he would remember that we had met also, face to face, not too long ago. Obviously he did, for he said with a smile, "And do you now obey our civil defense rules, comrade Ryan?"

I nodded, "Yes, I do; and do you, comrade Dimitroff?"

He laughed, "Frankly, not as often as I should."

It had been on a night Molly and I were working late. The air alert interrupted the last of some translation she was completing and I was editing a remaining few pages for our chief. We ignored the alert and kept on working. A half hour later we hurried towards the shelter, the dimmed, empty corridors echoing our footsteps. Through the heavy blackout curtains we heard the staccato ack-ack of anti-aircraft guns and the roar of planes. We turned a corner and, in our haste, bumped into Dimitroff and a group of his aides. He stopped us and asked sternly what we were doing out of the shelter during an air raid. Molly started to explain, but Dimitroff interrupted.

"Nothing, no document, is more important than the safety of our comrades. Remember that. You must not place your lives in jeopardy again. Is that clear?"

I nodded, speechless, but Molly replied, "Yes, but you, comrade Dimitroff, what are you doing out of the shelter? Surely, you know that your safety is important to all of us."

He smiled, and then said somberly, "You are right, comrade. I, too, am in violation of civil defense rules. Let us agree we will all do better in the future. Now, off with you, to the shelter." And we hurried away.

Now, at the small table, his smile did not obliterate the tired lines in his face, but his eyes were friendly and interested.

"Well, comrade Ryan, it is time you went home. We must keep our promise to comrade Tim. We will send you on your way tomorrow."

I gasped, "No, you can't!"

His eyes measured my stricken face, and he said, quietly:

"I know how you feel. You think you are deserting the struggle here, forsaking the beleaguered Soviet people, yes?" I nodded. He continued.

"It is good you feel this way, but you need not. There are many ways to serve the struggle, as you well know. Also I will tell you something you should not repeat, but because you feel as you do, I want you to know." He hesitated. I sat silent.

"The city has been slowly evacuating according to plan. Mainly factories and their workers. Now the Comintern and most of the government leave for Kuibyshev in two weeks. You will not be deserting Moscow, you would leave with us if you stayed. But it is needless to sit in Kuibyshev when you should be home. We must not delay any longer, if you are to go at all."

The import of what he was saying seeped slowly into my consciousness. Our worst fears were coming true. Moscow was in retreat too.

Dimitroff leaned forward, his arms resting on the low table, hands clasped. "We know a great deal about you and comrade Tim. Yours is a unique relationship and we respect it highly. Comrade Tim is one of our most valued comrades. He needs you and you need him for each of you to work at your best. Two like you should not be long separated."

I sat, speechless. In all my years in the Party I had not heard such personal comment from a leading comrade. I was surprised and grateful; but agitated at the decision to send me home. Dimitroff went on:

"About the child, we will take good care of him; after the war, perhaps then we can send him to you."

Throughout the thirty day voyage across the Pacific, life and work on the Soviet freighter were geared to round-the-clock blackout and Alert regulations as we ploughed slowly through Japanese-mined waters. A few days before we docked, Pearl Harbor was bombed, and I went ashore in another blacked-out city, this time an American one.

In New York I found Gene at the address given me at Party headquarters. That night, after the first hours of reunion, almost simultaneously each of us said to the other, "I've got something to tell you."

I told him I wanted a baby; he told me he might be going away again.

The day after Pearl Harbor he had volunteered in Washington to go to the Philippines as liaison with the revolutionary movement with which he had worked in 1931 and 1932. He was awaiting confirmation of an appointment to that war theater.

I told him I wanted to become pregnant immediately, all the more so if he were going away. "No political arguments, Gene. I want a baby, and with you or without you, I intend to have one." I was only half joking.

My train had crawled its way from Moscow to Vladivostok, taking seventeen days for the usual ten-day trip. Sidetracked for hours each day, I watched the right-of-way given to train after train filled with young Red Army men being rushed to the 2,000-mile-long Western front. Also in priority towards the west sped long trains of flat-cars loaded with tanks and giant guns guarded by young, straight-backed armed sentries.

Moving eastward as I, but with green light precedence that shuttled our train into more long waits, were lines of freight cars of machinery and coaches filled with workers, mainly women and their families. Whole factories and working personnel were being evacuated deep into the east beyond the Ural mountains where they were re-assembled and continued to produce the sinews of war.

Sidetracked with me, but under less comfortable conditions and with a lesser priority than our train, were boxcars of refugees and their bundles. Some of these faces became individual as we met again and again at a station's outdoor faucet or exercised weary legs between the waiting trains. They had been on the road for many weeks.

Out of the jumble of all these impressions, out of the memories of the war months in Moscow, out of the frustration of my unwilling departure, there grew each day on the long and endless land-trip and sea-voyage the need to affirm the future. Surrounded by death, I needed a personal act of creation. A bit corny, perhaps, but I knew that this was what I needed. Not as a substitute for Tim, who was now lost to us in the seething cauldron of war; not even as any reaffirmation of my love for Gene. This was for me and my need alone.

VII

Gene, Junior was born on December 7, 1942, on the first anniversary of Pearl Harbor Day. The United States was at war. The anti-fascist war alliance of the U.S., the Soviet Union, and Britain was one year old. Gene had been turned down in his request to go to the Philippines. The U.S. military was not interested in the revolutionary people's movements in Asia and the Pacific as active allies. Obviously not all components of the anti-fascist war coalition understood the character of that war in the same way.

Unlike Tim's birth in Los Angeles, now there were no adoring aunts and uncles and admiring comrades, no attentive grandmother and gentle grandfather to love the new grandson. Gene and I were alone with our baby, and so became closer in our need to cope together. He scrubbed diapers each morning before going to his Party office, while I sterilized feeding bottles. On weekends he aired the baby on Riverside Drive, when he was not out of town on Party work, while I escaped for a few hours into the gallery of a Broadway matinee or into the reference room at the public library on Forty-second street. In our tiny, scrubby apartment on West 135th street, off Riverside Drive, we battled cockroaches and banged uselessly on icy radiators that sent the three of us to bed each night dressed as though we were off on a snow trip.

And I lived in wartime Moscow. A wailing ambulance siren six flights down or a tooting ship's whistle on the river a half-block away froze me into air raid alertness. The roar of a plane overhead paralyzed me into waiting for the whooshing shriek of a bomb coming ground-ward.

I was contemptuous of what passed for "the war effort" here at home. I snorted angrily at exhortative civil defense articles in the morning newspapers as I recalled the action-filled Moscow days and nights. Gripes and jokes about food and gas rationing appalled me. I knew that for nickels and dimes at the neighborhood shops and for millions in Washington all rationing problems were solvable. "There's a war on, lady," became the facade behind which little people got pecked clean while war profits of big industry soared.

If our Party veered at times too much towards subordinating labor's interests to the war effort, I nursed a bitter anger at the American people who did not seem to know what war was really like. At times I wished a few of the bombs falling on Moscow and London would fall on New York too. I wished that New Yorkers complaining about ration coupons were compelled, instead, to worry about space on a refugee train.

But there *was* a war on, and American Communists, as Communists in all countries, became the most determined, politically aware fighters in that war. Fifteen thousand American Communists were in the armed forces. And because the other seventy thousand were actively and influentially inside the labor unions and people's organizations, our Party was able to quickly re-establish its relations within the mainstream struggle, despite its brief isolation from August, 1939 to June, 1941.

The struggle for the anti-fascist character of the war was, at times, no less arduous than the military battles. Throughout the war years there were Americans and Britons in high government and industrial levels who sought the enemy's victory, who felt we were in the right war but on the wrong side. The Right wing claimed that Roosevelt's war alliance was a sellout to Russia, while on the Left some shouted that the Soviet Union's anti-fascist war alliance was a sellout to capitalism.

Our Party's all-out involvement was suspect, at first, in light of its abrupt change, once again, from its claim from August 22, 1939 to June 22, 1941, that it no longer differentiated between "the camps of democracy and fascism."

Four days after the Hitler invasion, however, Party chairman William Foster told the national committee:

"Hitler's attack on the Soviet Union changes the character of the world war, and thereby makes necessary changes in our Party's attitude toward that war. . . . Whoever fights Hitler, helps the USSR, helps to defend American democracy, helps to guard world freedom and civilization."

Once again, this time in twenty-two months, we made a full-circle about-face. This time it had the full support of the membership. Once again, our comrades responded with vigorous leadership that made them the pivots in mass organizations whose breadth in support of the war now exceeded that of the 1930s.

After the U.S. became a fighting partner of the Soviet Union, Foster delineated more specifically our new national win-the-war unity. The goal was "the strongest possible collaboration among all classes and organizations in American life, that are ready to fight the Axis enemy." The trade unions, Foster wrote, had responsibility to "push for maximum production, in closest cooperation with the employers and government." He called for "avoidance of strikes," labor's assurance of "continuance of production," and labor's equal responsibility with employers to increase production through its full representation on all management, government, and industry boards.

Fighting for labor's greater involvement in the war was, in reality, a call to break corporate sabotage of the anti-fascist character of the war. The influx of Black workers into defense plants became stormy struggles against job discrimination, housing covenants, poll-tax laws and for anti-lynch legislation. Unions brought charges against whole industries, including auto, to force the monopolists to convert to war production. Involved here was not only anti-fascism, but simple survival on the economic front. Priorities for government contracts and rationed raw materials were going to defense industries; more than five million were among the "priorities" unemployed, that is, workers laid-off in non-war-related industries. "All for war production" became a political cry to assure the anti-fascist character of the war and an economic demand for the jobs that such production would create. The unprecedented recruitment of women into the wartime labor force aroused demands for equal pay, child care centers, job discrimination charges. The fight for price and rent controls to stop profiteering became a bitter struggle in the neighborhoods, struggles that forced public hearings on unfair profit gouging by the giant Atlantic and Pacific and National Foods chains and also the Milk Trust.

Even our apartment house on West 135th Street caught the fever. Our twenty-four families held frequent tenant meetings, organized a council, instituted a rent strike and took our slumlord to court. There, as spokeswoman for the group, I stood before The Bench. In speeches richly sprinkled with references to the war being fought abroad and our determination it not be lost at home, I proclaimed our group's refusal to pay rent until our demands were met. These included replacement of an old furnace which left us heatless on every cold day and night; regular extermination services to augment our daily war on cockroaches; repairs in specific apartments. Our rents were impounded by the court and released to the landlord only four months later when our council returned *en masse* to verify that our demands had been met.

It was not quite equal to fighting firebombs on the roofs of Moscow, but it was a satisfying battle. A pleasant aftermath was the new camaraderie as Italian, Puerto Rican and Jewish neighbors now met each other warmly in the hallways and rang each other's doorbells with taste offerings of some ethnic dish.

VIII

In larger arenas, we Communists actively supported labor, New Deal and third party campaigns and tickets, at the same time that the well-known Communists, Pete Cacchione from Brooklyn, and Benjamin J. Davis from Harlem, were elected to the New York City Council.

Despite coalitions and national unity, Harry Bridges on the West Coast was battling a second attempt of the shipping interests and the government to deport him as a Communist, and William Schneiderman's challenge to the lifting of his citizenship for the same reason was still being fought. Earl Browder, however, was released from prison by executive order "in the interest of national unity," while the Un-American Committee ignored the President's action and continued to witchhunt in the labor unions, the political coalitions, the anti-fascist groups.

No, all was not peace and harmony in the years of anti-fascist alliance. They were years of contradictions, years of struggle, years of trying to isolate the most rabid reactionaries from the diverse motivations of all those willing, for whatever reasons, to participate in the alliance.

Gene spent little time in New York, working out in the midwest states and in Washington, coping with realistic everyday problems of the movements. At home he wrote prolifically, offering analyses of the political-military situation abroad, exposing the imperialist mentality which held up the Second Front in Europe which, he showed graphically, could have made "1942 the year of the end of Hitler Germany."

He emphasized "the increasingly vital importance of providing all the East Asian peoples fuller opportunity to participate actively and fully in the war for the defense of their native soil and countries."

Japan's "demagogic pretensions [at being] the liberator of the Asiatic peoples," he warned, "can create temporary confusions, especially if certain sections of the East Asian peoples should get the impression that the united nations are not giving them a full opportunity adequately and resolutely to defend their land and country and are not given recognition to their right to national independence."

In 1943 he welcomed the "profound changes" in the anti-fascist military alliance created by the Soviet offensive on five fronts; the development of guerrilla warfare in Yugoslavia, Poland and Norway; the sabotage activities of French factory workers; the appearance of some organized opposition inside Germany, the real possibility of people's armed struggle in the Hitler-occupied countries.

Under pressures of shoring-up the coalitions at home and abroad and defending them from those using divisive tactics to destroy national unity, the tendency grew to muffle criticisms of the weaknesses of the alliance. In the interest of unity our Party tended to go along with actions which, in hindsight, are unexplainable and indefensible.

We condoned as "necessary" the herding of 110,000 Japanese-American men, women and children in detention camps in California, Arizona, Oregon and Washington state. We remained silent as their homes and property were confiscated or forcibly sold at outrageously low prices. It was not so much that we consciously believed this was valid and necessary, our chief concern was that there be no "boat-rocking" over any issue. Everything, including our independent thinking, was subordinated to support to the country's commander-in-chief of the antifascist war alliance.

Together with almost everyone else in the country and abroad, our Party received too calmly the news of the U.S. atom bomb killing and maiming of 200,000 of Hiroshima's 340,000 people and the levelling of Nagasaki in the last days of the war.

In fact, so one-sided was our view, we saw nothing ludicrous in Foster's statement in the *Daily Worker*: "Three days ago Japan suffered the great shock of the first atomic bomb; now it staggers under the still heavier blow of the Soviet declaration of war."

Eight:
BROWDER DREAM, TRUMAN NIGHTMARE

I

The war was practically over. In San Francisco a new international organization was formed at a conference of forty-six nations—an embodiment of the transformation of the anti-fascist war alliance into a postwar unity to secure the peace.

The issue now was, what kind of peace; what kind of new world on the hot ashes of the old. Everywhere the Communists emerged with undisputed anti-fascist records. From the underground resistance movements in the newly liberated countries they came forth to play a significant role in the struggle to reconstruct new governments and democratic institutions. Here in the U.S., too, by the mid-1940's our Party reached the apex of its political influence and organizational growth.

By 1943 we had some 83,000 members, 15,000 of them in the armed forces fighting fascism; 40% of our members were industrial workers, 14% Black, 46% women, 25% professional and white collar workers. A year later, 24,000 more joined, 30% of these Black. The majority of our comrades were activists in labor unions, in every type of people's organization. They helped mold national and local social policy, their participation in struggle was maximal, and decisive in many cases.

True, this influence and growth was not based primarily upon our revolutionary goals for socialism, but on our daily activity to affect the country's democratic direction. The anti-fascist war had just been won in collaboration with the liberal sector of U.S. capitalism. Socialism was not the order of the day, securing the continuing progressive direction of the country was. In contemplating postwar perspectives we again took our lead from the smoke signals coming out of Moscow, as we always had in the past.

Roosevelt, Stalin and Churchill had met face to face for the first time in November, 1943. At Teheran they projected a postwar world of cooperation, friendship and unity which would assure peaceful development for all countries. *Pravda* editorials and Stalin speeches emphasized again and again, "the vital lasting interests of the great powers which have borne the brunt of the war against aggression." The key word was, for us, "*lasting.*"

The Comintern had dissolved a few months before Teheran with the statement that it could no longer determine policy and tactics for Communist parties operating in such widely divergent conditions of historical and social development, and on different levels of class consciousness and maturity as exists in each separate country. Communist parties were being told to develop their own policies, tactics and activity based upon the unique national features endemic to their own country.

If all of these smoke signals were merely diplomatic maneuvers, as we were later told, our whole political experience had conditioned us not to see them as such. We had accepted in 1939 the Soviet view that the Nazi beast had changed its spots—how much more viable to believe now Teheran and Moscow's proclaimed belief in postwar alliance cooperation with liberal, bourgeois-democratic capitalism.

The "spirit of Teheran" became the slogan with which our Party projected the struggle to continue the unity of social purpose so evident during the war. The dissolution of the Party into an educational organization to dramatize our full partnership in this national unity evoked little reaction within the Party.

November 1943 to February 1944 was a four-month period in which creative, contradictory ideas, many of them alarmingly erroneous, agitated the national committee. For example, the majority of the committee members, including Foster and Gene, embraced "Teheran" as a popular goal to fight for, as a rally-cry to keep intact, if possible, the old wartime unity of action. Browder, on the other hand, developed "Teheran" into an already achieved state in which an "enlightened capitalism" was being led by "men of vision [and] intelligence" who in their own self interest were leading the country into a postwar world of "planned economy, peaceful industrial expansion and resultant well-being for all the people."

Similarly, changing the Party into an "educational association" was seen by the majority of national committee members as an insignificant change. They agreed with Gene's view expressed at a national committee meeting that Communist parties around the world often have changed structure and name to meet specific circumstances. What was decisive, he said, was that we retain our working class character, our Marxist-Leninist science, and that we work publicly as Communists.

Browder, on the other hand, offered the organizational change as dramatic proof that we were now a "loyal opposition," not a contending political force. He said that Communists now "loyally support the existing system of private enterprise which is accepted by the overwhelming majority of Americans."

As was its custom, the leadership did not categorically vote these differences up or down. Party members read published reports of Browder, Foster, Dennis and others that emphasized one or another aspects of a "general line."

In February, 1944, however, Foster wrote a long and angry letter to the national committee demolishing the extremes to which Browder's views had distorted original policy. He rightly accused Browder of negating the class struggle, the contradictions between capitalism and socialism, the very character of the capitalist system.

The national committee, in the main, agreed with this criticism; they had already begun to disassociate themselves from the most flagrant of Browder's views behind closed doors. They believed, however, that now, as in the past, Foster tended to oversimplify the class contradictions he emphasized. They felt he ignored the need for flexibility in tactics, that he minimized the role non-working class allies could play in the post-war era. They felt that in his polemic he swung to the opposite extreme of negating the "spirit of Teheran" as a popular struggle tactic.

Foster was prevailed upon to withdraw his letter and, as in the past, Gene and the others assured him that the worst aspects and crassest formulations of Browder's views would be modified in daily practice.

Later, when the crisis erupted and Foster's letter was published, he claimed in a subsequent article that he had agreed to the suppression of that letter "in the interest of Party unity," and also because he was afraid he would be expelled if he had taken his letter directly to the membership. If this had happened, Foster would have been a victim of a sacrosanct Party procedure he had always upheld and had used against others.

II

This period lasted only sixteen months. By early 1945 the objective scene began to change rapidly. The transference of the presidency from Roosevelt to Truman signified a sharp shift in U.S. foreign and domestic policies, a shift that became evident immediately. That postwar shift may have come in any case. It may not have. Roosevelt was no Truman, just as Truman was no Roosevelt. A new and different reality began to emerge internationally and at home. Within the national committee of our Party some began to demand a re-evaluation of the national unity concepts. Criticism of Browder's positions became sharper and more direct, but these were contained within the top leadership echelons.

Political intervention from abroad at this crucial moment intensified the problems inherent in a time when a shift in analysis and policy is in process.

The French Communist leader Jacques Duclos levelled a scathing attack upon our Party for what he termed "a notorious revision of Marxism." He countered Browder's positions to those of Foster and commended the latter's letter to the national committe, the letter no one outside the national committee supposedly knew anything about.

The Duclos criticism was in the form of a lengthy major article in the theoretical journal of the French Communist Party. It was published by the commercial press here in our country while it was still being translated from the French for our leadership.

Despite the non-existence of the Comintern, we knew that the Duclos blast against the U.S. Party was not a personal viewpoint. While conceding the basic premise of the criticism, Gene was furious at the public form it had taken.

"The wrong impression has been created that our reassessment comes now only as a result of pressures from abroad," he said. "Not only is this not true, but this impression complicates our coalition relations. Of all parties, the French should be sensitive to such questions."

At the moment, however, immediate concern was not so

much for our coalition relations as for the internal crisis that exploded inside our own organization. What should have been a rational shift in political gears became, for some unexplainable reason, a recriminative explosion that toppled leaders.

No one was prepared for Browder's bitter opposition to the correction campaign nor for Foster's vitrolic attacks upon Browder personally. The two months' discussion period preceding the emergency convention in July 1945, called to reconstitute the Communist Party and to officially reject the old "Teheran," national unity policy, became a period in which Browder and Foster wrote prolific polemics against each other in tones that exposed the deep-rooted, longstanding animosity between them.

The membership turned against all leadership with anger and cynicism; anger at the suppression of the original Foster letter, cynicism toward a leadership depicted as having been pied-pipered by Browder into the morass of reformism from which only a Duclos had saved them.

Leading comrades around the country resigned their state positions in the Party, claiming in *mea culpa* humility that they did not deserve them. Gene was furious and countered bitterly:

"Not breast-beating, but analysis is needed. Not a sick humility, but a Marxist scalpel. We have to examine together where and why we were wrong; we have to demonstrate our ability to learn from our mistakes."

Foster could have mitigated some of the anger and cynicism which was preventing objective analysis. He was the hero of the day and he chose to remain silent for too long on certain facts which only he was in a position to offer. Later, when it hardly mattered any more, Foster did officially admit that before the Duclos criticism had appeared there had been important differences between what Foster called Browder's views that "American reaction [was] no longer a danger" and "Dennis' emphasis on a perspective of sharp struggle ahead;" also, that even before the Duclos letter Browder had been challenged by a few comrades in the leadership, among them Gene, Gil Green, Robert Thompson and John Williamson. Foster added that "of all the comrades, Gene had been the least influenced by Browder's views."

Despite my angry disagreement, Gene had refused to make those facts known himself. He referred to them officially only after Foster did. He said the issue was not "degrees of responsibility" for the mistakes but the correction of them. Even as the correction process unfolded, those comrades rooted in the mass and coalition movements expressed concern that we would pendulum swing into a sectarian over-correction of revisionist policies. Gene had this concern too, and his reports emphasized that the mistakes being corrected had not been rooted in our coalition policies or in utilizing as effectively as possible the divisions within capitalism to defeat the most reactionary sectors. The mistake lay, he wrote, "in *relying* upon sections of capital to carry out consistently anti-fascist, democratic and progressive policy at home and abroad, during and after the war."

He wrote that in our commitment to the anti-fascist war we did not clearly differentiate between the motives of our bourgeois democratic allies and those of the Soviet Union together with the working peoples in all countries, including our own; that within those coalitions we did not sufficiently safeguard the independent role of labor, the interests of all working peoples, nor sufficiently put forward the policies of the Left and the programs of the Communists.

III

Having rejected the Browder dream of class peace and revisionism, and confronted now with the first indications of what was rapidly to become the Truman nightmare, our Party emerged with sharp, more realistic perspectives. Because Browder continued to actively oppose and obstruct this new political line, he was expelled in February, 1946. Gene's election as general secretary came as no surprise, although I had fervently hoped it would not happen. As in 1938 in Moscow I pleaded he not accept the new responsibility thrust upon him.

Over the last eight years, culminating in this year of consolidation-during-crisis, Gene had emerged as the leader of our Party. Not a popular, mass public figure, but a leader known and respected by movement cadre around the country, in and outside the Party, as a masterful tactician and strategist, a thoughtful leader who left the histronics and flamboyancy to others while he quietly analyzed, listened, questioned, worked and helped movements and struggles to materialize.

In his nomination speech Foster said, "His election will, in fact, be a recognition of a situation already in existence."

The only national woman Party leader at the time and an extremely popular one inside and outside the organization,

Elizabeth Gurley Flynn in a feature article on Gene's election wrote:

> "To those of us who work with this calm, rather shy, handsome big man with a youthful face, greying hair, blue eyes and a warm smile—this is a natural, an inevitable confirmation of the work he has actually done for the past year.... His knowledge, judgment and ability to coolly analyze situations and subjects, to think things through and to arrive at a rounded-out, balanced and correct Communist decision, are unfailing. ... He has performed yeoman service to create what he correctly estimated as our need, 'the achievement of greater independent Marxist thinking, genuine democracy and collective work, and a higher type of inner Communist unity'."

I was proud for him, but I also was afraid. I did not want this to happen. The eight years in national leadership had taken their toll. A newly developed minor heart condition would probably now become aggravated. His carefully controlled tensions, which others foolishly praised as "remarkable calmness," would now become more tightly coiled. The bureaucracy and sparking animosities on top which he tried to cope with by refusing to become a part of them, could now either consume him or destroy him. I feared the tautness of the tightrope he would now walk. I was uneasy at those deeply rooted personality traits which blocked him from being a back-slapping, smooth and glib popular figure the membership wanted. Our Party had a difficult healing process to go through. Gene would have the position and the responsibility, but he was taking over at a time when a healthy anti-leadership skepticism was dominant. Never again would we place blind faith in any leader. Yet I did not want Gene to be victimized by that healthy attitude. I wanted for him some of the adulation and confidence which Browder and Foster had had benefit of for so long. I knew my fears and concern could not keep him from being selected as general secretary. I could only stand by and be uneasy for him.

IV

The effect that the rifts and differences within the capitalist class may have on the people's struggles and the lessons to be learned about the need to utilize these rifts for the struggles were never clearer than in the contrasts between the Roosevelt and

Truman administrations. Both Democratic, each sought different methods in serving the interests of the class they both served. Under Roosevelt, the dominant sector of capitalism adjusted to a changed world reality by seeking detente with the Soviet Union abroad and detente with the American people at home. It responded with compromises, concessions and adjustments forced on it by a militant people's movement.

With the advent of the Truman presidency this changed. He had no use for this anti-fascist, progressive unity nonsense which, in his view, had weakened the United States' hegemonic role in the world. The atom bomb was dropped on Hiroshima and Nagasaki to dramatize that hegemonic role. At Fulton, Missouri, Truman and Churchill scrapped the old U.S.-British-Soviet cooperation and replaced that alliance with an "English-speaking" one based upon "joint naval and air force bases all over the world." U.S. aid was given to help France re-establish her pre-war empire in Indo-China. U.S. troops helped the British crush the postwar Greek revolution, and the West German state was established in violation of the Potsdam Agreement. The United States' divine right to intervene militarily into any country was proclaimed, becoming officially known as The Truman Doctrine. The Marshall Plan was inaugurated, wherein billions of U.S. dollars were used, in the guise of reconstruction, to control the political direction of the countries newly liberated from fascism. The North Atlantic Treaty gave the U.S. military bases and troop concentrations "up to the very borders of the Soviet Union," as former Vice President Henry Wallace charged.

At home President Truman midwifed McCarthyism some four years before Joseph McCarthy, junior senator from Wisconsin, came to the fore. Roosevelt New Dealers in and outside the government had become suspect as the Truman administration sharply changed the country's course. All who had or still urged cooperation with the socialist world and the reality of the liberation struggles of China, all Asia and Africa became suspect. A cold war, "Communist menace," had to have its counterpart in a similar "menace" at home.

Problems of peacetime conversion evoked a wave of strikes involving over four million people, the largest number in any one year in U.S. labor history up to that time. Hit hardest were the basic industries of auto, railway, mining, maritime. Militant strikers became suspect and part of the "Communist menace."

President Truman's Executive Order 9835 initiated the

witchhunt in government. Some four million federal employees were "investigated" for their "loyalty." Liberals, progressives, former anti-fascist New Dealers were fired as "security risks;" others resigned to avoid the harassment of investigations into their private lives. Thousands were hounded out of federal agencies.

In the restive labor movement the Taft-Hartley anti-Communist affadavits served the same purpose as Executive Order 9835 did in government. "Communist" was now synonymous with "militant," and the dour headhunters were not even aware of the ironic compliment they paid the Communists. Or maybe they were. Refusal of any labor activist to sign the I-am-not-a-Communist affadavit was read as admission to being a Communist, and they were booted out of the union. Militants who in good conscience signed the affadavit were prosecuted for "perjury." The lever used against the unions was that unless their organization was purged, it would be denied the services of the National Labor Relations Board.

Three years before Joe McCarthy meteored upon the scene, Gene appeared before the Un-American Activities Committee, popularly called the Un-American Committee, to oppose legislation to outlaw the Communist Party. He warned that these bills were not directed against Communists alone. "Undefined and undefineable" persons labelled as Communists were threatened, he said. "Anyone who holds the same view as Communists that the Negro people are entitled to equal rights or the fundamental view that all people are created equal could under the proposed legislation be prosecuted for the crime of being a Communist fellow traveller."

In 1947 there were 212 bills on the Congressional calendar to limit labor's bargaining power, abolish the union shop, abrogate the right to strike, legalize the labor injunction, cripple the Wagner Act.

By the summer of 1948 three government committees were simultaneously conducting separate hearings on "Communism" in the labor movement, in the organizations of the farmers, veterans, youth, and peace groups. The courage of those who refused to cooperate with these committees ran into the many hundreds, and they were blacklisted out of jobs and professions, indicted under various charges.

None of these Congressional committees, however, investigated the 142 lynchings of Blacks by whites during 1945-1951.

They did not investigate the legal murder by execution of the seven young Black men in Martinsville, Virginia, or Willie McGee at Laurel, Mississippi. They did not investigate the long imprisonment of Mrs. Rosa Lee Ingram and her two young Black sons for the crime of defending her from a white employer's rape.

V

Unlike those who had been unwillingly subpoenaed, Gene had battled for his right to testify before the Un-American Committee. He was a voluntary witness against the proposed legislation to outlaw the Communist Party. We Communists were not alone in opposition. Eleanor Roosevelt and president of the A.F.L., William Green, condemned those bills, as did thirteen leaders of Ford and Buick locals of the United Auto Workers Union, the secretary of the Alabama Federation of Labor, and Wisconsin state C.I.O. leaders. The U.S. Department of Labor admitted the mail was "running 19 to 1" against the bills.

On March 26, 1947, according to *Time* magazine (April 7):

"Into the committee room strode a big, tweedy, pipe smoking man. He looked like the editor of a college press. He was Eugene Dennis, general secretary of the Communist Party. Appearing at his own request, he was armed with a 21-page document. He had scarcely settled himself in his chair before he was in trouble...."

The *New York Times* account described what followed as "a scene of confusion and uproar" in which "voices and emotions rose" immediately after Gene sat down and identified himself.

From that moment the transcript reveals a sparring bout in which committee investigator Stripling and chairman J. Parnell Thomas insisted that before he could testify Gene had to answer a barrage of questions, each of which, while differently worded, asked whether he had gone under any name other than Eugene Dennis.

To each question Gene responded, with little variation, "I am Eugene Dennis. I am known as Eugene Dennis. I pay taxes under the name of Eugene Dennis. According to the Constitution of the United States a man may change his name under oath of law or under common usage." He insisted these questions were "quite irrelevant and immaterial" to his intent to voluntarily testify against the pending anti-Communist legislation. The stormy session ended with:

Chairman: Serve a subpoena on this man and he is through for the day.
Dennis: I insist on submitting this [indicating statement] into the record.
Chairman: You are excused.
Dennis: Do you accept this as the testimony before the Commitee?
Chairman: You are excused.
Dennis: Mr. Thomas, on behalf of the American people I hold this committee in contempt.
Stripling: Let the record show that he is being served with a subpoena.

Newsreel film in theaters around the country showed a subpoena being thrust at Gene, he throws it to the floor, chairman Thomas is pounding his gavel, armed police rush in, grab Gene by the arms and, pushing and pulling, they drag him out of the committee room.

Sitting in the dark movie house in our neighborhood, our four-and-a-half-year-old Gene Jr. watches this film in tense silence, fists gripping his chair arms. For months afterwards, pulling his toy cowboy guns out of their holsters, he points them at every traffic officer we pass, snarling under his breath:

"Bang! Bang! My daddy and me, we don't like cops!"

Party comrades and progressives generally understood and approved Gene's refusal to be intimidated on the witness stand. They recognized the effort made to prevent Gene's exposé of the committee. But few undertood why, as some put it, Gene "played into the committee's hands" by refusing to answer so simple a question as to his name.

Throughout the long witchhunt years many good people succumbed to the news media's campaign to depict anyone who took the Fifth Amendment—that constitutional right against self incrimination—as being obviously guilty. Unless one were deeply involved in these events, few understood that, under questioning, one could not choose which questions one would or would not answer; that one lost the Fifth Amendment right to not answer if some questions are answered.

Gene had appeared voluntarily to state his views regarding pending legislation. He refused to be subjected to diversions from the issue at hand. There was another consideration, too. In the small top Party committee where the question of who should represent the Party at the hearing was decided, Gene had suggested Ben Davis, former New York City councilman. Ben insisted that Gene, as general secretary, be the one. Others sat silent, and at one point Ben challenged "this mystery stuff that keeps Gene from taking on these kind of hearings." Ben accused Gene of being a "coward, afraid to go into these hostile situations." At that point Gene curtly closed the discussion, saying he would go to Washington.

At home that night when he told me what had happened I asked, both curiously and somewhat worried, whether he would answer the Committee's questions.

"Of course not. That's not the problem. It is the kind of questions they will ask. Names. Passports. Travels. My work abroad. They will be a diversionary smokescreen."

I exploded in anger, "Then you're letting Ben provoke you into a jail sentence!"

He shrugged, "No one at the meeting objected, why should I?"

"But it's not just personal," I insisted. "It will weaken the impact of your challenge, which you'll never get to make."

"That was my objection to going. But if the comrades can't see it and everyone sat silent as the whole issue was turned into a charge of my *fear* of going, that settled it."

VI

Having gone before the Committee that March 26, Gene unleashed a militant offensive. Refusing to recognize the subpoena thrust at him at the end of that hectic session, he did not appear on April 9 as ordered. Instead he called together a small group of capable research workers and our Party lawyers. He put before them the task to give him the facts and the legal grounds to support the charge he wanted to make. As a result, his letter to the Un-American Committee, in lieu of his appearance, challenged that body's legal and constitutional validity.

Gene charged that committee member John E. Rankin of Mississippi "is not a lawfully elected, or duly seated member of the House of Representatives of the United States," having been elected in violation of the Fourteenth Amendment. Corroborating his charge statistically, Gene declared that "no less than

750,000 Negroes in the state of Mississippi of voting age failed to vote (November, 1946) for reasons that cannot be assumed to be voluntary."

Black spokesmen were quick to embrace this unprecedented challenge to racist power in government. Former Dean of Howard University Law School, Charles Houston, agreed to represent Gene when he was indicted on charges growing out of this challenge, saying, "This case, I believe, blends into a defense of the rights of fourteen million American Negroes. I welcome it."

Earl Dickerson of Chicago, Black president of the National Bar Association, argued the case in the appeals courts, together with white conservative Louis F. McCabe of Philadelphia. Some seventy-five Black leaders filed an amicus brief expressing their intense concern in this first constitutional challenge to the illegal practices of the South condoned by Congress and the government in the North. All Black newspapers in the country commented editorially and in column features in a vein similar to that of the *Baltimore Afro-American*:

"If these constitutional arguments are upheld, Mr. Dennis will have done more than vindicate himself. He will have struck a vital blow toward unshackling the disfranchised masses in Dixie—a blow which Congress, by its refusal to pass a federal anti-poll tax law, has studiously refused to strike."

In its April 9th session with Gene absent, the Un-American Committee heard investigator Stripling summarize a dossier describing Gene's past activities and arrests in Los Angeles, his travels to China and a list of the names he reportedly had used. The Committee voted to ask Congress to indict Gene for "contempt."

Committee member Richard M. Nixon said if Dennis returned to California he would be arrested and prosecuted as a fugitive. Meanwhile, Nixon urged, he should be charged with the stiffer *"conspiracy* to commit contempt" which carried a two-year sentence instead of the one-year term for simple contempt. Congress voted the original charge by a vote of 196 to 1, with American Labor Party Congressman Vito Marcantonio warning his colleagues in a speech on the floor explaining his lone vote.

"One fact you can't deny. If the people of Germany had defeated

Hitler's effort to destroy the constitutional rights of the Communist Party, he [Hitler] would never had gained power, and there would have been no World War II."

Gene was convicted in a Washington, D.C. trial, June 27, in which Judge David Pine denied him the right to introduce as evidence the letter he had sent to the Un-American Committee stating the Fourteenth Amendment reason for his refusal to appear before the committee. Pine reduced the whole case to the obvious issue of whether Gene did or did not appear in response to a subpoena.

I.F. Stone wrote from the nation's capital that summer: "Washington is living under the shadow of terror." Five hundred fifty C.I.O. and A.F.L. union officials warned in a joint statement that the Un-American Committee was "spearheading Big Business' drive against labor in the name of hunting Communists." Thirty-eight leaders of the Auto Workers Union in Detroit protested Gene's conviction. Four hundred picketed Attorney General McGrath in similar protest when he appeared at the Palmer House in Chicago. Five hundred delegates at a jobs conference in York, Pennsylvania, passed a resolution against the conviction. In Hollywood, where the Un-American Committee ran public extravanganzas that surpassed in fantasy those produced for the screen, Judy Garland urged people to "tell Congress how much you resent the way Mr. Thomas is kicking the daylights out of the Bill of Rights," and Frederic March warned, "They're after more than Hollywood. This reaches into every American city and town."

VII

Early in the 1948 presidential campaign, media polls showed Truman an unpopular candidate; analysts referred to the fact that he was running scared before a new kind of opposition. He had lost the solid social base Roosevelt had had, while his get-tough policies were being trumped by the Republicans.

The new third party with Henry Wallace as its standard bearer crested early as an impressive vehicle that revitalized the political charisma and unity of the old coalition movements. The Left and the Communists had actively supported its formation. Truman, however, played a well-plotted poker hand and won the election. Confronted with the ghost of Roosevelt to haunt his digressions, the President belatedly but energetically embraced that ghost. Brushed with his own Red-scare campaign by the Republicans who leaked stories about pending grand jury indictments of Administration officials on espionage, Truman finessed by escalating his own " Communist menace" drive to new levels.

Two days before the Progressive Party opened its national nominating convention in Philadelphia, the leaders of the Communist Party were arrested on charges of "conspiracy to teach and advocate the overthrow of the government by force and violence," that is, alleged violation of the Smith Act. Newspaper headlines immediately linked the new third party to the arrested Communists and to the key words "conspiracy" and "force and violence."

Simultaneously Truman draped himself vigorously in the Roosevelt mantle and energetically wooed labor back into the Democratic fold. He passionately argued the lesser evil theory, addressing himself "to those whose worry over the state of the world has caused them to lean toward a third party." To these, he pleaded that "a wasted vote" would "play into the hands of the Republican forces of reaction whose aims are directly opposed to the aims of American liberalism." Of the grand jury leaks about "spies" in his Administration, the President cried he was the victim of "a Republican red herring campaign."

On that same day, Gene held a press conference to note:

> "President Truman's belated discovery that the current spy scare in Washington is a 'red herring' sounds like the sad wail of a man who has been hoisted by his own petard. . . . Now the Democratic Party candidate for the presidency finds that the G.O.P. has turned his own red scare against him in a neat campaign trick. Now it is his ox that is being gored."

The Progressive Party attracted to itself a large core of devoted, tireless, militant activists around the country. It was definitely Left of the old New Deal coalition and was, as Gene noted, "anti-imperialist and anti-monopoly, not merely anti-fascist."

The Un-American Committee witchhunts, the government loyalty purges, the Taft-Hartley straitjacket, the growing number of trials and convictions for "contempt," "perjury" and the first "spy" case indictment—that of Alger Hiss—all these took their toll as they were intended to within the labor and people's movements.

Labor officials who had been part of the old Center-Left coalitions in building the C.I.O. and the New Deal alliances, now embraced Truman's cold war foreign policies and succumbed to Red-baiting activities within their own unions. Anti-Sovietism within the context of the Cold War and the Progressive Party as the new militant opposition to Trumanism became the chief issues.

Within our Party, many comrades, including Gene, felt that the Party's new dogmatic tactics exacerbated the divisive polarization taking place. A self conscious fear of being labelled recalcitrant Browderites by Foster who kept that ghost actively alive as a bogey pushed our comrades into positions which weakened our labor and coalition relations.

With no official Right wing Browder trend to lock horns with and with a new credibility growing out of his role in the 1943-45 internal crisis, Foster moved tenaciously from Left field. He succeeded in establishing the policy that Communists make as a precondition for continuing unity relations the endorsement of the Progressive Party, denunciation of the Truman and Marshall Plan Doctrines and support to the foreign policies of the Soviet Union. Communists in the trade unions and people's organizations were under instruction to make these the main issues in their activity; coalitions relations were severed when they failed.

However, in articles and reports Gene insisted:

"We oppose any sectarian tendency to convert the political struggle within the trade unions in behalf of Wallace and the new people's party into a movement to split or withdraw from the established trade union centers."

He emphasized the Party's duty "to champion its own Marxist point of view on all current questions, as well as bring forward its fundamental program for the eventual socialist reorganization of society."

"However," he said, "in doing this, we must reject the sectarian concept and practice that the maintenance of our independent positions means, or must result in our self-isolation, the separation of the Communists from the masses of the working class or the alienation of us Communists from our progressive non-Communist allies, especially in the labor movement."

A few years later, when the Party was re-evaluating this period, Gene argued in 1956 against Foster's claim that the expulsion of the Left unions from the C.I.O. had been "inevitable" because of the cold war, anti-Soviet policies of the officialdom. Gene replied:

"The question is not what the top leadership of the C.I.O. did. The question is how we Communists and the Left worked to stay with the rank and file, on what basis and on what issues did we seek to unite them to fight that leadership."

In a similar vein, during a political post-mortem in 1953 on whether or not the formation of the Progressive Party had been a sectarian, leftist withdrawal from the mainstream, Gene wrote in a letter from Atlanta prison:

"The Progressive Party as an anti-war and anti-fascist alignment of certain Leftwing and other independent labor and progressive forces arose out of the specific conditions, trends and needs of the 1947-48 period."

Among its many weaknesses, he singled out that Party's:

"failure to combine an independent policy and tactic with activity in the mainstream . . . its failure to work with the great masses of working people who have not yet broken electorally with the major parties of capital around a whole number of very specific issues."

Paraphrasing the Lenin precept which always had guided his style of activity, Gene reiterated that the struggle must be on specific issues agitating the mainstream, a struggle waged "among the people and their established organizations, not from the ivory-towered sanctuary of a simon-pure Progressive Party."

The differences over these tactics in 1947-48 and efforts to correct them were sidetracked abruptly for some seven years. In January, 1949 the eleven members of the Party's national board began a nine-months-long court trial defending themselves and the Communist Party.

VIII

The eleven (plus Foster who was severed from the case early due to ill health) were indicted on two counts: conspiracy to teach and advocate the overthrow of the government by force and violence, and membership in an organization that teaches and advocates such forcible overthrow. They were now on trial on the first count. With these convictions, the State sought to outlaw a legal, minority political party by so-called "legal" process. All minority opinion and action would then be intimidated and strait-jacketed.

Interesting, but momentary, differences surfaced among the eleven defendants regarding trial strategy questions. One or two urged passive non-participation in the whole procedure to dramatize the illegality of the trial. The majority rejected this as foolish leftist posturing. They argued that every channel of democratic and legal due process must be utilized to fight for the legal, constitutional rights and very existence of the Communist Party. This together with the right of Americans to read and hear all political ideas, including those of the Communists, they decided, was the main issue of the trial. In passing, one urged that the right to teach and advocate what the Smith Act prohibits, forcible overthrow—that is, the right to revolution—be defended. The majority decided that the right to revolution would be defended as a theoretical, historical concept; the main task was to combat the government's intent to portray our Party as a secret, foreign agent involved in adventurist coups d'etats. The defense, they decided, should be as much as possible within a context that could solicit the widest support. This was in the spirit of Congressman Vito Marcantonio's warning on the floor of the 80th Congress that "The defense of the constitutional rights of the Communists is the first line defense of the democratic rights of all Americans."

This strategy enabled us to solicit and secure a highly versatile team of attorneys, a combination of knowledgeable Left and conservative, constitutional democrats who, in the process of the nine months' trial, received a political education.

On opening day, January 17, 1949, newspaper headlines screamed: "400 POLICE ON DUTY AS COMMUNISTS GO ON TRIAL." On the second morning: "COMMUNIST LEADERS ON TRIAL AS ENEMIES OF U.S." Defense attorneys protested as prejudicial the police cordon around the courthouse and reports that "the largest detail in policy history [will be] assigned to every session of the proceedings."

Judge Harold R. Medina peered down from his high bench, the American flag at his back, and with raised eyebrows claimed he saw "no armed camp." He did protest, however, at the discreet picketline in support of the defendants on the small traffic island across the street from the courthouse.

For the first three months our defense was an unprecedented offense against the whole U.S. system of jury selection. Meticulously researched and introduced through expert witnesses, our challenge proved the class and racial bias used by courts and judges to keep Blacks, workers and the poor off jury lists. This detailed challenge, substantiated by official statistics, charts and graphs, became a classic presentation studied and used in subsequent political trials. It opened the way to the partial breakthrough made in the 1960s, although in 1949 Judge Medina ruled against us.

The prosecution's case was as simple as it was grotesque. It would prove, prosecutor McGohey claimed, that Marxism-Leninism was merely a synonym for the forcible overthrow of the government. The eleven defendants being Marxist-Leninists, reasoned McGohey, meant that they conspired to teach and advocate the overthrow of the government by force and violence.

The prosecution's star witness was Louis F. Budenz, former Party member, former editor of the *Daily Worker*, and now a professional witness testifying, for a good price, at hearings and trials of Communists around the country. He lectured for three weeks from the witness box, upholding the government's definition of Marxism. He supplied the bizarre twist that anything the Party did or said that appeared in conflict with his definition was "merely window dressing asserted for protective purposes," "an Aesopian language" understood by the "in" membership.

Acting as his own attorney throughout the trial, Gene challenged the Budenz testimony:

"If the Court pleases, I must object most strenuously to this line of questioning and these allegations. This witness cannot speak for any defendant or any Communists. Would you hear Judas Iscariot on the Sermon on the Mount or Benedict Arnold interpreting the Declaration of Independence?"

Judge Medina, however, adopted the Budenz nonsense as

his own and throughout the trial he constantly kept closing the door to defense efforts to offer what the defendants actually did teach and advocate and do.

Judge Medina upheld prosecutor McGohey' objection to one interruption by defense attorney Richard Gladstein during McGohey's opening statement to the jury. However, the Judge himself interrupted Gene's opening statement twenty-nine times. Each time Gene started to tell the jury that the defense would show what the Communists did advocate and do, Medina intervened to sarcastically comment: "That's what you think." "Oh, no, you won't." He instructed Gene to get off these subjects and when Gene persisted, the Judge exploded in the jury's presence.

Medina: Now, Mr. Dennis, that is the end, that is enough. You are not going to go on any more with that and you will kindly desist. . . . You have it in your mind that you are going to go into wage increases, the Spanish war, the Chinese war or how you are going to get the rich to pay more taxes, and it is evident enough that that has nothing to do with the case here. The case here is whether you conspired in the way that is charged by the government.

Dennis: I am trying to establish my intent, my political conduct and what we really advocated and taught, and the question of peace, the question of defense of the Bill of Rights, the question of living standards of the people—these are the things.

Medina: You see, after I tell you to stop, you look me right in the eye and you say it all over again.

After all defense opening statements were completed, the Judge instructed the jury to ignore "all you have heard in the course of these openings about ideas and things of that kind." He re-read the indictment to the jurors and when defense attorneys Gladstein and Harry Sacher objected to this judicial rebuttal of the defense case, Medina retorted:

"Well, I'm not going to sit here like a lump on a log [while] defendants' counsel tries to convey to the jury that such a conspiracy as charged here was perfectly all right."

For months the jury heard prosecution witnesses—all of them F.B.I. agents either sent into the Party or recruited after they were in—testify to what, in their opinion, Marxism-Leninism is, and relate that what they heard at Party meetings and in classes constituted force and violence advocacy.

As he did during Gene's opening statement Medina curtailed efforts of defendant witnesses Robert Thompson, Henry Winston, Gil Green, John Gates and Carl Winter to testify what Marxism-Leninism meant to them, what their years-long activity flowing from that understanding was all about. Medina ruled such efforts "self serving" attempts to "show what good guys you are." All they had to do on the witness stand, he said, was to confirm or deny "under oath" whether they did or did not "entertain such intent as has been charged here."

He reiterated again and again throughout the six months—sometimes angrily, sometimes menacingly—that this was no political trial and that he would not allow the defendants to prove otherwise. At one point, chafing under these restrictions, Gil Green on the witness stand remarked, "I thought we were going to get a chance to prove our case." Medina became livid. "You are hereby remanded [to jail] for the balance of the trial."

Defense attorneys constantly objected in vain to the tainted testimony of FBI agents and renegade Party members as the sole base of the prosecution case. At one point Gene said:

"Your Honor, even the Court must take into account that a person who, let us say, works for a Pinkerton Detective Agency and testifies against trade unionists surely cannot be considered an unbiased witness. Nor for that matter could any FBI agent. They are not impartial observers. They are sent into unions, they are sent into workers' organizations, like our Party, with a purpose to distort and disrupt and, in fact, to attempt to destroy our organizations."

Medina replied, "How are you going to detect crooks and criminals if you don't have detectives and persons to watch them?"

Not only did the Judge allow the entire prosecution case based on this informer-type testimony, he actively supported the prosecution's efforts to force defendant witnesses to play that role as well.

Instructed by Medina to answer the prosecutor's questions regarding names of individuals other than the defendants, John Gates said:

"It would degrade me in the eyes of my associates and the labor movement . . . to act as a common stool pigeon. . . . These people are people who work in private industry and I will not disclose their names because it would lead to their loss of work, probably, if I did so."

In a heated exchange that followed between attorneys and Medina on the instruction, the scene erupted.

Dennis [concluding a lengthy discourse on Gates' right not to answer the question]: Mr. Gates testified, among other things, that he attended conventions of our Party in Texas and Alabama and North Carolina, and I assume that following this line of question Mr. McGohey will be asking questions, who was there, whom did he see, etc. . . . To give any information . . . would be to put anyone mentioned by Mr. Gates in a position where he would be subject to lynching in the South. And I say that this line of question, among other things, is an un-American effort to infringe on our basic rights and to try and compel the defendants to act as police, as FBI informers [and] would be a violation of the traditions embodied in our Bill of Rights; this would be acting in the traditions of Edgar Hoover and Herr Himmler because such rulings could only be conceived and executed in the spirit of a police state inquisition."

Medina: I think I have heard about enough, Mr. Dennis.
Dennis: I would say in conclusion, your Honor, that no court or no legislative body can kill ideas, political doctrines, movements of the people, such as the Communist movement. They can't do that by force, whatever the form of compulsion. And no court by force or compulsion—
Medina: I would rather not hear any more, Mr. Dennis.
Dennis: —can compel any Communist or any reputable working—
Medina: Don't you think it would be better—
Dennis: —to bear false testimony and act as an informer against his associates.

At another point in this exchange, defense attorney George Crockett told the Court:

"I am particularly anxious to address the Court on this subject because I am mindful that if the abolitionist of another day had not taken the same position as Mr. Gates has taken today. I probably would be a slave instead of a free American citizen."

Medina angrily cut Crockett off, turned to Gates in the witness stand and sentenced him to jail for thirty days.

Bedlam broke out in the courtroom. Spectators groaned loudly, some shouted, "No, No!" All eleven defendants jumped protesting to their feet.

Defendant Winston: If your Honor please, may I now be heard? More than five thousand Negroes have been lynched in this country for such
Medina: Now, Mr. Winston—
Winston: —and the government of the United States should be ashamed for
Medina: Mr. Winston, I herby direct that you be remanded for the remainder of the trial.
Defendant Gus Hall: It sounds more like a kangaroo court than a court of the United States. I have heard more law and more constitutional rights in kangaroo courts.
Medina: Now let me see, this is Mr. Hall?
Hall: That is right, this is Mr. Hall.
Medina: Mr. Hall, you are hereby remanded for the balance of the trial.
Dennis: I wish to protest most emphatically this outrageous decision on the part of the Court. I must say all honest men must view this action of remanding as a contemptible action, a violation of our traditions and our Bill of Rights—
Medina: I shall treat you, Mr. Dennis, as one of the counsel as indeed you are. . . . I do not state that as a guarantee that I will not take some action against you if you become too disorderly, but I want you to realize that I understand the character of the expression which you have just used, but I will take no action on it.
Dennis: I wish the Court to know that I seek no special rights or privileges, but the rights I exercise an as American citizen, as an American worker, as a Communist.

With four of the defendants already in jail for the duration of the long trial, Medina remanded a fifth, defendant Carl Winter, when he too refused to give the prosecutor names of individuals in no way related to the trial proceedings. At one point the Judge threatened to send Ben Davis to jail as well. From the witness box Ben objected to a Medina ruling barring testimony showing what the Party advocated and actually did in the Negro rights struggle.

Medina (to Davis):   I have penalties at my disposal if the defendants insist upon interrupting the proceedings and holding forth—
Davis: It is pretty hard for the defendants to sit here like a lump on a log, as you say, while a lot of rulings are made which are practically cutting the guts out of what our Party stands for—
Medina: I consider that an extremely offensive statement.
Davis: Well, the whole trial is offensive to me and should have been thrown out a long time ago.
Medina: Now, Mr. Davis, do you realize that you may be forcing me to remand you during the remainder of the trial?
Davis: Well, I can't help that. All I want to do is say the truth.... If you wanted the truth you would let our Party say what it teaches and advocates.

For nine months we sit through this macabre trial in which the "crime" is meetings held, classes taught, public speeches made, books read and recommended to be read. Again and again Prosecutor McGohey ominously confronts a witness:

"I show you Government Exhibit Number so-and-so, is that what defendant Stachel [or another of the defendants] gave you?"

You watch with bated breath. The murder weapon? A bloody knife? A gun with the tell-tale fingerprint on it? The witness examines the exhibit and replies, "Yes, sir, that is the book."

Lenin's *State and Revolution.* Stalin's *Problems of Leninism.* Marx and Engels' *Communist Manifesto.* Pamphlets by Foster and Dennis. Articles by one or another defendant.

The defense objects again and again over the long months at this procedure of putting books on trial. Medina peers down at the court and says very somberly:

"This book is, as I understand it, part of the paraphernalia, one of the implements that are alleged to have been used by the defendants in forming the conspiracy that is alleged in the indictment ... the point is how did these defendants use this book."

Another day, another defense objection, and the Judge goes into a long soliloquy comparing the Marxist books in our trial to a bank robber's tool kit. Defense attorney Harry Sacher heatedly protests, "I tell you that the culture of the world will not long survive with that approach to books."

Medina: You are not going to say any more, Mr. Sacher. You are through with your argument on this. . . . I have never heard such propaganda in a trial in my life. I am not going to have this trial carried on for the purpose of pushing out propaganda.

Sacher: I object to that. That is what the prosecution is doing. We are trying to prove the truth here and we are being stopped from proving the truth.

In mid-October, 1949, after seven hours of deliberation on a case that took nine months to present, the jury returned the expected guilty verdict. Expected because of Judge Medina's blatant prejudicial conduct in the presence of the jury and his whittling away of the crucial aras of the defense case; expected because of the mounting nightmarish quality of the political atmosphere of the time.

Immediately upon the jury verdict, Medina denied bail to the eleven (which they got weeks later on appeal) and sentenced all the defense attorneys, including Gene, to prison terms on "contempt of court" charges.

Nine:
POLITICAL PRISONER/ PRISON WIFE

I

We close the apartment door and walk in silence down the dim, narrow hallway towards the living room that doubles as bedroom and study. I have the feeling that this particular moment is very important. Perhaps I should allow the tears to break through, to let the youngster know we adults, too, are vulnerable, that he need not meet some stoic standard. Or perhaps I should force myself to smile, to reassure him that mommy is a strength to lean on. Instead, I bungle this critical moment. I inadequately and too casually suggest, "It's still awfully early. Let's rest for awhile."

In the rumpled bed there emanates the warmth of the long night during which Gene and I had talked and laughed and talked without words, but had not slept. We had shut off the alarm before it could ring, rose at dawn, and the youngster had come out of his tiny hall bedroom, sleepily asking, "Is now the time, daddy?"

Gene had said, "Yes, son, now is the time." Now he was gone and I lay quietly beside our seven-year-old whose face is burrowed into the pillow. He half-turns, says hesitantly: "Mommy, let's you and me always pretend that daddy is away on one of his trips to Chicago, that he'll be home in a few days, okay?"

I agree. There are six and a half years ahead, but I make the pact to live each day as though Gene were coming home tomorrow. He had left that morning to start serving the year's sentence on the Un-American Committee contempt charge. Then there would be the five-year Smith Act sentence, plus the six months' contempt of court penalty Judge Medina had imposed. After those six and a half years there could be another trial and another five years' conviction on the second count of that Smith Act indictment.

However, on this May 12, 1950, at my son's request, I concentrate on getting through the first day. For purely selfish reasons, I convince Young Gene to stay home from school. "Let's get those new shoes you need, then we'll go to the zoo and we'll have lunch on the terrace in the park," I bribed.

We cut through the north end of the Columbia University campus and walk west to Riverside Drive to catch the Fifth Avenue double decker bus. It is a familiar route. Since moving to the apartment on West 119th Street off Amsterdam Avenue in early 1947, Young Gene and I had walked this way each morning to and from his half-day playschool at Riverside Church, that handsome monument to the Rockefeller dynasty. It was a good school, progressively experimental, tokenly inter-racial. Its director, Miss Perry, was a tall, sparse, Eleanor Roosevelt type both in physical appearance and in social outlook. She and her staff radiated a genteel equanimity our youngster sorely needed.

Now as we walk, I recall a session with her soon after Young Gene had been enrolled. Responding to her request for a consultation, I had listened as Miss Perry extolled my son's "fine attributes," and then I bristled defensively as mothers do at outside criticism, when she added, "but Eugene is a persistent liar." When the children talked of their fathers and "what they did," our not-yet five-year-old claimed his father was a professor at nearby Columbia.

Reprovingly the school director added, "Now we know that isn't true. Yet when we try to get him to admit he is lying, he gets angry and stubbornly insists his father *is* a professor at the University."

"You, of course, know what Mr. Dennis 'does,' don't you?" I ask quietly.

She falters self-consciously, "Well, yes. His name and photograph is constantly in the newspapers and on the radio. That is exactly my point; why does Eugene lie?"

I've got to make this gentle child educator face our reality. I urge her to get our original application form, then I ask: "What is listed there as Mr. Dennis' occupation?" I prompt.

"Journalist," she reads.

I press my point. "You did not accuse me of lying then, Miss Perry. You don't do so even now. Did Young Gene do any differently than you and I did?"

She sat at her desk, eyes downcast, toying with her pencil. I continued. I want her to understand.

"Our only desire was to get him into this school. We wanted no publicity and we wanted to save you any harassment or embarrassment. You accepted our little subterfuge because you then could officially claim that you did not know we were *that* Dennis. My husband and I are grateful to you. Young Gene is happy here; he's getting something he needs badly."

"But think of the traumatic effect on him when you teach him to lie, to disown his father," she protested weakly.

"We did not instruct him in anything, Miss Perry. He is not denying his reality, nor disowning the father he loves. Actually, he is coping in his own way with survival in a hostile world not of his making. Obviously, in this nursery-school world of his, he still does not feel secure enough to openly claim his father. Let's not put the onus of our adult world on a five-year-old child."

Our consultation ended politely.

Fall registration for the first grade at the neighborhood public school coincided with a new flurry of publicity for our family. The arrest on the Smith Act indictment and the weeks-long fight for the right to bail catapulted Gene back into the headlines. Radio newscasts and newspaper stories recapsuled, too, his earlier skirmish with the Un-American Committee and the conviction that followed. His photos in the media became so common that often while walking with him on the street or waiting on a subway platform, I saw people nudge each other, "There's that Commie leader." I smiled at Gene's embarrassment when loud whispers usually added, "He's handsome, isn't he?"

But not all was humorous compliments. A red rubber rat hanging on our apartment door knob was turned into a, "Look at the toy someone left you," for the benefit of a child who did not yet recognize the meaning of that ugly message. Threatening notes appeared in our mailbox and under our door. Obscene phone calls wakened us at night. Teams of FBI agents sat outside our building, followed Gene downtown and walked behind me as Young Gene and I moved about the neighborhood.

The home of Bob Thompson, head of our New York state organization and one of the Smith Act eleven, was invaded by a drunk who tried to attack Bob's eight-year-old daughter, boasting he'd give "that damn Commie" a bad time. Young Gene was no longer allowed to play on the street; reluctantly we had to tell him the reason. He had become angry at the new and insulting restriction, charging tearfully that we didn't trust him. We decided it was important that he know that it was not lack of our trust in him, but the threat of an evil, sick, political beast. That explanation he appeared able to accept, even if grudgingly. Our problems were not unique. All known Communists were coping with similar personal problems in varying degrees.

As the opening of school approached, I was uneasy but resigned and Gene and I talked of both the practical and emotional supportive steps we'd have to institute as our six-year-old mvoed further into that hostile world. When a wealthy friend of the Party said he wanted to pay Young Gene's tuition to a parent-cooperative, progressive school downtown, Gene immediately accepted. I was conflicted with the "principle" of special privilege. Gene argued emphatically:

"Neither my child nor anybody's child is the advance-guard of the struggle. He'll have plenty of battles to fight in which we will be unable to protect him. We've given him a rough row to hoe, let's at least help him where we can."

Relieved and grateful, I enrolled Young Gene into the Downtown Community School on East Eleventh Street, sometimes called the poor man's annex of the more prestigious Little Red School House, famous private school on the west side of Greenwich Village. The school bus picked him up each morning, delivered him each evening, and there were permanent instructions at school that he was not to be released at any time to anyone who might claim they came from his parents to get him.

Young Gene remained at Downtown for the full eight years. In the summers he went to the camp in the Catskills operated by the school director and his wife, Norman and Hannah Studer, two warm, very supportive human beings. For eight years director, teachers, counselors and the majority of the parents surrounded our youngster in safety, protected his right to be publicly known as his father's son, and repelled FBI harassment as more Smith Act defendants' children sought security in that school.

In sympathetic and historical terms understandable to the children, teachers explained in each classroom why Young Gene's father was in prison. He became a hero-image to most of them. In the two ugly experiences in all those years, the parents involved were told that unless they accepted the democratic premise of the school, they should withdraw from it; that Young Gene remains.

In 1951, when the long five-year pull started, Young Gene and I moved into a tiny apartment on East 12th Street, just around the corner from his school. It then became in every sense of the word a neighborhood school for him, with school-mates coming over to play, stay for dinner, and often to sleep over.

All this was yet in the future that May 12, 1950 when Young Gene and I rode on the top deck of the Fifth Avenue bus. In the park above the river children played in sandboxes. Mothers gently rocked baby carriages. Students walked with books under arm. No one really cares, I mused. What purpose is served by Gene's going to prison? From the small face pressed against the bus window, came the words:

"I guess daddy doesn't really love us as much as I thought he did."

My heart pounds. I look about me furtively at the passengers sitting near us. I want to stop the words. I want to urge, not here; wait, we'll talk at home. But for the child there is no proper time, only his need.

"If he really loved us, he'd tell the judge he was sorry." The head turns, the eyes accuse. "I heard you and daddy talking. The judge said if he'd say he was sorry, he'd not have to go to jail. Then he'd be home with us now."

It is true. Judge Pine had offered Gene the opportunity "to go before the House Un-American Activities Committee and purge yourself of contempt. If you do, I might take action which would be just and proper under the circumstances."

In the courtroom on that day in 1947, Gene had replied:

"There is one thing I would like to make clear. I do not, and would not, change one iota of my judgment that this Committee is a pro-fascist instrument, a Committee which has usurped constitutional power. And with every means at my disposal I would challenge the authority and constitutionality of this Committee and its activities which are inimical to the interest of our country. [These views] I will not concede nor abandon. My liberty as an individual is, of course, dear to me. But more dear is the liberty of the whole American people."

Riding the bus on the morning he had gone to prison, I

falteringly paraphrase these words for our son. He interrupts impatiently.

"I know all that. But he could have said he was sorry and not mean it. We would know he didn't mean it. His friends would know he didn't mean it. And he could have stayed home with us."

I fumble for words as I try to explain why there are men and women who choose prison, even death, to defend what they believe, hoping that others will understand and, understanding, will act to right the social wrong.

Under my encircling arm, the sturdy body shudders with the weight of a deep sigh as he turns again to the window, pressing his face against the pane.

"I know," he says softly, as though explaining the problem to the children he passes by, "Other people wouldn't know, if he lied. They'd think he was really sorry and that the Committee was right."

Fierce pride in a daddy willing to go to prison for his ideas. Fierce love for each other, a love that supports each of us in what we have to do. Fierce hatred of those who imprison men and women for their social commitment. These are the emotions that sustain us for the next years.

II

While not a staff member, I had covered our 1949 Smith Act trial frequently for the *Daily Worker,* writing mainly feature "mood" pieces about the incongruities of Judge Medina's efforts to fit the prosecution of a political party into the format of a criminal trial and the government's need to rely entirely upon police informers and agents to do it.

With other defendants' wives, I accepted speaking dates. Our theme was, "Your freedom is in jeopardy as long as our husbands are persecuted for their political ideas and activity."

In Detroit I spoke at a civil liberties banquet where, according to the news account, I "forcefully flung the false charge of 'force and violence' back into the teeth of the warmakers." In Connecticut I spoke at the factory gates of General Electric in Bridgeport and Winchester Guns in New Haven and at a banquet in Fairfield.

These speaking dates increased during 1950, the year Gene was in prison. Civil liberties conferences in Boston and Philadelphia, indoor and street corner rallies in Harlem, a day-long nationalities' picnic outside Chicago where among the six thousand people I met three young couples—Black, Jewish, and Slav—each of whom proudly introduced their newborn infants named either Gene or Dennis.

In New York Young Gene's eyes shone brightly as he watched eighteen thousand people in a Madison Square Garden rally rise to their feet applauding as I brought greetings from his father in prison. My not-yet eight-year-old was sure Daddy would be home the next day after such a demonstration of support. His mother, however, was wiser, but kept plugging.

The women's commission of the Party asked me to initiate and become volunteer editor of a woman's page in *The Sunday Worker*. I accepted with some trepidation. I did not fully agree with all of the commission's views on The Woman Question; also, no one had a clear idea what kind of page they wanted.

With a fluctuating group of three women volunteers, I started to experiment, after winning agreement for full autonomy over the page from the paper's male editors. Responsible for article planning, editing and layout, I also alternated each week doing a column with Claudia Jones, a Jamaica-born young black Party leader who later served a Smith Act sentence, was deported to London in the mid-1950s, and died there shortly after.

Claudia's column, "Half the World," dealt with the political women's movement, especially with the peace movement. Mine, more personal, was entitled "Comradely yours, Peggy Dennis", and ranged from problems of raising children in a hostile McCarthyite era to polemics against a brand of feminism that saw the female gender alone, regardless of socio-political outlook, as all-decisive.

Our bulging mailbag of letters, questions, and unsolicited articles impressed the puzzled male editors. My own somewhat ambivalent views on The Woman Question were reflected in our page, "Woman Today." Mine was neither the solely economic interpretation of our Party nor the too subjective "consciousness-raising" that was to become so popular years later. I bristled at the men-are-the-enemy advocates, yet I was bitter at the male chauvinism blatant in our Party, in my own life, and society as a whole. I scorned the reduction of the complicated problem into complaints about whether or not the working husband helped the housewife with the supper dishes, yet I fumed at men who superciliously believed household chores were women's work.

I liked the members of our Women's Commission personally, but I felt they were not typical women and knew little of the problems of ordinary women. They were political career-women, without husbands and children. They were neither housewives nor on-the-job working women. They spent their time in political circles, intent upon leading and recruiting women into existing organizations. They seemed oblivious, almost as much as our men comrades, to the practices in these organizations which made it difficult, sometimes impossible, for most women to participate unless they, too, were ready to become freed from emotional/family ties or entanglements.

Once again I felt there was an assumption of either/or choice that was unacceptable to me personally and which I knew was unacceptable to the majority of women. I knew that in form, if not in content, I was no truly emancipated, independent Woman, but I felt that the whole issue was more complicated than that of holding an outside job or having an independent career. Human relationships, and certainly male-female relationships, were more complicated than our Party could admit. Aside from on-the-job economic issues facing women, our Party, including its women activists, responded with built-in male rhetoric.

I was, I guess, a contradictory, confused combination of my mother's feminist influence, my Party's economic determinism, and my own emotional commitment to a unique husband whose consuming needs as a fulltime revolutionary leader determined our whole life style. All of these merged into a fiercely independent spirit which fought within that relationship but always within the limitation of the belief that his needs came first. They came first, however, only because together we merged into one total devotion to that revolutionary commitment. I knew that I could not allow my peculiar life-needs to influence my views on The Woman Question as a whole. But I also knew that neither my Party nor its leading woman comrades understood the complex scope of the Question, however glibly and simplistically they claimed they did.

My own ambiguities and personalized forms in my columns and articles evoked more discussion than did the formal Party resolutions and documents on the subject. Some women wrote, "I object to being segregated to a special page." Others expressed "pride in our new page which treats us as politically-minded individuals." Some wanted "working class oriented household hints." Others were "insulted at such concepts of women's interests." We blazed no innovative trails, but our readers responded to the first attempts to deal with the subject in simple human terms.

III

So the year 1950 passed, with a widening activity and new involvement. However, my days were counted as mere intervals between the Saturday half-hour visits with Gene.

He had chosen to serve his one-year term at the Federal House of Detention on West Street in the city. As a result of having been his own attorney in the Smith Act trial he had the right to consult frequently with lawyers and co-defendants while working on appeals briefs. By serving his time in New York City these valued consultations were frequent, and our own weekly visits were a spin-off bonus from that choice.

West Street was not an easy place to serve extended time. It was a stop-over prison for those awaiting trial, on trial, awaiting sentencing, or waiting to be shipped to penitentiaries around the country.

Gene worked as clerk of the second floor, and his duties brought him into contact with all incoming men. He assigned them cells and helped them get settled. He served as personal adviser to many, legal expert to all, urging each to use every legal and constitutional recourse open to them.

In his autobiography, *Dangerous Scot*, John Williamson describes the arrival of a group of Smith Act prisoners at Lewisburg federal prison a year later in the summer of 1951, in transit to their assigned penitentiaries:

"When six of us first arrived... and marched single file into one of the big dining halls for our first meal, a terrific cheer went up. From all sides came shouts, 'Hello, Gene!' Guards came running immediately but all was quiet, as if nothing had happened."

However, from May, 1950 until early March, 1951, the old barracks-like West Street prison on the edge of the river on the far west side of the city was the focal point of my life.

Each Saturday Young Gene sent me on my way, "Tell Daddy I love him," but he would not visit with me. Gene understood the child's fear but insisted it had to be faced.

"Tell him to come. This is part of our reality, he has to face it. He has to see for himself that I am well, that the prison doors will not close on him too if he comes."

Young Gene finally agrees. Frightened, he sits tensely in the crowded waiting room, pulls back when our names are called. He slides stiffly onto the stool in front of the glass barricade, gripping my hand tightly.

Gene comes through the door on the other side. Thin (he had lost twenty-nine pounds the first month and is still losing rapidly), his faded blues and white t-shirt give him the youthful air of some twenty years ago, except that now in prison his hair is turning white. He hesitates, looks for us in the line-up. His eyes crinkle with pleasure as he walks towards us. He picks up the telephone and eight-year-old and forty-four-year-old obliterate the glass wall between them as each thrusts his body forward, presses palm to glass, and across the phones come a simultaneous, grinning, shy "hi." Gene had prepared well for that first visit with his frightened son. The boy soon is chuckling and laughs out loud as his father regales him with the funnier aspects of that macabre, stupid life Inisde.

Gene was not the only political prisoner at that time. Exercising their rights under the First and Fifth Amendments not to cooperate with various congressional witch-hunting investigations, fifteen others are in prison. In the West Street visiting room I saw, but was not allowed to talk to, Doctor Miller of the Spanish Anti-Fascist Committee and the Rev. Richard Morford of the American-Soviet Friendship Council.

Despite my new activity editing the woman's page, writing my column, speaking at meetings, writing articles on behalf of the political prisoners, 1950 was a lonely, frightening year. It was a dress rehearsal for the five years that lay ahead. To Gene's colleagues in the Party leadership officially I was an important symbol, the wife of their imprisoned general secretary. But none of them asked how I or Gene's son were making out emotionally. Not one of them opened his family circle to us or offered to play surrogate father for a weekend's afternoon to a child who, chunky and boisterous by day, whimpered at night, "I want my daddy." They sent Gene's weekly pay envelope but they gave nothing of themselves. During that year my walls of self-sufficient reserve and aloneness grew higher around me.

By contrast, Young Gene and I spent much of the prison years warming ourselves in the bedlam of the sprawling household of my friends Barbara and Bernie. Far removed from the milieu of national Party leadership, both were activists on the neighborhood levels. Barbara and I had met at the sandbox on Riverside Drive when our youngsters were toddlers. Now we were made part of a family in which the children welcomed my son as brother.

No one, however, could help me fill the void in my life. At night I lay in the dark alone, willing myself to almost physically reach out across the sleeping city and touch Gene as he lay in his cell bunk. I concentrated upon making my presence felt by him. At other times I panicked and tossed, fighting the fear that he was irreparably lost to me, never to return. I lived for that weekly half hour when we embraced with our eyes through that glass barrier, when we sat alone on our island, talking quietly underneath the shouting, straining voices of inmates and visitors around us trying to use those damnable phones as bridges to loved ones.

The weekly half-hour visits that first year and the two hours a month visits the next five years became the center of our existence; letters were a frustrating substitute. In those visiting rooms I found what I badly needed. Exchange of political opinions illuminated my activity. A caressing glance assured me that I was still, despite the passing years, needed and desired. Overcoming all obstacles, for a short time Gene brought the component parts of our relationship together, a process I too often lost sight of in my lonely existence on the outside. For some five years this is what our relationship grew on.

Gene came home in early spring, 1951, and as a family we did not have to cope with the problems of readjustment—he was going back into prison shortly and he remained for that brief interval a very special guest. On July 2 he returned to prison to serve the five year Smith Act sentence and the six months contempt of court sentence Judge Medina had imposed.

IV

The taxi sped through the Atlanta streets, away from the center of town. My stomach heaved as I was rushed toward the unknown. I was in alien territory. That morning I had cringed when for the first time in my life I saw a "Colored Waiting

Room" sign at the railway station and the "Colored in Back, Whites in Front" sign on the bus.

The cab turned in at a long circular driveway surrounded by lawn, low shrubs and flower beds. High, concrete walls extended from either end of the massive Administration Building. Perched in watch towers with gigantic searchlights stood armed guards. I had arrived at the Atlanta Federal Penitentiary, maximum security complex which a 1948 report of the U.S. Bureau of Prisons had described as: "A walled institution, heavily-barred and bolted fortress-like bastille which reflects the general 19th century philosophy of prison design. . . ."

To Atlanta prison, according to that report, were sent "men with an extensive criminal record, or those serving long sentences for serious offenses. . . . [men who are] major escape risks, given to violence, serious troublemakers."

In Atlanta prison were Gene and John Gates, editor of the *Daily Worker*. Later other Smith Act political prisoners were incarcerated there—Bob Thompson, Alex Bittleman, Phil Frankfield.

Nervous and tense, I waited in the corridor after signing the entry-book. After a half-hour, I was told by a clerk that Warden Hiatt wanted to see me. Ears pounding and throat dry, I entered the office where the Warden sat scowling. I was not asked to sit down, so I stood at his desk. He began without any preliminary amenities.

"You and youah husban' are violatin' ouah rules heah, an' we caihnt alloah that."

So started a thirty minute session that had me inwardly quaking with fear and seething with anger. Outwardly I remained polite and very careful, because early in his tirade the Warden threatened:

"Noaw, you jus' remembeh, neithah you nor youah husban' has any rights heah. Only privileges we give you, no rights at all. We can and we will take away these privileges from both of you, youah co'espondence privileges and youah visitin' privileges."

At another point, "Youh jus' remembah, we have youah husban' heah, youah remembah that, an' we'll get along jus' fine. You two betteh learn to cooperate, we have him heah, you know."

I kept assuring Mr. Hiatt that I wanted to cooperate. I just wasn't clear what I was not cooperating about. He picked up two sheets of paper and waved them in my face. I recognized two of my letters to Gene. His face reddened as he fumed:

"You jus' caihnt write all this cowminist stuff. It's illegal. That's the crime youah husban' has committed an' you caihnt write or talk to him 'bout this criminal stuff."

I recalled having written bits of news about trade unions passing resolutions for a Korean ceasefire, the fight of the second-round of new Smith Act defendants for bail, conversations with various Socialists and liberals to initiate an amnesty appeal on behalf of the imprisoned Communists.

With a sarcasm lost on the warden, I asked, "What am I permitted to write and talk about to my husband for the next five years?"

"Weel," Mr. Hiatt leered, "why doan' you jus' keep tellin' him how much you love him, but this illegal cowminist stuff is out."

I was curtly dismissed and sat again in the long corridor. Frightened. Angry. Helpless.

My name is called and I walk slowly through one, a second, and a third heavy iron grate door which is unlocked for me. A short distance down the long, wide, tile-walled passageway, the armed guard at my side stops, unlocks still another door, this time a solid one. I enter a bare room in which stands a long table. At the narrow head sits a guard and on the farther side, so close to the guard that their elbows touch, sits Gene. I walk forward hesitantly. I had been instructed earlier that we may embrace briefly upon arrival and departure, but we are not to touch each other at any time during the visit.

I sit gingerly into the chair across from Gene and notice for the first time the wooden partition, about a foot high, dividing the table down its length. The guard tells me that I am not to reach across that partition at any time. I am not to open my bag nor hold any object in my hand. For the next two hours the guard follows our conversation across the barrier, his head bobbing right and left like a spectator at a ping pong match.

Gene talks quietly against my anger and fear. I see the controlled thinness of his mouth lines, the narrowed tightness of his eyes. His hands are clenched into fists and they keep tapping the table as he talks. Only when he breaks into his own words to ask about The Kid do his eyes smile, his fists open. "I miss him. Bring him as soon as you can."

He talks of that which disturbs us both. He too had had some bad sessions with Warden Hiatt. Many of his proscribed three letters a week were being returned by the official Censor as "unacceptable" because he had written opinions on current national and international happenings.

He says, "I could no more acquiesce to this unconstitutional, despotic form of thought control and be silent on any social issue I wish to write about than I could stop thinking or breathing."

He has written his attorney to take legal action and now he adds, emphasizing each word: "But you are not in prison, you have other ways of protest. Use them."

Buried inside the concrete walls of maximum security Atlanta prison where wardens threaten "cooperate, or else," where mere existence is a "privilege, not a right," Gene really believed that struggle decides everything. He really believed we could win, if we fought.

That night as the train sped northward, I did not share his courage or his faith. Bruised at the indignity of the visit, burdened with the frightening realization that much of his well-being Inside depended on my ability to fight on the Outside, and overwhelmed at the guilt of being free while he was locked in that small, crowded, eight-man cell with its dim, unshaded single light bulb, its open toilet, its open-barred sides denying a moment's dignity of privacy, I wept noiselessly into the hard plush of the coach seat that smelled so strongly of insecticide.

V

Censorship of our correspondence was lifted after a heated session in Washington with James V. Bennett, Director of the U.S. Bureau of Prisons, at which Congressman Vito Marcantonio, our attorney John Abt, and four of us prison wives presented grievances on behalf of our husbands. A rider was attached to this victory, however. If any of Gene's letters were published or quoted in public, our correspondence and visiting privileges would be taken away, and Gene would be thrown into solitary. Gene filed a protest with Bennett, charging this proviso was a veiled frameup threat, since he had no control over his letters once they left him. Gene urged that I test that unconstitutional ruling by violating it. I hotly refused. I did not share his implicit faith that a "people's movement" would prevent the application of the penalties Bennett threatened to impose on us.

The conditions of our visits, however, remained unchanged, and Gene served notice that he would not participate in them. He told me, in the guard's presence in the visiting room, that I was not to come again. He would refuse to see me until our visiting arrangements were improved. I was to publicize these inhuman restrictions in my speeches and articles.

When Gene wrote that I should again visit, I was ushered into a lounge with large windows, potted flowers, long sofas where we now sat side by side holding hands, surrounded by groups of other inmates and their visiting families. Only one guard sat behind a desk off in the corner across the room. We assumed we were still being monitored, probably electrically now, but we didn't care. The changed circumstances, still within the prison walls, made our reunions less grim. And when Young Gene was with us, the room rang with the warm sound of laughter. Other inmates smiled and even joined in without knowing the particular joke that had passed between father and son.

On each train trip down Young Gene suffered violent stomach upset; during the visit he laughed with his father, but on the trip back he was pale and silent. Gene and I, on occasions when the child was not with us, often discussed whether we should stop his visits, whether they were too hard on him. We agreed that it would be worse if he were encouraged to block out his father altogether. He was part of our life, we could not shut him out.

One time, while we were home in New York, I casually suggested to Young Gene that perhaps the trips were too rough on him. I told him his father would understand if he decided not to make them. My nine-year-old looked coldly at me, "My dad needs me." His visits continued every two or three months throughout the five years.

VI

Despite our victories on correspondence and visiting, we were unable to make even a dent in the regulation forbidding the Smith Act political prisoners from receiving radical magazines, newspapers or books. They were able to order books, at our expense, directly from publishers, but the warden had to approve every request. Since to the mind of Mr. Hiatt every book on history, philosophy and political science was suspect and "cowminist," Gene's requests were turned down constantly throughout the years in Atlanta prison.

Most families of prisoners are, and especially were then, frightened and intimidated and therefore submissive to the "no rights, only privileges" threats of wardens and guards. Most families, Black and poor white, were unable to make the long, costly trips to visit; they knew little of what was happening inside and they did not feel they could do anything, even if they had known.

The Communists in prison were a new breed at that time. They were proud political prisoners, knowledgeable of their rights, and with active families, organizations and publicity on the outside to support them. Fellow inmates knew this and admired them. Wardens and guards knew this and hated them for it, but moved warily. Bennett and the U.S. Bureau of Prisons in Washington recognized this and moved cautiously.

At Atlanta maximum security prison our fight was censorship, visiting conditions, book rejections—all fought within the context of constitutional rights of the individual in or outside the prison. At minimum security federal prison at Terre Haute, Indiana, Ben Davis bent segregation boundaries imposed on Black prisoners. At Leavenworth, the issue was denial of certain job rights to Irving Potash, leader of the Fur Workers Union. Our demands were always not for special privileges, but against special discriminations.

The original threat, "remember, we have your husband here, you'd better cooperate," struck fear in all our hearts; yet we had no choice but to fight.

Anti-Communist hysteria was at its crest. Bob Thompson was attacked with an iron bar in West Street prison and lay for days near death; he pulled through after brain surgery and with a permanent steel plate in his skull. The inmate assailant claimed as his defense, "anti-Communist duty." William Remington, a "perjury" victim of Truman's "loyalty" investigations, was killed in a prison-yard brawl that appeared suspiciously engineered. While having good relations with their fellow inmates, our political prisoners had to be alert at all times for stool pigeons planted in their cells, provocateurs in the free areas, guards who sought to create incidents that would justify shake-downs, lock-ups, solitary, loss of good time. Our fears were valid, but, as Gene kept emphasizing, their safety depended on our fight for them on the Outside.

Returning from a West Coast speaking tour in late summer,

during Gene's second year at Atlanta, I arrived at the prison to be told I could not see him because he was in the prison hospital. I stared at the warden in disbelief.

"You're crazy if you think I will leave here without seeing my husband, particularly if he is in the hospital."

He insisted and I told him I would telephone Mr. Bennett in Washington and my attorney in New York and that I would call a press conference on the prison steps within the hour with the international wire services.

Ten minutes later I was escorted by armed guard deep inside the prison compound, my legs trembling and my heart pounding. Gene was seriously jaundiced from a neglected gall-bladder infection, and surgery was being urged. After visiting at his bedside and being told that the prison doctor was out of town, I returned to New York and called him the next day.

I expressed shock and anger at not having been notified of my husband's illness, and the voice over the wire replied, in genuine surprise.

"Youh mean youh wahnt us to in'fom youh ev'ry time youah husban' isn't well?"

"That's exactly what I mean. I want a telegram or a phone call from you or the warden any time anything the least bit out of routine happens to or involves my husband."

"Tha's highly irregulah, Mrs. Dennis, otheh fam'lies doan make such demands on us—" I started to interrupt but Dr. Janney hurriedly concluded, "but if tha's the way you wahnt it—"

When surgery became unavoidable, I tried and failed to negotiate Gene's transfer to a hospital outside the prison and to have the operation performed by a surgeon of my choice. Mr. Bennett told Marcantonio in Washington he would be "crucified" for molly-coddling the country's Number One prisoner if he granted the request. A Dr. Ernest Poer of Atlanta would be called in, however.

Driven by the nightmare of all the "mishaps" that threatened, I battled on every procedure. In one of many telephone exchanges, Dr. Stanley E. Krumbeigel, chief medical officer of the U.S. Prison Bureau in Washington, assured me:

"Mrs. Dennis, your husband is the most liked man in that institution. That is his greatest guarantee as far as his postoperative care under the trusty aides."

As in West Street prison, Gene was well-liked in Atlanta too. Called "Pops" or "Professor" by the younger men, he moved among them quietly, helpfully. He taught young Blacks and Latinos and Chicanos to read and write. He wrote legal briefs for men forgotten for years. He advised on personal family problems and encouraged each into action.

I visited Dr. Poer in his downtown Atlanta office, having decided our only security was candor. The Doctor sat quietly, hearing me out, then said:

"I appreciate your concern and your honesty. But what you don't seem to realize, Mrs. Dennis, is the fact that everything you have done around your husband's case since he entered that institution works in his favor now. The light of publicity has been on him at all times. Believe me, your husband is the last patient in the world I want to lose under my knife right now."

I had accomplished the only assurance possible. I had alerted Mr. Bennett and Doctor Krumbiegel in Washington and Doctors Janney and Poer and Warden Hiatt in Atlanta of the political implications inherent in the issue of Gene's medical care. I could do no more.

Surgery was successful. Dr. Janney telephoned me at the hotel as soon as it was over. That afternoon and for the next four days I stayed at Gene's bedside, walking through the inner prison yard compound at the guard's side on steady legs. It was now familiar territory and I even smiled and nodded to prisoners as I passed them in the yard, and once I passed within three feet of Johnny Gates, the *Daily Worker* editor, each of us grinning broadly.

VII

Having won his fight against censorship of our correspondence, Gene's letters became sharp, cogent essays of political analysis. Impatiently, torrents of ideas and demands burst forth. Urging organization, actions, building of united fronts against the Korean war, to brake McCarthyism, to defend constitutional and democratic rights, to utilize all forms and means in the electoral struggle, he could not accept the fact that so little was being done.

Despite his outward serenity, he served his prison years doing what the prisoners called "hard time." He lived each minute "on the outside." That was hell, prisoners told me. The only way to survive, they said, was to forget the Outside, roll loosely with the Inside. But Gene couldn't do that. He worked in the greenhouse; he played cards; he read his way through the limited library; he squeezed every bit of political news out of the newspapers and magazines which the men traded around; he demanded from me letters relating facts and analyses appearing in political and theoretical journals that he was not allowed to receive. He lived in minutiae the problems of the Outside movement.

The prison censor must have had a boring chore reading our letters. We each held our emotions tightly in rein. Inhibited by the censor peering over our shoulders, repelled by the warden's leering instruction that I spend the next five years proclaiming my love for my husband, there arose another problem. During one of the interims between visits, my need became greater than my reticence. My nightly letters poured out cries for help and love, wanton despair and fear and longings. Then I apologized and Gene carefully replied that he wanted always to be a part of "all unsolved difficulties, trials and tribulations." He hoped he could "sometimes even contribute a little to working things out, even though confined and restricted" as he was.

In our next visit, however, he explained his too controlled response to my letters which echoed his own pent-up feelings. As soon as those outpourings of mine began to reach the censor desk, the prison psychologist interviewed Gene to discuss "this obvious emotional breakdown" of mine and, he said, to explore with Gene what would be my "breaking point." Gene had furiously objected to this interference and to the interpretations and he stalked out of the office. I listened and internally cringed as this bucket of filth slithered upon us. We agreed we could not give the authorities the ammunition they were obviously fishing for, distorted as their search was. The leering warden, the peeping-tom censor, the gleeful psychologist had done their work well. Unlike other prisoners, we could not ignore them, nor their watchful, trap-like observations of everything we said and did. So now, only in a treasured phrase at the beginning and close of our letters did we touch lightly the throbbing wounds that lay deep inside, carefully concealed.

To his son Gene wrote humorous jingles, riddles and poems. He described in scientific detail his work at the prison greenhouse. He jokingly argued baseball predictions. With the passing years, the letters reflected a more serious vein, meeting the growing maturity of the child and the father's need to remain a part of that growth and to keep the relationship from becoming statically isolated from the boy's life.

To me Gene continued ceaselessly to pour out his political frustrations, demanding reasons why movements were not moving, analyzing brilliantly the fissures and divisions within the enemy camp that, he said, must be utilized in every way possible. While these letters were not publicized because of the Prison Bureau's threat, copies were circulated privately among many comrades. Some bristled at the implied criticisms, others agreed but appeared as helpless on the outside as Gene was in prison.

Finally, during one visit I angrily told Gene he was battering a stone wall; it was time he faced the political facts of the Outside. I talked rapidly, but practically in a whisper. I used our veiled, oblique, almost code-like contexts and references. But what had happened was no secret. The FBI knew, the news media knew, the remnants of the people's movements knew. Our Party had taken a severe beating under the assaults of McCarthyism, the Smith Act arrests and imprisonments, the continuing anti-Communist hysteria. It was reeling on the defensive. But the almost fatal blow was self-inflicted when the Party leadership took the whole organization underground, placing control of daily operative financial and political decision-making into the hands of this subterranean structure.

Those of us left above ground cynically called ourselves the "expendables." Included in that small group were the 160 Smith Act defendants in various stages of legal litigation, their wives and families; also those few around the country who had resisted going underground, including the California Party organization, and individual comrades who for various reasons had not been instructed to go illegal. Above ground, we became a Party unto ourselves, the only visible Party activists fighting for the constitutional and civil liberties of Communists as part of the fight against McCarthyism.

Who, then, were the expendables? I rhetorically argued in that prison visiting room. Who needed those absent, faceless leaders and their decisions made in faraway hideaways, relayed to us through channels which brooked no discussion, no exchange of views. We made our own decisions in the heat of our activity and we functioned without that leadership.

For me that old mystique of the omnipotence of "The Party" was badly shaken. The invincibility and infallability we had imbued in those two words, "The Party," was dissipated. The "Party" had become merely a conglomerate of individual persons, some good, some bad, some inconsequential. The Party was me and the small group of women with whom I worked. Absent leaders held no special attributes. No longer would I allow these individuals to determine my political opinions or my personal life as I had in the past.

Gene listened in silence, his eyes narrowed. He did not respond to my bitter outpourings. He cut through, instead, to the heart of the immediate problem which agitated him. Couched in the usual scrambled ambiguity with which we discussed things political in that visiting room, his words said:

"I don't understand. It was not intended that way. We planned to safeguard a few, select cadre for the future, never to take the whole organization into illegality, to take decision-making control underground; that is impossible to believe. Legal, constitutional processes still exist, they must be used. Those very few to be secured for the future were to be 'on ice,' with no contact with the Party. I don't understand what happened."

He wasted little time in recrimination or speculation. "If this is the situation, then you and the others who are around have to develop your own activity." I told him that was what we were doing, and he replied cryptically, "Then do it harder; there are obviously fewer of you to do all that needs to be done."

VIII

After the McCarthy years were safely behind us (defeated finally not so much by people's opposition as by McCarthy's over-reaching charge of the Democratic Party with twenty years' treason and the U.S. Army with being riddled with "Comunist spies"), a popular view developed that we Communists had exaggerated the threat of repression. In more comfortable hindsight, some pundits claimed we Communits had been paranoiac in translating the attacks on us into an attack on the whole democratic, liberal society. These views were expressed inside our Party as well, *after* everyone was safely returned from the underground.

I did not agree then and I do not agree now. The very costly error on the part of our Party was the *over-reaction* of the leadership to a very real threat. The error lay in the sectarian policies engendered by Foster's campaign to so obliterate what he saw as the remnants of Browderism, from 1947 onward, that Communist relations with the Center-left democratic, liberal trends within the labor movement and the people's organizations were destroyed. In the political hysteria that escalated, Gene's reports and articles urged that united action with all small "d" democrats—whatever organization label they may wear— was essential to defeat the repression. He had pleaded, "Our Communist Party is not doomed to burrow in the dark like a blind mole." But that is exactly what it did. Within a few months after the first round of Communist leaders had gone into prison, the Party was taken underground.

Despite these hindsighted claims, we Communists were not alone in feeling that the Supreme Court decision upholding the imprisonment of the leadership of a legal political party created "a profound constitutional crisis in our country," as the Party's statement at the time said. Samplings of non-Communist reactions to that Supreme Court action reveal similar concern.

St. Louis Post Dispatch: "The logical consequences of this decision would be for the Department of Justice to throw perhaps as many as 75,000 or more people behind bars for their political and economic beliefs. . . . Six men have amended the U.S. Constitution without submitting their amendment to the states for ratification."

New York Post: "Now the court has given its blessing to heresy-hunting. . . . Never was it more vital for Americans who value their liberties to speak against repression."

New York Times: "This disenfranchisement of a political party is not an easy price for America to pay for any sort of internal security. . . . It is for us, the American people, to keep alive the habit of free and full discussion, to tolerate differences of opinion no matter how distasteful to the great majority. . . ."

New York City Black councilman Earl Brown: "My interest is not the Communist eleven, but all Americans. The Court's decision cannot curb the Communists without hurting all of us."

Tom Blair, Black columnist, Boston Chronicle: "Six men in black robes have touched off the biggest witchhunt in modern history. . . . This may be the beginning of the end of all civil liberties for all political racial and religious groups who speak out against injustice."

I.F. Stone: "The forces which gave the New Deal vitality under FDR are being immobilized by striking at their periphery. This is where the Red hunt pays off. It's in the rent bill and the tax bill and the grocer's bill that you will begin to see its price."

Labor officials and local trade unions issued statements and resolutions calling the Supreme Court decision against the Communists a threat to labor's rights.

All this was in early 1950. The political climate deteriorated rapidly. The conviction of Ethel and Julius Rosenberg and Morton Sobell as so-called "atom bomb spies" in March 1951, and the entry into federal prisons in July of that year of the leaders of the Communist Party as advocates of forcible and violent throw of the government set the stage for the frenzied years that followed. Courage to stand up and say "No" was hard to come by.

In Hollywood stars and technicians and directors and stage hands, in their fight against a new invasion by the Un-American Committee, coined the slogan "Courage is Contagious"—but the contagion was not widespread, the fear and intimidation was.

It crept into every sphere of American life. Behind the headlines about name-people dragged before The Inquisition, there were thousands hounded, harassed, denied the right to jobs and professions once their names were even mentioned in those congressional witchhunts or whispered to neighbors and employers by slithering FBI agents. The Department of Immigration arrested four hundred non-citizens and held them for deportation, claiming it had three thousand more whose crime was that of "Communist sympathies." The Attorney General released a "subversive list of two hundred fifty organizations" and the Un-American Committee topped that with one of seven hundred thirty-three, making every member of such an organization suspect.

Thousands of militants—in the labor movement, former anti-fascists, New Dealers, Progressive Party activists, former Communist members—went into a personal "underground," dropping out of all activity, rebuilding new lives in enclaves of suburban and urban obscurity. Their children grew up in the 1950s in a vacuum of political silence, unaware of their parents' past, deprived of their heritage.

The nation stood mesmerized and during that first summer Gene translated the political into personal terms. On one of my early prison visits he said we had to face the possibility that I too might be arrested. We had to take legal steps to protect Young Gene, to keep the social agencies from stepping in to claim him as a neglected or abandoned child.

Armed with Gene's practical suggestions, Young Gene and I that summer took a "vacation" out to the West Coast, where he met for the first time his grandparents, my sister and her family, cousins whom I had not seen in some twenty years. As he basked

in this unfamiliar family attention, I explored the possibilities—
Who would "buy" my child, give him safety and security and love
should his mother, as well as his father, be taken from him? I was
shocked to find Mama and Papa now as old, old people. My sister
was in trauma, a newly-discovered cancer threatened her life.
The cousins, with families of their own, were all relatively afflu-
ent and far removed from our once common radical origins. Yet,
as I candidly placed my problem, two immediately responded.
The legal papers transferring guardianship in the event of my
arrest were signed and deposited with an attorney. He advised
me, because I was in New York, and the new guardian in California, to make some intermediary arrangement to prevent the
government from stepping in at the moment of arrest.

Back in New York Bernie and Barbara readily agreed to that
role. Another legal document was drawn up; one copy was filed
in our attorney's office, one Bernie put in safekeeping at their
home, the third I carried with me at all times. I told Gene all that
had been done. He was satisfied, but said tentatively, "Perhaps
we should send him to join his brother." I rejected it without
hesitation. "Not yet. If the worst happens, the guardians could
still do that for us, couldn't they? Let's wait."

We did not tell Young Gene of all these legal machinations,
but I casually mentioned one day all the friends and family he
now had: "If anything should ever happen to me, you're surrounded by people who love you." My nine-year-old looked
soberly at me and asked: "Will I be arrested too, when you are?"

Gene and I were determined that I should not be. In prison
he impressed upon me again and again that my public activity on
behalf of the constitutional issues involved in the fight we were
making, and my complete separation from internal Party underground structure, were my greatest assurances against arrest. I
recalled this admonition a year later when I got a message that I
was being considered for going underground. Without consulting Gene, I refused. I was opposed to that whole set-up, I wanted
no part of it, and I felt, as Gene did, that I was doing more for the
Party out in the open. Also, unlike in the 1930s, I would not give
up my son nor contact with my husband for an assignment made
by some individuals whose judgments were no longer sacrosanct
to me.

IX

The steps taken by the leadership in early spring of 1951 to safeguard against the unpredictable future were not drastic. A few comrades were selected across the country to make themselves "unavailable" to FBI arrests, and of the eleven due to surrender into prison July 2, four did not show. Gene was to have been a fifth, and I often wept at night for that lost moment when a quirk of circumstance landed him in prison instead.

During the short time that he was home between his release from West Street prison and July 2nd, Gene played devil's advocate, probing my feelings about that possibility. In Los Angeles in 1930 I had been uncertain—now twenty-one years later I was sure of my views. I was convinced that the government efforts to decimate our Party and imprison our cadre had to be blocked. I believed that Gene had to be one of those saved. He was too capable politcally, too experienced in such important ways to waste away in prison. He was particularly qualified to continue his activities in any situation, at home or abroad.

Gene tested me, emphasizing the difficulties. "It would be rough on you and The Kid. It's the FBI, not local police, this time. They'll hassle you hard."

"We'll survive."

"I may not be able to send for you two, like last time. It may be for a long time."

"If it's a long time, all the more reason for you to get away. If you go abroad, maybe we'll be able to get there too. If not, we'll wait."

"If I come back, there'll still be prison."

"The whole purpose is to avoid prison now, isn't it? If the political climate gets worse, then you won't come back at all, not openly anyway. If it gets better, you'll decide when to come back, right? You'll probalby go to prison then but at a time of your choosing and when the Party will be in a stronger position."

Relieved at my acceptance of that which he would have done anyway, Gene participated in constant sessions as the day approached. I asked no questions; I didn't want to know specifics, and Gene offered none.

Two nights before the July 2nd surrender date, he left home at midnight. Zero hour had arrived for us. However, five hours later he returned, worried. During the day he sent me to the homes of two comrades with the message that something had gone wrong; he would try again. He left a second time. He was back at dawn and at ten o'clock that morning he surrendered into prison with the others. The scheduled rendezvous had failed twice.

As we rode downtown to the Federal courthouse Gene asked me to find out what had gone wrong. Had it been a plausible breakdown in arrangements or had the sharp differences within the leadership provoked someone to want him isolated into prison?

I was at a loss as to how to start such inquiries, and I was relieved when in one of his first letters Gene indicated in his usual code-like double-talk that I should not pursue the matter. He wrote that this was too critical a time to raise questions of suspicion or recrimination.

Although relieved at the moment, a few years later I regretted Gene's decision. In his campaign in 1959 to oust Gene as general secretary, Gus Hall revived a weird version of that 1951 incident. Travelling about the country garnering support for himself in the Party's top post, Hall spread the story that in 1951 Gene had deliberately violated the decison that he was to go underground, opting instead for what Gus called "the security and safety of prison."

When these stories came back to us, Gene merely shrugged, saying if anyone believed Gus' tale, then a denial on his part wouldn't make any difference. I was furious. Hall's sick view of prison as a haven of safety and security appalled me and, I asked Gene angrily, "How does Gus presume to know what happened to you on that night?"

Of the four who did not surrender into prison July 2, 1951, Gus Hall was apprehended within a few weeks while drinking in a bar across the Mexican border. Robert Thompson was arrested a year later in a comfortable summer resort cabin in the Sierras. Gil Green and Henry Winston successfully eluded the FBI for five years and chose their own day on which they announced to the news media the date and time they would apepar at the Federal courthouse in New York City to voluntarily surrender. During those years, too, none of the comrades around the country who had made themselves "unavailable" to FBI arrests were apprehended. They returned from the underground at the moment when the Party decided they should.

X

On June 20, 1953 the morning after young Ethel and Julius Rosenberg were legally murdered by execution, Gene wrote from his cell in the Atlanta prison:

"Millions of people the world over will long remember Ethel and Julius Rosenberg. And June 19, 1953 will go down in history as a day of infamy when a barbaric crime was committed against humanity.... As the sun set and the Rosenbergs burned, an electric shock was felt around the globe. In Europe and America, in Asia and Africa, people cried in anguish. They demonstrated in anger. They vowed that these two young martyred dead shall not have died in vain....

"Not a few Americans will ask in hopelessness, why was it not possible to prevent this ghoulish Hitlerite execution? The answer lies partly in the advanced process of fascistization that has developed in our country as part of the cold war program.... The other part of the answer lies in the dangerous and costly fact that the weakest link in the worldwide movement of the peoples for clemency and human rights, for democracy and peace is here in the USA.... Too many people and mass organizations, including many opponents of McCarthyism and atomic warfare, as well as numerous adversaries of capital punishment, remained aloof from the struggle. The objective and subjective factors responsible for this heartrending defeat must be examined searchingly. The sooner this is done the sooner the barbarism of June 19th will be avenged."

On the night of the execution I lay tossing in my bed, empty and numb from the tears I had shed. Suddenly screams from Young Gene's room brought me to my feet. His eyes glazed, my ten-year-old screamed over and over again, "I don't want to die!" In my arms, only half awake, he sobbed, "They'll kill him, too. Bring my daddy home; they'll kill him, too."

This was a spin-off of a recurring nightmare. On those other nights I awaken to his sobs, "I tried! I couldn't stop him! I tried!" I wake him and each time he flings his arms wildly around me and has to retell what happened before he can be reassured it was a dream. He is walking down the street with his father; they are laughing together. Towards them comes Rickey—in real life the school bully who taunts him with "Commie bastard, Commie jailbird" epithets. They come face to face. Rickey whips out a gun and shoots. Young Gene throws himself in front of his father, who falls dead at the boy's feet. And the child sobs, "I couldn't save him, mommy. I tried, but I couldn't save him."

My own recurring nightmare I tell no one. I walk in darkness. I hear Gene calling me. I cannot find him. He keeps calling, in helpless pleading. I run through thick forests, down strange streets, through walls and rivers. Always in darkness. The voice calls. I hear it. I cannot answer. He needs me, I cannot find him because he is nowhere. I wake, hearing his calling plea. In the dark, he stands in my doorway, large as life. I press the bedside light. He is gone. I am alone, Always, unalterably alone.

XI

At night we each weep and surrender to the fears that grip our lives, while during the day Young Gene is a chunky, self-reliant, boisterous, over-active ten year old. And I by day am the efficient executive, chairman of the national committee called Families of the Smith Act Victims, and a public representative and member of the National Committee to Win Amnesty for Smith Act Victims.

Our Families Committee grew rapidly, unfortunately, as Smith Act arrests of one hundred sixty Communists took place in Los Angeles, Baltimore, San Francisco, Honolulu, Pittsburgh, Philadelphia, Detroit, St. Louis, Chicago, Seattle, Denver, New York, Boston, Cleveland, Buffalo, Butte, South Carolina, Puerto Rico. Forty-one served prison terms ranging from three to eight years.

Our committee was launched in late September, 1951 at a public reception. It brought into a difficult amalgamation the three divisions of families of Party leaders: the prison wives of the political prisoners, the wives of "unavailables," and the families of those in various stages of litigation.

In California the fourteen defendants remained in jail four and a half months, fighting for reduced, "reasonable" bail rights. In New York, the second round of defendants—the New York Seventeen—moved through West Street prison as through a revolving door for three months in their bail fight. Persons who responded to the wives' appeal for bail loans were in turn themselves hauled into court, their political pasts scrutiinized, their money rejected. The Civil Rights Congress sought to buy bail bonds with its five-year-old Bail Fund, but the courts demanded the names of every person who had ever contributed to that Fund over the years. The Fund trustees—Dashiel Hammett, noted mystery writer; Black educator Dr. Alpheus Hunton; millionaire radical Frederick Vanderbilt Field—refused to release these records and they were imprisoned for "contempt."

In her autobiography, *Unfinished Woman*, playwright Lillian Hellman recounts that she had asked Hammett why he did not admit to the court that he did not know any Bail Fund contributors' names, instead of going to jail for refusing to release such names. He had replied:

"If it were more than jail, if it were my life, I would give it for what I think democracy is, and I don't let cops or judges tell me what I think democracy is."

Our Families Committee was national in its obligations and organized around itself active groups in St. Louis, Chicago, Los Angeles and Baltimore. We were all wives who had at one time been politically active in our own right and who, over the years, had become highly politically-oriented wives of Party leaders. Now we emerged, through necessity, to fight for the very existence of the Party, for our husbands as political activists. Among the Smith Act defendants and prisoners were a number of women. In the case of the Winter and Frankfeld families, both mothers and fathers were arrested.

The guideline we set for our Families Committee was a unique kind of political activity. We created a channel whereby the widest spectrum of people could participate in a fight-back against McCarthyism in humanitarian terms, in protective support of the individual victims and their families. Given the political climate of the time, such simple acts were affirmations in the constitutional and democratic issues involved, acts of political solidarity.

The human terms in which we placed these activities included protection of our children; watchdogging the needs and problems of the prisoners, including the fight for their release—unconditional amnesty; participation in defense activities of those on trial.

In the first traumatic weeks, when the bloodhound-like search for those who did not show on July 2nd reached terror proportions, two radical summer camps abruptly expelled an entire group of our children. The FBI, under the guise of hunting the fathers, kept these camps under twenty-four-hour surveillance, harassed staff, children campers and their parents. The administration asked our children to leave.

Out of this experience arose one of our most successful

efforts—to assure each of our one hundred twenty-five Smith Act child victims, a score of other children whose parents faced deportation, and Black children of civil rights cases a positive summer in safety and acceptance. Over the years, the number of liberal, progressive camps to take our children grew, as did the scholarships they offered. Our annual spring appeal for financing this summer project became a popular campaign in which tens of thousands participated.

In 1952 the author Albert Kahn, who now lives in Glen Ellen, California, wrote a booklet, *Vengeance upon the Young: The Story of the Smith Act children*, based upon many hours of interviews with our families. The theme was the FBI harassment of the children. Kahn interviewed Communist wives and their children who were under twenty-four-hour surveillance, followed to playgrounds and into supermarkets; their classrooms invaded and the children singled out by FBI agents, identified as children of "fugitives," and teachers and classmates asked to cooperate in spying on them; employers visited, wives "fingered" and then fired by embarrassed employers. Two Black children, aged four and two, were expelled from city child care centers after visits by FBI agents. Out of these harassments grew delegations of neighborhood parents to city and state FBI headquarters

We sold two printings of 25,000 each of that booklet in a few months. Money came in with the lists of whole organizations, asking that the booklet be mailed out to their memberships.

Enabling every Smith Act prisoner to have a regular monthly visit with his or her family, regardless of the travel cost to faraway prisons, was a simple human need. It was also a political act of support and was understood as such by the prison and government authorities. The arrival each month to every Smith Act prisoner the allowed commissary money, the prompt arrival of every magazine and newspaper and book request of each of our prisoners, the supply of whatever special medical and orthopedic aids each needed—all these were aspects of servicing political prisoners made possible only through the response of thousands to our appeals. Each dollar that came in was a bold affirmation that these prisoners were not forgotten, that the political reason why they were incarcerated was well understood.

Our appeals were made in simple terms at public meetings, small house parties and most effectively through what was a little known form in our movement at the time—the use of direct mail appeals. Twice a year, spring and at the winter holidays, we reached out to fifty thousand homes with the political message of the fight-back, news of each Smith Act prisoner, the status of various trials, the problems of individual families and the organized way in which we were trying to cope with them, and, mainly, news of our children.

For six years, from lists given us gratis by liberal magazines, newspapers and organizations, we reached six hundred thousand homes. The responses came in single dollar bills, with notes outpouring emotional support. A group of farmers in the midwest wrote they had little money, but would like to give a farm-summer to a few of our children. All they had to offer, they wrote was "plenty of fresh air, lots of milk and our affection."

The National Committee for Amnesty to Smith Act Victims was an ad hoc group which advocated unconditional amnesty to the victims of McCarthyism in prison. The Committee's chief activity, in addition to meetings and conferences, was solicitation of letters and petitions to President Eisenhower.

Eleanor Roosevelt, in *McCall's* magazine, 1956, explained her signature to one of our petitions:

"I wished to call attention to the fact that the Smith Act under which these people were sentenced, is from many points of view a dangerous Act.... To curtail our right to discussion may be only a step from accusing people for what they think, rather than for what they do. This is dangerous to the traditions of a free country. If you don't approve of a law, then you don't feel that anyone is rightfully convicted under that law."

Many hundreds of lesser prestigious—and perhaps therefore more courageous—persons gave their names to cables and petitions on behalf of freedom for the Smith Act prisoners.

The Families Committee. The Amnesty Committee. Local defense committees around individual defendants in various cities. A Trade Union Committee of One Thousand to Repeal the Smith Act. These were the only open channels we "expendable" Communists worked with for the period of the six-year reign of McCarthyite terror. A slim reed to lean on personally, but I learned that in personal terms there was no one to lean on, except for Gene in the prison visiting room.

Immersed in the technical, organizational, political problems of the two committees I concentrated on—the Families and

Amnesty—I drew little personal solace from either. Except for a small group of us who carried the daily chores of the group, in the Families Committee we women did not work well together. In our outward political activity we did spectacular, gratifying things. Internally, we became the recipient of all the tensions and emotions which had no outlet. With husbands gone and the Party organization we had always relied upon absent, living with insurmountable family problems and fears and apprehensions, we were thrown upon our own resources and upon each other.

We were not equipped to help each other because we had no experience in the Party to meet each other as individuals, only in impersonal political concepts. As chairman of the committee, I was held politically responsible for its activity. As to the personal problems each of us had, none of us was equipped by our Party experience to respond to each other on a simple human level. Like the other wives, officially and outwardly I was too calm, too impersonal, too political. Within myself, I cried silently. Only Rose Perry, our committee's executive secretary, became a personal friend during this time and our friendship continues today.

XII

Each summer Young Gene and I went to the West Coast where I combined meetings for the Families and Amnesty Committees with restful visits with my own family and their friends—a different, secure world. In Chicago, Detroit, Seattle, Spokane, Bellingham, Los Angeles and San Francisco while I worked, Young Gene was delighted to learn that all these strangers admired his father and, perhaps more important, "They like me, too, don't they, mommy?"

To and from the West Coast, we travelled via Atlanta, for our visits with Gene. The news I would bring him of where we had been, where we were going, whom I had talked to, the responses to our activities interested Gene in every detail. But it was never enough. He demanded more activity.

On the lower West side in New York City I spent a quiet hour of discussion with a Catholic priest and came away with an invitation for one of our women to speak to his congregation. He also gave his signature to our amnesty appeal.

In New York, too, I found a delightful friend in Royal W. France when I first went to his office to solicit his aid in the amnesty campaign. Tall, slightly stooped, white haired, gentle of face and voice, France had left academia in Florida to offer his services in New York as an attorney in various Smith Act cases. In his first conversation with me, and later in his autobiography, *My Native Grounds*, France explained he had to do this "not because I believe in what you say, but because I believe that you have the right to say it. To me this is basic democracy."

Of that first meeting, he wrote in his book:

"I had been approached by Peggy Dennis, wife of the imprisoned Communist leader Eugene Dennis, to try to enlist support for a petition to the President for amnesty for the Smith Act victims. I was attracted to Mrs. Dennis by her vigorous personality, her understanding of my points of difference, as well as of agreement, with the Communists, and by her unflagging loyalty to her husband."

Imbued with the constitutional issues involved, France was confident he could get a number of his liberal friends to join him in initating a new amnesty appeal. His refreshing lack of political inhibitions was tonic to me in those days. We met and talked often in his midtown office or together with his wife at their home on the East side. He was puzzled and hurt when his old friend Roger Baldwin, head of the American Civil Liberties Union, turned down his request to join the amnesty appeal. Undaunted, France plugged on. He worked tirelessly with the Rev. A. J. Muste, director of the Fellowship for Reconciliation; he got his old friend Norman Thomas to agree "our main job is to make democracy work," despite Thomas' virulent anti-Communism.

In Chicago Abe Feinglass, international vice presdient of the Fur Union, and Herbert Marsh, president of the Packing-house Workers Union, separately put me in touch with various union officials with whom I talked amnesty, political prisoners, Smith Act repeal. In Denver the Mine, Mill, Smelter Workers' Union sent $10 every month for the entire six years to the Families Committee, and labor councils of two New England cities sent us money and a list of three hundred local union officers to whom to send our *Vengeance on the Young* booklet.

In San Francisco, Party leader and Smith Act defendant William Schneiderman spent an afternoon arguing against the validity of my tour. He claimed "amnesty is an unrealistic possibility at this time," therefore I should not be advocating it.

That Sunday morning, however, I spoke from the pulpit of a

Black church in the Fillmore district and was interrupted with enthusiastic "amen, sister" approval when I called for the unconditional amnesty of imprisoned Ben Davis, Pettis Perry and Claudia Jones, and compared political fugitives Henry Winston and James Jackson to the refugees riding the freedom train out of slavery.

In Los Angeles another Party leader and Smith Act defendant, Dorothy Healey, arranged for me to talk with interested editors of liberal magazines, groups of rank and file trade unionists, activists in the Progressive and Democratic parties, and to a Hollywood group deeply involved in fighting their own battle with the Un-American Committee.

In Spokane I got heckled by a group of young Trotskyites, and my speech became a polemic about coalitions to save American democracy versus their meaningless "Revolution Now" slogan. In Bellingham I was the honored guest of the Fishermen's Union at a baked salmon dinner.

Harry Bridges, maverick radical labor leader, took me to lunch in San Francisco and spent the time disparaging the amnesty campaign. He said being in prison was an "expected hazard" of the "profession;" he was sure Gene knew it and "can take it." Responding to my argument that it was not a question of being able to take it but a form of mounting the struggle against McCarthyism, Bridges said: "This is not a good time to fight."

I recalled, but did not tell him, an incident that occurred two days earlier. I had been guest of honor at a Women's Brunch attended by thirty-five women, mainly wives of organizers and leaders of Harry's I.L.W.U. union. The women listened appreciatively as I described the work of our Families Committee, the problems of the politial prisoners, the reliance upon the support we were getting. There were many questions. One woman, however, sat silent. She was Harry Bridges' wife who, with their two young children, was the brunt of a public harassment campaign around the government's third attempt to deport Harry as a "Communist." Nancy Bridges finally spoke.

"You make it sound like you are all amazons of strength and paragons of objectivity," she said bitterly. "Tell me, aren't you ever afraid? Don't you ever lay in your bed at night and cry?"

There is an embarrassed silence. I look at the women around me. How can I share what it really feels like without being maudlin, non-political. My tears at night. My nightmares. My child's dreams from which he wakes up screaming. I look at the women, waiting silently. And I reply, "Yes, I'm afraid. And I cry at night. But I've got to keep fighting back. And we all need each other, fighting together, otherwise we will all drown together in an ocean of tears."

Ten:
UNRESOLVED CRISIS

I

With six others of the original eleven, Gene was released from federal prison in early March, 1955. For the next ten months they were on "CR," conditional release for the remainder of their sentence. Parolees on "CR" may not consort with individuals or circumstances related to their original crime. These national leaders of the Communist Party were forbidden to see each other or any other Communist, nor could they participate in political activity. They had to get jobs acceptable to the Parole Department, report their finances and their every personal movement.

As in prison, Gene challenged these restrictions as violations of his constitutional rights. He finally won the right to become a salaried political consultant to the attorneys working on the Party's court fight against the Subversive Control Board efforts to outlaw the Party. As political consultant, Gene met freely and often with the clients in the case, the Communists around the country, including those who, like he, were on "CR."

He researched the Party's history and ideology which the attorneys used in preparing their briefs and arguments against the Board's charges. He sought out and talked with hundreds of Party and non-Party people—each of whom had experienced the last five years from different disadvantage points, each impatient to talk of their particular political frustrations. He saw or wrote to each of the many hundreds of diverse persons who had signed amnesty appeals, and he urged them to continue their support of amnesty for those still in prison.

The "CR" period which kept Gene out of the daily routines

of organizational tasks, was good for us personally. It gave us time to deal with the tensions at home sparked by the problems of adjustment. Between Gene and myself these problems were surprisingly minimal. We were even closer, and there was an added note of new respect on Gene's part for my political independence. There was an undefined recognition of a new self confidence I seemed to radiate without being aware of it. There were, too, moments of resentment when I forgot to consult him on little daily matters. I had become accustomed to considering only a son, not a husband too. But mainly we revelled in the fact that he was home again.

Between father and son, however, the situation was more complex. The thirteen-year-old found that the image he had idolized from afar for so many years was in fact simply an ordinary man who in daily contact often became an irritant. Gene had returned, after five years of sublimated memories, to an unavoidably close relationship between mother and son. He often felt excluded from references of shared experiences, and we found that living daily routines together was different than our emotional relationships based only on prison visits and letters. Slowly, however, after recurring stormy scenes there emerged a less idyllic but more realistic relationship between them. The pent-up love and mutual need began to settle into a normal enjoyment of each other.

During these months I continued my Families Committee activities and I worked on a book of Gene's prison letters International Publishers was to release after "CR." Until then we were still bound to the 1951 decision that his letters could not be publicly quoted or published. I accepted this project only after getting an agreement from Gene and the publisher that I had sole authority to select and edit the letters, write the introduction, make all production decisions.

"CR" ended in December and on January 20, after five years, the Party went public. The anniversary of the *Daily Worker* was celebrated in Carnegie Hall where Gene and the paper's editor, John Gates—the Atlanta prison graduates—were billed as main speakers. On stage sat the other newly liberated parolees. From the underground comrades had begun returning home.

II

Sedate Carnegie Hall rang with camaraderie as people

embraced and laughed and cried. Most of them had not seen each other in five years. Back from the underground and out of the prisons, returned from a protective self-isolation, comrades now mingled emotionally; and those of us who had carried on as best we could above-ground saw this night as our special celebration.

Some of our comrades were still in prison but the rash of arrests had stopped. McCarthyism was in decline. There was a new Communist Control Act but we were challenging it in the courts. The Korean War was over. Racial segregation in the schools had been declared unconstitutional. The first conference of twenty-nine African and Asian states at Bandung had placed Third World liberation high on the international agenda. The heads of state of the U.S., the Soviet Union, France and Great Britain had met peacefully in Geneva, after Moscow broke Washington's atom bomb monopoly.

New winds were blowing and our being in Carnegie Hall was part of it. We were euphorically confident that, unlike Humpty Dumpty, we could, we had to, put it all back together again. We were proud of the courage so many had displayed and we were proud of the tenacious way in which we had fought back. However, we also were aware there was an accounting to be made. Many things had gone wrong organizationally. Many mistakes had been committed politically. It was a time for celebration but it was also a wary time. We were waiting to see whether we would only congratulate ourselves on having survived the last five years or whether we would face up to the fact of the isolation and sectarianism that had almost destroyed the organization during those five years.

Gene stood at the podium, his hands gripping the edges of the lectern. He was, as always, a poor public speaker, devoid of dynamic oratory. Imapct of ideas, not gimmick histrionics, was his style. Most audiences wanted to cheer and applaud, not to think. Tonight, however, Gene radiated a confidence that, muted as it was, fed the euphoria of the crowd.

He called for a bold re-unification with the American people and the audience applauded. He said that the last five years had taught us all, Communist and non-Communist alike, that if we don't hang together, we'd surely hang separately, and that this needed unity presumes differences of opinion. "We Communists respect the rights of others to disagree with us," he said. "All we ask is an equal right to voice our beliefs and to try to convince others that our ideas have merit." The audience cheered. This was clearly no ordinary speech. They leaned forward to catch every word. The bombshell came undramatically, as Gene quietly said:

"We admit we have not had all the correct answers to every problem in the past, nor do we have a monopoly on wisdom today. We have, like others, made not a few mistakes. Our American Communist Party, guided by the socialist principles and scientific outlook, is going to take a new look at all problems . . . [it is going to] learn from any wrong judgments, tactical mistakes or theoretical errors we may have made."

A massive, collective gasp, then thunderous applause and cheers. From the podium had come the promise we needed.

Six weeks later, in a similar vein, Gene told a Party activists' meeting that the courage we had shown in going to prison, into the underground, or staying behind to fight must be translated now into a new kind of courage; a courage "to go among people who disagree with us, to engage in friendly debate with our adversaries in the battle of ideas . . . to think more deeply, more independently."

The end of "CR" in December; the Carnegie Hall "New Look" pledge in January; the activists' meeting in March; and on April 28, a long, microscopic analysis of "the state of the Party" to the first national committee meeting in five years. Published as a forty-eight page pamphlet entitled "The Communists Take a New Look," with this report Gene opened up a new era in our Party. He called for a wide-open, freewheeling examination of everything with no holds barred, no sacred cows exempt. His political characterizations were too startling for some.

Unlike Foster and others who attributed the Party's isolation to the beyond-our-control repressive measures against us, Gene claimed our mistakes were the result of a "deeply ingrained Left sectarianism" dominant for the last decade. This pinpointed the period to the pendulum-swing that occurred after the fall of Browder, and also the years of the underground. Gene now charged that we had become "a prisoner of Left wing centers" instead of "a part of the peoples' mass movements."

He placed this sectarianism within a completely new context—new for our Party at least—when he said this sectarianism was due, in large part, to "the mechanical and doctrinaire fashion" in which we adopted as our own "the experiences of other parties." He called for a "creative" interpretation of Marxism based upon "the experiences, circumstances and tradiitons of our country," and said that only we and we alone would determine that creative interpretation.

Rejecting the lifelong custom of following Moscow's lead in all matters theoretical and tactical, Gene declared that our policies and tactics must be based on solid objective analyses of reality in our own country; these analyses should evolve out of consultation with "broader circles" in and outside the Party; they should be the result of discussion derived in "an atmosphere in our Party where individual members feel free to dissent from the majority and to submit alternative and unorthodox policies and proposals."

He urged not a revision of Marxism but a use of the Marxist-Leninist method to explore new phenomena and new theoretical concepts. On questions of internal Party structure, Gene offerd what was for our Party a daringly new concept of the Party's vanguard role, saying we should no longer cling to the old idea that we and we alone have all the answers and that "all those who really want socialism will have to come to us." He urged instead a "most positive approach to all honest Socialist and Marxist oriented groups and individuals." He projected "friendly debate and cooperation" combined with "sharp political and ideological struggle" that could lead eventually to the unification of all socialist-minded persons into a "new and broader mass party of socialism." He rejected the established use of democratic centralism which, he said, in practice, stifled democracy and perpetuated bureaucracy.

Using this body of new criteria, Gene examined each area of mass issues of the past years and found our Party sorely lacking, all due to that ingrained sectarianism and rigid methodology which, although some had opposed, dominated the organization.

Gene's views fell on fertile soil—excitement permeated the Party's ranks. Not everyone, however, welcomed this political iconoclasm. Foster and a hard core of oldtime comrades were horrified at what they saw as heresy. Shocked at the public candor of Gene's analyses, Foster claimed its effect was to "lower seriously the Party's prestige." Instead of recognizing the relief and enthusiasm with which the "New Look" was welcomed, he predicted that such open debate would "undermine its [the Party's] morale." Deaf to the membership demand for reappraisal and unrestricted discussion, Foster branded the new atmosphere as "revisionist" and "anti-Party."

It us unlikely that Foster's opposition, nor that of his followers, would have seriously affected the outcome of that healthy discussion and re-examination opened in late April. Unfortunately, other circumstances intervened, and we were soon catapulted into a four years' long destructive crisis that surpassed the early factionalism of the 1920s and the 1944 crisis. The undertow that dragged the Party down at a moment when it was beginning to rise to new heights was the explosive reaction to the revelations of the Stalin crimes admitted by the Soviet leadership only after his death. This changed the whole character of the "New Look" campaign. And yet in a bigger sense, the two were related. What we were undertaking to do within our Party under American conditions, the new Soviet leadership started to do at its 20th congress that same year; that is, break with old mistakes and face up to new circumstances.

III

Shortly before the text appeared in *The New York Times*, Gene brought home a typed copy of the secret Khrushchev report. Late that night I retreated into the bedroom of the large, shabby apartment I had found on the edge of West Harlem on 151st Street when Gene had come home from prison. It was a dark, rundown, roach-infested apartment with an elevator that broke down often and a furnace that conked out during every cold spell. But we had controlled low rent and it gave us, for the first time, two bedrooms and a study—space for the three of us to get away from each other.

I lay in the half-darkness, the typed pages illuminated only by a bedside light. The cold printed words recocheted like bouncing pellets. Without analysis and in no political context, Khrushchev's admissions stood naked, unadorned, beyond comprehension. These were no regrettable "excesses" committed in the heat of revolutionary overthrow of the class enemy power. These were no unfortunate over-zealous "distortions of socialist legality" in pursuit of class justice against remnants of that class enemy. The new Soviet leadership was admitting, three years after Stalin's death, to what had been a years-long, deliberate extermination by execution and imprisonment of hundreds of thousands of socialist, Party and non-Party, cadre—scapegoats for a misfired economic or political policy which could not be admitted to have been wrong; sacrifices to the ill-conceived belief that to question leaders' policies is treason or foreign agent provocation. Khrushchev now admitted that the charge "enemy of the people," which sent those so accused to prison and execution, was actually a deliberate hoax to eliminate "the possibility of any kind of ideological fight or the making of one's views known on this or that issue, even of a practical character."

This annihilation on a mass scale was carried through by Stalin, the Soviet leadership now admitted:

> "at a time when the revolution was already victorious, when the Soviet state was strengthened, when the exploiting classes were already liquidated and socialist relations were rooted solidly in all phases of national economy, when our Party was politically consolidated and had strengthened itelf both numerically and ideologically."

The last page crumpled in my fist, I lay in the half darkness, and I wept. For Tim in Moscow. For Gene's years in prison. For Young Gene's years in a hostile world. For the years of silence in which we had buried doubts and questions. For a thirty-year life's commitment that lay shattered.

I lay sobbing low, hiccoughing whimpers. Gradually the tears dry stiff on my face. I rise and go out into the dark apartment. Young Gene's door is closed. Gene is in the small study, his head resting against the old armchair's high back, a cold pipe held loosely in a hand that hangs limp over the chair's side. I crawl onto his lap, his arms hold me and we cling to each other, wordlessly, in the dark. The night passes and with the morning comes, once again, the reality of the struggle.

I get my political bearings. I agree with Gene that the exposures and the processes of correction are expressions of the stability of the Soviet Union and the intent of the post-Stalin leadership to rectify these crimes. A new admiration evolves out of my tears.

Letters begin to pour into the *Daily Worker* bemoaning "the waste of fifteen, twenty years of my life," declaring our Party was "now discredited beyond repair," that it should shamefacedly disappear altogether. Uncomfortably, I recognize these as my first reactions, but I know them now to be false.

The greatest assurance for our continuing viability was this new era of candid admission and correction of errors that we here at home and the comrades in Moscow were launching. We had immaturely over-idealized the road to socialism. We had been incapable of facing reality and incapable of admitting mistakes along the uncharted road. And we were each of us responsible. We had followed leadership blindly, simplistically allowing them to do, in our name, the terrible things they had done.

Khrushchev had parried that question of responsibility. This disturbed me but I hoped that answers would be given. We here also had to answer that question within the context of our own problems. But now from Moscow to New York, all over the world, the Communists were moving to a "new look" at old formulas, challenging old relationships with Moscow as the single fount of all political wisdom, searching for new approaches to their own countries, their own Parties.

We could be on the eve of an important transformation. If our gods now proved to be mere mortals with feet of clay, we were released from blind obeisance. We had the responsibility to think for ourselves. Never again could leadership command instant allegiance by claiming omnipotence and infallibility. The main task was still the fight against the class enemy, and in this fight Gene and others were committed to some heavy rethinking and bold action. The Soviet comrades were also. The going would be rough, but we could make it.

However, the convergence of our original "New Look" campaign and the shock of the Stalin crimes was more than we could easily absorb. The positive effort at re-examination of all theory and practice became a four-year destructive battle.

Since the beginning of the 1960s the official Party version of that four-year period has been that it was a struggle between Browder-like revisionism led by John Gates, the editor of the *Daily Worker*, and a staunch, victorious defense of the Party led by William Z. Foster. Documents of that time and the personal experiences of thousands who went through that fight, however, contradict that version.

In reality, the period from 1956-1960 was a struggle of the majority of the Party against both the revisionism of the Gates group and the sectarianism of the Foster group. It was a struggle for bold, innovative, dialectic change in the organization's concepts, actions and methodology within the frame work of the principles of Marxism-Leninism.

Within a different context, and in a more critical situation, it was the continuation of the efforts begun in the late 1940s, and continued ineffectually by some comrades in the underground in 1953, to overcome the swing to sectarianism after the defeat of Browder's revisionism. Those efforts at correction were aborted by the McCarthyite repressions and by the isolation of the underground leadership from the Party membership and the mass movements. Now that unfinished business was tackled by a resurgent membership under the aegis of Gene's "New Look" report.

There are many "ifs" one could speculate about, in hindsight, concerning that 1956-1960 struggle. *If* Foster had not opposed the effort in the abusive and condemnatory way he did, *perhaps* a large number of comrades would not have been pushed into the extreme views of what became the Gates group; *if* many in the Gates group and those it influenced had not ended up advocating the liquidation of the Party and expressing a virulent anti-Sovietism under the guise of "independence," *perhaps* Gene would not have retreated by late 1958 from some of his original innovations; *if* the leading Black comrades had not been stymied by the issue of Black unity into trying to minimize their differences with Ben Davis, who was in the Foster camp, *perhaps* these comrades would have more aggressively advocated those positions in Gene's program with which they agreed; *if* Gene had been a good factionalist, *perhaps* he could have more decisively and more quickly combatted and isolated the Foster and Gates groups. Instead, he refused to fight for his views and he refused to actively fight factionalism with a factionalism of his own.

IV

Most of us were not surprised at Foster's opposition. After all, it was primarily his policies and their aftermath that was being officially declared costly mistakes. We were not prepared, however, for his vitriolic methods. We had forgotten his factionalizing expertise displayed in the late 1920s and again in 1944. He was a master at it.

Even so, we embarked upon this venture with confidence. Foster and his stalwarts were a minority. Gene wrote enthusiastically to John Williamson in London who had been deported after serving his five years' Smith Act prison term:

"The reports [of the April 28 meeting] can't begin to convey the significance of the new atmosphere that is being created in our deliberations; the give and take, the sharp and pointed debate.... In the process of this, certain irresponsible things are said and projected. Nevertheless the net and overall effect is healthy and positive. And believe you me, at long last we are beginning to come to grips with some old and unresolved questions, as well as moving forward resolutely to tackle that which lies ahead."

Within four months the situation had changed. Foster's intransigencies began to repel many, his labelling as "anti'Party" and "anti-Soviet" all who disagreed with him angered everyone. Claude Lightfoot, popular Black leader of the Illinois Party organization and member of the national committee, angrily declared at one meeting that he would not participate in any further discussions "if I am going to be branded a right wing revisionist every time I express an opinion."

An influential grouping called for the liquidation of the Party. There were three trends within that faction: one developed the theory that the mass movements needed no revolutionary vanguard, that they would spontaneously and instinctively move towards socialism; another embraced Browder's view of a liberal, enlightened, reform capitalism that made unnecessary either revolutionary struggle or a vanguard, Communist Party or otherwise; the largest grouping felt that Foster's stubborn sectarianism, coupled with the shock of the Stalin crimes revelations, so discredited the Party and socialism that we could not regain our credibility nor be depended upon to institute the changes we now advocated. Foster seized upon all these views and accused his critics of being liquidationists.

Gene wrote again to Williamson, this time in a more worried vein:

"Unfortunately the struggle against the Right and the avowed liquidationists is complicated and impeded because of the untenable position adopted by the Old Man [Foster]. He has opened a fundamental assault against the main political direction of the April plenum and the draft resolution adopted, combining this with an all-out attack against diverse rightist elements. He has lumped together the entire national committee and the dissolutionists, revisionists and various shades of Right. [But] methinks the line of the draft resolution will prevail over and against the Right and the Old Man."

From the beginning Gene opposed Foster's attempt to stop the free-wheeling debate. Instead he told a meeting of the New

York state committee early in the debate:

> "I don't agree with most views expressed here, but I have no desire to label those political positions. I would rather examine what may be valid in their criticism and argue and try to persuade you on those questions I believe erroneous."

Soon, however, he became concerned with the growing liquidationist views emanating particularly out of the New York organization. By the end of January, 1957, he wrote Williamson in London that the struggle was intensifying against the positions of "both the Left and Right factional alignments." In an article titled "What Kind of a Change," he wrote:

> "I do not agree with those who believe the Party cannot change or with those who think no change is necessary. The question is, however, what kind of a change."

This debate over the direction and content of change encompassed all areas of Party theory, policy, tactics. The one area that became the most divisive, however, was that of our Party relations with the socialist countries and with other Communist Parties, particularly that of the Soviet Union. In June, 1956 during the first horror at the Stalin crimes revelations, Gene wrote a major analytical article trying to place the Soviet phenomenon in an historical context which the Khrushchev report did not, without condoning the events in any way. He wrote, in part:

> "We defended and accepted the indefensible and unacceptable with uncritical attitudes.... We too often treated criticism from sincere trade unionists and liberals as though it came from the professional anti-Communist and anti-Soviet baiter. For all this we feel profound regret, without reservation or equivocation."

At the same time, he wrote: "I do not agree with approaches that minimize the errors now revealed. I cannot agree, on the other hand, with sweeping anti-Soviet indictments that fail to take historical fact and perspective into account and that, regardless of intent, foster hostility toward socialist countries. I share the attitude of a frank and honest self critical apology to honest people we have mistakenly condemned. But I cannot accept the viewpoint that wipes out and undermines pride and confidence in the socialist countries."

In an earlier symposium in Carnegie Hall with the arch anti-Communists Roger Baldwin of the American Civil Liberties Union and Norman Thomas of the Socialist Party, Gene argued that what appeared at the time to be a deep-going correction of the Soviet errors by the Moscow leadership should now make possible, in his opinion, improved relations and united action in mass struggle between the Communists here at home and those whom we had vilified in the past for their criticisms of the Soviet Union.

When the Soviet troops occupied Hungary in 1956 the *Daily Worker*, under Gates' leadership, denounced the action without giving the readers a factual analysis of what was happening inside Budapest at the time, and it did this in inflammatory anti-Soviet and anti-socialist terms. Gene disagreed with the *Daily Worker*, and sent in a letter for publication. In his view, the editors had concerned themselves only with the Soviet response to a crisis after it had exploded. They did not place prime responsibility where it belonged, in his opinion, upon the Hungarian Stalinist leadership for the crimes which forced the people to rebel against a socialist government. Nor had the editors recognized, Gene wrote, that the Rakosi regime had collapsed, and that the fascist elements grouped around Cardinal Mindzenty had turned the people's rebellion into a bloodbath.

V

The 16th national convention, in early 1957, after a year of devastating in-fighting, faced a real possibility of an organizational split in the Party. This threat was defused through adroit compromises engineered primarily by Gene, although most of us were cynical of the durability of the facade of unity achieved at the convention. Yet some basic guidelines were established, officially, at least, and by majority votes.

Despite Foster's opposition, the convention reaffirmed the belief that the main obstacle to the Party's revitalization was Left sectarianism and dogmatism, not revisionism as Foster claimed.

Despite opposition of the hard-core of the Gates group, the convention rejected any type of Party dissolution and it reaffirmed the organization's commitment to the universal character of Marxism-Leninism.

Over Foster opposition, the convention at the same time emphasized adherence to the application of Marxist-Leninist principles to the realities of the American scene, and to our own interpretations of those principles independent of those made by other Communist parties. On various organizational precepts, the convention adopted the new relationship between the Party and other socialist-oriented trends, and sought new interpretations of the concept of democratic centralism, which would strengthen the democratic processes.

The inherent differences among all the groups was dramatized in the responses to a long greeting to the convention by Jacques Duclos. Once again, as in 1944, he wrote a lengthy critique of our Party and its convention documents.

Foster demanded the convention vote endorsement of the Duclos document. He saw it, as in 1944, as a vindication from abroad of his own position. Many in the Gates faction demanded the convention officially condemn Duclos for interfering in our internal affairs. Other comrades wanted to avoid the whole issue by not having the letter read to the convention at all. Gene and others insisted it had to be read together with all other official greetings received. In his keynote report, however, Gene referred to the Duclos letter, and he told the convention:

"Our decisions will be our own, made by the collective judgment of this convention and will be based on our Marxist understanding of American reality and the needs of our people and our nation."

Neither the Foster nor the Gates group was satisfied with the convention results. The unity and compromise achieved was a surface one, yet Gene and others felt that in avoiding a split and having established minimal guidelines that rejected the extremes of both factions, time was won in which to isolate these extremes further.

However, six weeks later Gene wrote Williamson that "a resurgence of factional activity still threatens to split the organization." He added that "neither Bill [Foster] and Ben [Davis] on the one hand nor the Gates-[Joe] Clark forces on the other seem able or willing to learn anything from the convention in this respect."

From London Williamson urged that he ally himself more clearly with Foster, and Gene replied:

"Bear in mind that we cannot play 'favorite' with either faction, especially in the post-convention period. Both factions endanger the life and unity of the Party and impede the further unfoldment of the struggle against doctrinairism and revisionism which the convention only began."

In another letter, he vented his impatience with Foster:

"It should be borne in mind that nothwithstanding his noteworthy contributions, recent as well as past, Bill has become very rigid and inflexible on tactical and personnel questions and is intensely subjective and bitter. This, of course, is grist to the mills of the Right opportunists, especially the revisionist elements."

In the year following the convention, many left the Party. Most of these were connected in varying degrees with the Gates group. Some left in frustrated disagreement with the convention decisions, others in disgust over the factionalism, many because they did not believe the Party could re-coup itself.

Foster merely shrugged "good riddance" and demanded punitive organizational action against those who remained and did not agree with him. The majority of those leaving were a whole generation of state and national activists who had come into the Party from the Young Communist League. Many were our most effective workers in the mass movements. A number had fought in Spain with gun in hand.

Gene was disturbed by the exodus and saw as many as he could personally, urging them not to leave, asking them to stay and help institute the changes needed to make the Party the viable organization it could and had to become. Replying to a question from Williamson, Gene wrote four months after the convention:

"You ask 'who is taking a walk?' . . . The heaviest losses of membership took place after the publication of the special report of Khrushchev on Stalin; there was another notable exodus after the events in Hungary. Following the convention, quite a few left the organization in New York, in the first place those who were associated with the Right wing. This process continues and one of the big factors was the damaging role of the protracted factional struggle which affected many comrades regardless of their previous political positions. . . . A helluva lot of damage has been done and the going will be rough for quite some time."

Six months later he continued to write of the threat of "a

real split in the Party," and he expressed the belief that "a showdown is fast approaching."

Such a showdown did come. It triggered the last big exodus from the Party and it caused Gene to retreat somewhat from his earlier positions regarding our attitudes towards relations with the Soviet Communist Party.

VI

This was a time of great upheaval in all Communist parties. The Stalin crimes revelations, the Hungarian rebellion and the spectacle of workers striking against a socialist government in Poland, the Soviet military intervention, the admission of Soviet error in earlier condemnations of the Yugoslav Communist Party (condemnations which other Parties, including ours, had dutifully echoed)—all these created a wholly new atmosphere internationally. Gene followed closely the debates within the Italian, French, British and Spanish Parties. He constantly urged Williamson to send him packets of all unpublished materials from these Parties; also to rush to him copies of the drafts still being worked on in those countries regarding their independent, national road to socialism, their new concepts regarding the type of socialist democracy now being envisioned for the developed countries as different than the Soviet experience; and their changed definition of international solidarity based upon equality, friendly criticism, and no longer acceptance of a hegemonic role for any single Communist Party within the international movement.

Within the Soviet Union there were counter-pulls regarding how deep-going the correction of the Stalin crimes should go. There was alarm, too, at the Hungarian and Polish events, and there was consternation at reactions to the Soviet events within the international movement.

At the end of 1958 the Communist parties of twelve socialist countries met in conference, and in a final communique declared, among other significant things, that revisionism and not sectarianism was now the main danger within the international Communist movement.

The Soviet comrades obviously were unable or unwilling to follow through boldly with the full implications of their own Twentieth Congress revelations. They were going to restrict correction of the Stalin crimes to a humanitarian opening of the prison and labor camp gates. They were not going to cope with the Stalin methodology and precepts nor their own compliance with them. They were obviously more afraid of the eruptive period of open debate that would have to precede real correction. They were going to freeze the thaw before it had really begun. They now declared the bold correction of the mistakes to be the main danger, and in the old style they proclaimed this to be so not only for themselves, but for the whole Communist movement.

Once again the influences from abroad exploded upon us here at home. The Foster group revitalized and seized upon this statement as full vindication from abroad, the only high court it ever recognized. They demanded immediate endorsement of the statement of the conference of socialist countries and they demanded official correction of our national convention decisions to bring them in accord with the new *ukase* from Moscow.

Among those who had formerly made up the Gates faction there were, as usual, differing views. Some demanded that we condemn the twelve Party statement as an interference in the internal affairs of other Parties and that we reaffirm once again our independence from Moscow. Others were as violently critical and for the same reasons, but they proposed no official action be taken by our national committee on the matter.

The anger and frustrations after three years of in-fighting became centered on the issue of our independence from Moscow's views and its presumption to make analyses for us.

As in 1939, and again in 1944, at home I beat hard at Gene's silent pacing. The promise held out by the new Soviet leadership in 1956 was dissipating. All right, that's their problem, I argued. If the Soviet people can live with such a superficial adjustment of the wrongs done them for more than twenty years, let them. But here, we had not even begun to pull out the roots of that damnable sectarianism nor faced up to the many mistakes of the underground years. His whole political premise had been based upon just that need. We couldn't accept Moscow's views as ours. And if we didn't meet the issue of non-interference from abroad each time it specifically occurs, I taunted, then what good were the fine convention resolutions and speeches?

Gene would not be baited. He sought from within himself plausible explanations for the Soviet viewpoint. He found it difficult to put into practice that new independence of action he had proclaimed. This was conditioned, too, by his aversion to the pronounced anti-Sovietism that surfaced in the debate. I urged that he go behind the misguided rhetoric and try to understand the intent of those comrades. That was part of the problem—he did not trust that intent.

Characteristically, again he steered a course between all these pressures. He sought to analyze the international experiences that must have influenced the thinking of our Soviet comrades. As for our Party in the United States he claimed:

> "While the struggle against dogmatism and sectarianism has only begun, our Party is not immune from revisionist influences and trends and they have become more, not less, prevalent, especially in regards to a lack of faith in the Party, questioning the validity of all Marxist principles, a distorted concept of proletarianism internationalism and an opportunist approach to many aspects of mass policy."

He said that our convention in 1957 had determined for a struggle against both sectarianism and revisionism, and he was sure our 17th convention in 1959 would also. He reiterated that only our Party alone would decide for itself, on the basis of the specifics of any given moment, when one or the other was the greatest threat to our performance in mass activity. As usual, neither group was satisfied with his positions. Foster charged that Gene was a conciliator of revisionism, while the other group (formerly known as the Gates group and now led primarily by Dorothy Healey of Southern California, Sid Stein and Fred Fine in the national office) charged Gene was a prisoner of Foster's doctrinairism.

From the beginning in 1956 Gene had chosen a difficult role for himself, and he maintained it for the whole four years. I believed then and believe now that politically his views were the only sound ones in the whole factional crisis. I disagreed with him vehemently and angrily, however, on the way he refused to fight factionally for his positions, and his belief that people would be won over on the basis of the validity of his ideas alone. He had taken a similar view in the factional fight in Los Angeles in the late 1920s and now again.

He projected what he believed to be a valid political analysis. He worked to isolate the extremes of both the revisionist Right and the doctrinaire Left. He sought to consolidate the best elements influenced by both extremes into a majority unity essential to Party activity. These goals, so clear to him, were not understood in the heat of battle. His refusal to get sucked into polarity was interpreted as a sign of vacillation and weakness. He became the target of all the opposition, each group claiming he was conciliating the other. He refused to join either faction. He refused to organize his own faction. He kept his channels wide open to everyone, even those who maligned him the most.

When Foster and Davis tried to get Gates removed as editor of the *Daily Worker* in 1956, Gene blocked it. After the 1957 convention, when the large, newly elected national committee failed, in secret ballot vote, to elect Foster to the top seventeen-member executive committee, Gene forced the enlargement of that group by one to include Foster. When Foster and Davis in 1958 tried to remove from Party posts, and even talked of expelling, Claude Lightfoot of Illinois, Mickie Lima of California, Carl Winter of Michigan and Dorothy Healey of Southern California, Gene stopped these moves and instead nominated three of them to the national board of the Party.

The 17th national convention in December, 1959, no longer faced any threat of a split. But the Party was decimated by the time it consolidated on the basis of the main precepts Gene had offered in his "New Look" report so long ago. Foster opposed the 17th convention as vehemently as he had the 16th, and as he had the original "New Look" report. While consolidation was the keynote of the convention, Foster still demanded purges, and he demanded that Gene be kept from any leading post. This demand was, of course, ignored by the small top committee considering leadership proposals for the convention. However, a secondary crisis did arise within the leadership as it prepared for the convention's opening.

VII

Gus Hall came into national Party leadership in much the same way Earl Browder had some thirty years earlier. Browder had returned from a two-year stay in China to be tabbed new national leader in the aftermath of the Lovestone-Foster factional fight. His main qualification at the time was that he had been, of all national comrades, least identified with that factional situation; it was hoped that he could bring unity to the Party.

Gus Hall was born into a revolutionary Finnish family in Minnesota. He became a Young Communist League activist, and a member of the C.I.O.'s Steel Organizing Committee in Ohio in the mid-30s, when thousands of Communists were welcomed into that organization. Later he became Communist Party state head in Ohio. When Gene went to prison in 1950 on the Un-American Committee contempt conviction, Gus was brought into the national center as a compromise choice between Bob Thompson, state chairman of the New York Organization, whom Foster and Davis wanted, and Gil Green, head of the Illinois organization, whom Gene wanted.

Gus was not involved in the big internal Party reappraisals in the struggle against Browder in 1945. He was in the Navy at the time. He was not involved in the 1956-1960 eruptions either. He was in prison most of the time; his "CR" period ended shortly before the 1959 convention.

Before Hall had even come off of "CR" Gene suggested that he be brought into some national post at the time of the convention. Gene had to convince some comrades, saying that Gus would be a fresh face, he had no involvement in old wounds, and as for many of his weaknesses and inexperience, a strong collective could help him.

Gus Hall, however, had more ambitious plans. In the weeks before the convention he travelled about the country organizing support to his election to Gene's post of general secretary. He played hard on the still-existing doubts and dissatisfactions of both Fosterites and former Gates people. He offered himself as being all things to all people; all he wanted was that top post.

Comrades of various political persuasions came in a steady stream to our home to tell Gene of Gus' trips into their states. They urged Gene to stop him. Gene, however, shrugged, saying if Gus was so avid for one title more than for another, something would be worked out.

Two weeks before the convention, the committee on personnel and leadership went into session. Gus Hall was adamant. He would take nothing less than Gene's post. The comrades felt strongly the need for a new face in the national leadership group, but they were not prepared to remove Gene as general secretary Gus remained firm, and finally Gene conceded the title to him, "in the interest of Party unity."

Gene then proposed a national slate which, he felt, in total would be a strong group. This included himself as national chairman; Hall, general secretary; Ben Davis, national secretary; Claude Lightfoot and Elizabeth Gurley Flynn, vice-chairpersons; and Foster in an honorary post of chairman emeritus. This proposal was gratefully welcomed by the comrades who were relieved that Gene had averted a crisis by gracefully stepping down before Hall's demand. Foster, however, quickly dispelled that unanimity. It became evident that in his desire to oust Gene completely, Foster had made an agreement with Hall that in exchange for Foster's and Davis' support to his bid for Gene's post, Hall now would support Foster's determination to oust Gene from any leading role and put Ben Davis in as national Party chairman.

The committee members were shocked, yet immobilized by the sensitivity of the issue of promoting Negro leadership. The committee deadlocked for days. Gene refused to step down a second time, accusing Foster of cynically using the Negro issue to re-open the factional fight. He said the Party membership for four years had rejected Foster's political policies and Davis' support to those policies. He said he would not make it possible for them to seize organizationally what they had failed to win politically.

Gene came home each night tense. Pacing the floor, a chain-lit cigarette in one hand and a tall drink in the other, he recounted how things stood. Then he went into the study and worked on his convention report until dawn. On the eleventh day he flew to Washington; he had been subpoenaed to appear before the Subversive Activities Board. He flew back that night and again worked on his report.

Finally, on the twelfth day, the Black comrades on the committee told Davis that the real issue in this instance was not "Negro Leadership," but Ben's leftist sectarian politics which they would not support. At that same session, Gene informed the committee he would not step down no matter how long they deadlocked. He said if his unity slate was not adopted he would take the issue to the convention floor and let the membership decide whether they wanted him ousted from leadership, especially when the Party was uniting on what was essentially his political programs, not that of Foster and Davis. The deadlock was broken; the unity slate was adopted.

Two days before the convention opened, Gene was finishing his convention report. I was in the bedroom reading when I heard a gasp, a rasping cry, a crash. Gene was lying face down on the floor, his report pages scattered about him, the desk lamp shattered at his feet. Police and doctor came simultaneously with oxygen tanks. He had suffered a mild stroke. No foreseeable after-effects. He was to stay in bed for a few weeks.

As he lay ashen gray with mask fitted to his face, it was just as well that no one asked me at that moment whether the twenty-two years Gene had been in national leadership, the last thirteen as the head of the Party during its most difficult time, had been worth it.

Gus Hall came the next day, affable and relaxed. He sat at Gene's bedside taking voluminous notes and when he left he had with him Gene's unfinished convention report. The following morning acceptance of Hall as the new general secretary was assured by his appearance as the chief convention reporter. The unity slate with Gene as national chairman was adopted despite last efforts by Foster and Davis to upset it on the convention floor.

Eleven:
THE LAST YEAR

I

The year 1960 started quietly. Outwardly we were in low key. Gene was recovering well and already chafing under doctor's orders that I hold him back. Between us there was a gentle closeness, but also an undercurrent of restraint that arises when good friends avoid talking about that which lay heavy between them. For the first time I had to seethe in silence. I could not argue or scream or howl as was my way. Gene was supposed "to avoid tension," inane instruction from a doctor who knew better.

I could not deliberately create additional tensions for him, yet there was so much unspoken between us about the weeks that led up to his stroke. The four years of factionalism I could understand. About Gene's having been everyone's scapegoat and fall guy I could even say, as I had, that he was partly responsible; he didn't fight back. But what I felt now was different. The conniving, unprincipled scramble for personal position by Gus Hall, Bill Foster and Ben Davis, and the manipulation of a prostrated, exhausted Party for their own purposes repelled me. I was contemptuous, too, of those comrades who, claiming for four years to have been Gene's political adherents, had sat silent as Gus and Bill and Ben sought to oust Gene altogether. The slow process of degeneration of my respect for leadership in the specific, which had been developing over the years, now exploded. But Gene was ill and I had to contain my fury.

From his bed Gene discoursed quietly on the subject of titles; they mean nothing, he said. It is what the individual puts into that title that is important. The real test of the convention decisions would come in putting them into practice. They were based on a number of important new theoretical and organizational concepts regarding the role, structure and work of the Party. As chairman, freed from routine matters, he would devote his energies to the much needed thinking and studying and continuing re-thinking of all these problems. If we didn't succeed in this, he concluded, the Party would not be prepared for the new decade ahead.

Within a few weeks Gene became involved gradually in meetings downtown, helping to get the national center reorganized and back to work.

In the spring a persistent cough led him to a routine chest x-ray which led to a biopsy which led to surgery. On May 23, at Mount Sinai Hospital, the surgeon tells me, "I'm sorry, it was inoperable; we just closed him up again."

To my hesitant question, he replies, "Eight months, twelve at the most."

I turn on him angrily. "Who the hell are you to say how long he lives, when he dies? You, God or something?"

Startled, he apologizes and hurries away. Stunned, Young Gene and I look at each other, uncomprehending; we walk silently out of the hospital. We need to prepare ourselves for seeing Gene when he is brought down from Recovery. On the hospital steps we meet two comrades we know well. They say they had been sent "to find out how the surgery's going."

"They couldn't operate," I reply dully. Without a glance at us, they turn to each other.

"He's through; damn it, now trouble starts."

"All hell'll break loose. Maybe we better sit on the news for a while."

"No, we better not; let's go."

Without a word to us, they hurry down Fifth Avenue intent upon their problems. At the apartment that night the telephone rings incessantly. From California and Illinois come scolding complaints: "You shouldn't have told the truth. You've given them ammunition for a new power struggle." From Booklyn and Manhattan come curt calls, barely concealing the hope for confirmation: "Is it true he is dying?" No one calls to just say, "I'm sorry; is there anything I can do?"

In the next weeks comrades tell me that Gus Hall had conveniently telescoped the time factor. Compelled to defend his usurpation of power five months earlier, he now was telling everyone that Gene's health was the main reason why he, Gus, had campaigned to replace Gene as general secretary. And the comrades, unclear as to time sequence and recalling that Gene at the last moment had been unable to attend the convention, now repeated Gus' claims. So even Gene's cancer, diagnosed six months after Hall's coup, was now used to Hall's advantage.

Gene knows nothing of all this; he is engrossed in a different struggle, a struggle to live. We are caught between divergent views of our internist who, true to his promise to be utterly candid, insists, "Nothing can reverse the course; time is proscribed," and radiologists and chemotherapists who say, "Surgery is proscribed; our possibilities are limitless."

Our days and weeks become governed by the daily trips to the hospital's tumor institute for treatment. Young Gene graduates Bronx High School of Science, but only after a confrontation in which he is threatened with denial of his diploma because he refuses to sign a loyalty oath. Without telling us about the incident, he solicits the aid of the American Civil Liberties Union and the threat is dropped. We hear of it only when someone from that organization phones to congratulate us on "your son's courage." When I ask him about it, Young Gene replies, "It's nothing much. And you and Dad have more important things to cope with right now."

Young Gene talks of cancelling arrangements to attend the University of Wisconsin in the fall. His keen pleasure at going is now tempered with hesitations. Perhaps he should stay home, go to City College or Hunter. I want to keep him home, to share with me the uncharted, frightening months ahead. But I urge him to go. I can't tie him to our death watch. He has to get away, perhaps now especially.

I knew, too, that Gene needed above all else normalcy in his days, not death watches around him. So Young Gene left, faced with new challenges and new situations at a moment when he was locked deeply into emotional concerns for what he was leaving behind him at home.

Late September. The final cobalt treatment. The large negatives are hung before us. Medically, scientifically, the tumor is gone. The radiologist beams. Like most people, we have a smattering of knowledge. It is gone—*if* the wild cells have not already escaped to some as yet untraceable parts of the body. Still bound to a promise I begin to wish Gene had not extracted, our internist, who is also our friend, sits in our living room and shakes his head. "Nothing has changed, Gene. I wish it had, but it hasn't."

I argue combatively, "You have no proof. Maybe the radiologist is right."

"No way."

Gene chides half humorously, "You don't leave a guy any fighting room, Doc. I can't just meekly curl up and die. Remember your dialectics, struggle decides everything."

Freed from daily hospital treatments, and with four weeks before the monthly check-ups begin, we take off on holiday. Montauk. Connecticut. Cape Cod. Only a delightful dress rehearsal, we say, for a return later to that fisherman's shack on Deer Isle in Maine where we had spent a memorable summer in 1959. We drive. We walk. We laugh. The sun, the sky, the stars, the ocean, the firelight—everything has new dimension, deeper color, special oneness with our search for eternity. Slowly, guardedly, we talk of Tomorrow. Hesitantly, Gene says, "There is so much I still can do. Our Party must absorb the lessons of these last years. It must not slide back. I can help."

Then suddenly, the pain. Moving in, taking over, becoming an arrogant, destructive, domineering member of the family. Perhaps naively, we are stunned. Behind the bathroom door I whisper into a towel held tightly to my face, not so soon, please god, whoever you are, not so soon. We are angry and belligerent. This can't happen to us. The hours and days and nights and weeks are measured now only by the level of pain. When it is under control and recedes, we laugh again and walk along Riverside Drive in the October sun, in the cool November mist, in the December snowdrifts. On good days Gene even goes downtown to a committee meeting, comrades come to the house to discuss their work. But mainly, his pain is now our reality.

The interludes between the brief but frequent returns to the hospital are no longer new beginnings, only temporary respites. Our reserve of hope is slowly drained, like a seeping hourglass. And still he fights. He refuses the full doses of demerol or morphine I had been taught to administer. In hospital and at home he refuses to become a comatose vegetable—the price for full release from pain. He refuses to curl up in an unconscious wait for death. A few days without pain and we walk again and plan again; more limitedly, true, as the future now is only the next day.

II

In mid-October Soviet Premier Khrushchev returns to the U.S., this time to address the UN General Assembly. We receive word that among his entourage is—Tim. I had last seen our first-born in 1941 as he sat in a crowded train waiting to be returned to the children's home, away from the war that threatened Moscow. He was eleven then; now he is thirty.

In early 1947, Paul Robeson had travelled abroad and on his return he spent a long, leisurely afternoon at our home. Interspersed with his political impressions of postwar Europe and discussion of the role he would play in the projected new Progressive Party, Paul talked glowingly about an evening he had spent with Tim in Moscow. He had a message for us, too. Tim's life so far had been predicated by the Soviet comrades on the premise that he might someday join his parents. Now he was a young adult. He had decisions to make and he was making them within the context of his Soviet life, the only life he knew. Gene was concerned that I was hurt by Tim's message. I assured him, no, here or there he's got his own life to lead; anyway, what could we say to him. We were no more ready to offer him choices now than we could earlier.

That had been fourteen years ago. The Truman nightmare. McCarthyism. Prison years. Party crisis. Years pass. One does not actively mourn the dead forever. Tim had become an irrevocable void. Now suddenly he was in New York, a Soviet journalist who was to remain for some months to cover the UN sessions; an assignment, we were told, he had sought as a way of visiting us, Soviet citizen though he now was.

The old mystique still prevailed, and the comrades downtown made surreptitous plans for getting the three of us together. Gene was in the throes of a pain-cycle, and it was decided I should first meet Tim alone. I was to arrive in the company of *Daily Worker* editor James Jackson, at a certain restaurant. Tim would come with the *Pravda* reporter and we were all to meet casually, a group of journalists at lunch. So after nineteen years, Tim and I went through the motions of being formally and casually introduced by our fellow newsmen.

I had been coached that this was to be a meeting of strangers; we were not to embrace or show emotion. We ate, drank, small-talked, and all the time Tim and I devoured each other's every facial expression, every word. No explanation was given for all these machinations, nor were we told why Tim could not visit us at home.

How Gene was to meet Tim, under these circumstances, became a difficult logistics problem for our comrades. We decided to go along with their contrivances for now, however; later we would work out our own ways for seeing Tim. In a few days, we decided, we would send for Young Gene to come home to meet his brother.

A non-diplomatic reception at the UN Soviet mission later that week was considered a good occasion for father and son to meet casually while circulating around the grand ballroom. It was obviously a gala event as more than one thousand guests converged on the mansion on Park Avenue. Cameras clicked as newsmen and FBI agents noted each arrival. With the palm of his hand pressing at my back, Gene and I walked through the narrow lane left open from curbside to front door. Reporters recognized Gene, called his name, asked if he was all right now. Gene smiled, waved and pushed me on.

The heavy doors opened, a young man led us into the foyer. "Comrade Dennis, yes?" Gene nodded and our escort opened a closet-like door. "Comrade Khrushchev is waiting upstairs for you." In the small elevator, Gene's eyebrows rose quizzically. This was not in the script, but I only grinned, intrigued.

We were led into a very large, square-like room where two men sat behind a long table at the far side. The shorter, stocky one rose as we entered and walked toward us with arms flung out high and wide. Nikita Khrushchev stretched to his toes to embrace Gene in a bear hug. Stepping back, he looked up at him, gripping Gene's arms.

"Comrade Dennis," he effused. "At last, at last we meet. We have for so long admired from afar your political courage and leadership, and now you show equally a physical courage—" I could not catch the translator's words. Without pausing, the Soviet leader said: "Tell us, is there anything, anything at all we can do? Is there something we can do in Moscow for you that is not being done here? Tell us, tell us what you need."

The short, flamboyant Russian and the tall, reserved American stood clasping each other's arms, faces wreathed in smiles that needed no translator.

A tall, thin man walked over from the table and stood quietly at Khrushchev's side. The translator said: "This is Comrade Gromyko."

Shaking hands, I noted that the Foreign Minister had a more gentle, mobile face than newspaper pictures indicated. We were led to the table laden with samovars, fruits, cakes, bottles of wine. Khrushchev said something to his translator, who left the room. Gromyko explained in English, "Tim will come now." Khrushchev waved expansively to chairs opposite his own and urged, "Eat, please, eat, drink." Gromyko said, "We are very proud of Tim. He is ours, you know," then laughing; "we have no intention of giving him back to you."

Tim came into the room and father, mother and son embraced as the Premier and the Foreign Minister of the Soviet Union smiled broadly.

Khrushchev dismissed his translator with a jovial challenge, saying Tim will translate. "We will show your parents how well we have educated you."

The Premier had recently returned from his first trip to the People's Republic of China and for the next three hours he related detailed angry complaints about the "stupid mistakes of the Chinese comrades." He chronicled instance after instance of what he termed Chinese misuse of expensive Soviet machinery, insults to Soviet engineers and specialists, ways in which Soviet know-how was being ignored, the "idiocy" of the "primitive" commune economy while sophisticated Soviet equipment rusted on rail sidings.

I listened fascinated, waiting for explanations for these "stupidities." Obviously, what he was relating were after-effects, not causes, for the deteriorating relations between these two great socialist countries. There was a missing link somewhere, and Khrushchev was not providing it.

Even as I listened, my mind wandered. Despite the profuse warmth displayed, there was insensitivity, too. Yet I could not ask the Soviet Premier and Foreign Minister to please excuse us, we want to be alone with the son we have not seen in nineteen years, the discussion on China could wait.

I glance at Gene. I feel his tension. He sits quietly. His fingers grip the tiny pillbox. His eyes flicker from Tim to Khrushchev and back again. Only the straightness of his back, the lines of his mouth, the restless fingers, the tired but alert eyes send their message along our private antenna. I touch his thigh under the table, he glances at me, I smile and whisper, "Relax, it's okay, relax."

I look at this thirty-year-old stranger across the table, our son with a wife and small son of his own. Tim and Young Gene. I visualize the opportunity they will now have to know each other. Young Gene will probably lose his semester at school when we send for him, but it will be well worth it. I whisper silently to Gene, hold on, the next months will be good ones; the four of us together finally; just hold on. Tim and Young Gene, brothers yet strangers from two different worlds. One a product of socialism, raised since age five without parents or family in a Soviet children's collective; the other a product of capitalism, raised in a revolutionary family. One growing up in the socialist land where being his father's son brought accolades and privilege and made him protegé of official Soviet leadership; the other growing up in the U.S.A. where being his father's son meant McCarthyism, years-long trips to prison visiting rooms, a child's watchful wariness, asking of each stranger, are you friend or foe?

Were there basic differences between these two in value judgments, personal integrity, sensitivity and concern for people in the specific? Was this "new socialist man" really so different, and if different was he necessarily better, than my younger son?

My random thoughts are interrupted as I hear Gene say somewhat wearily and with a testy edge to his politness, "But these are the internal affairs of our Chinese comrades. Perhaps, Comrade Khrushchev, they need to find their own way, based on their own experiences and their own history and their own culture." And I recall, fleetingly, our talks in Shanghai twenty-six years ago and Gene's impatience then with advisors who came to China with blueprints.

Under the table's edge he opens the pillbox and unobtrusively swallows the pain-killer drug with a polite sip from his teacup. Later, interjecting again into the monologue, Gene says, "All this concerns primarily relations between the Soviet Union and China, but these problems must be resolved soon, for they affect too the international revolutionary movement, the national liberation struggles and our efforts for world peace."

The grand ballroom was dark, the reception was long over, the coterie of newsmen outside long gone when we left the Soviet UN Mission late that night.

III

We were confident that we would work out less spectacular ways of spending time with Tim in the future, but within a few days of that strange night Gene succumbed once more to a new pain cycle which closed out the rest of the world.

On October 17th Hearst columnist George Sokolsky wrote an "exposé" piece about Tim. He claimed Tim's role in the entourage at the Soviet Mission was that of "Nikita Khrushchev's principal adviser on American affairs." He referred in conspiratorial tones to the fact that Tim most obviously was "the son of Eugene Dennis who disappeared in Soviet Russia between 1931 and 1935." With an innuendo which is always more damaging than the simple truth, he implied some sinister purpose for which this American son had been raised and educated in the Soviet Union, and now surfaced in New York at the United Nations.

Reporters seized upon the story. Telephones and doorbells rang constantly at our apartment and at the Soviet UN house on Park Avenue. At both places the stop-gap "no comment" was used. Demand grew that the Sokolsky story be confirmed or denied. From the Soviet comrades came the message that they did not care what we confirmed or denied; Tim was here, and the explanations were ours to make. But they wanted our public statement made at once—this silly fuss had to stop. The Soviet Premier believed there were more important global issues that merited serious press coverage of his presence in New York.

Through his haze of pain Gene sent me downtown, saying, "Tell the comrades we will issue a brief statement acknowledging our relationship to Tim. It's time this farce is ended. The fact that he is here indicates the Soviet comrades agree."

I went first to our friend and attorney, John Abt, who assured me there were no legal problems at all. At best, he said, "a one-day flurry of publicity; so what?"

As the thundering subway train hurled me uptown from Cortlandt Street, I tried to accustom myself to the realization that the old ghost was now suddenly and miraculously to be finally buried. I left the subway at 23rd Street and walked the three blocks north to Party headquarters to tell our comrades of Gene's decision and John's agreement.

I sat before them—three ordinary men with little but official authority going for them, and I heard in disbelief their adamant, "No." Adverse publicity ... political embarrassment ... revival of the Moscow tag. "No." Tim must leave at once, that was the only way to silence the whole unfortunate publicity mess.

I argue, I plead. For some twenty-five years we had accepted this situation. Now, Gene, our attorney, the Soviet comrades, all say it is no longer necessary. The answer is "No." I hear myself for the first time putting into words that which I had not allowed my consciousness to admit. "Gene is dying," I say. "Give him his son." The answer is "No."

On the long bus ride home I weigh the possibility of ignoring that decision. I had reached the point in my life when I could. I no longer had any qualms about making my own decisions, superimposing my "No" over theirs. And yet I knew I would not. I couldn't thrust this fight on Gene now as he battled merely for pain-free days and nights. The Soviet comrades would accept the official decision, not mine. And Tim would follow that instruction without question; in fact, he would be shocked at my rebellion. I couldn't win.

Tim left for Moscow in a couple of days, although for one moment we ignored all decisions and his last day was spent in our apartment at his father's bedside.

IV

After an overly sentimental and extravagant Christmas, Young Gene returned to Wisconsin and Gene was taken back to the hospital, in a heavy snowstorm. He was home in four days, blissfully without pain, but this time it lasted only three weeks. He returned to the hospital.

On January 31 the hospital day progressed slowly in its routine flow of desultory talk and long silences. We read the President's inaugural speech. We talked about the accelerating differences between Moscow and Peking. Gene told me of a confused night in which he wasn't sure whether it was dream or fact. He had wandered from room to room throughout the hospital looking, he said, for Young Gene and then for Tim, but each eluded him. They'd disappear just as he found them and sometimes they merged into one; he wasn't sure which one he was looking for, or which one he had momentarily found.

Around five o'clock I said I'd go down to the coffee shop, did he want anything? He took my hand, urged me not to go yet, "Wait awhile."

I stand silently at his bed, wanting but not knowing how to dissipate the strange mood that suddenly hangs heavily between us, not wanting to reject by a single reflex twinge the hand clinging to mine. Outside his window the early winter darkness obliterates the silhouetted treetops. He leans back on his highly propped pillows, looks quizzically at me.

"It's somehow different this time. I may not go home again, will I?"

With a brusqueness acquired over the months, I retort too quickly, too sharply. "That's crazy. You said last night the pain is receding. You'll be home in a day or two."

He smiles indulgently. "I guess you're right."

The months-long routine had become reflex action, each protecting the other, yet knowing that neither is fooled. But it is the only way we can cope with each other's agony and helplessness, and our own.

He lay smiling, holding my hand. With the other I brush back the thick, curling shock of white hair that falls across his forehead. Suddenly a convulsive shock transmits from his body through my arm. His hand jerkily tightens over mine. He stares at me in surprised accusation. I stand mesmerized as his life-force explodes and we suddenly drown together in the fountain of his blood.

Later that night television and radio around the world flash the news bulletin: "Eugene Dennis, American Communist Party Head, Is Dead."

Official condolence cables pour into Party headquarters. France. Italy. The Soviet Union. Germany—West and East. Denmark. Norway. Sweden. Finland. Poland. China. Hungary. Bulgaria. Israel. Spain. Czechoslovakia. England. Japan. Korea. Malaya. Vietnam—North and South. Ireland. India. Holland. Indonesia. Portugal. Philippines. Wales. Greece. Pakistan. Cambodia. Yugoslavia. Romania. Turkey. The African States. The Arab lands. Latin American and Central American countries. Canada. From cities and towns and Party committees and Party clubs across our own country.

But at 5:30 p.m. on January 31 he lay alone in that hospital room turned morgue, and I can neither stay nor leave. There is no one there to pull me away from that blood-spattered room, to force me back among the living.

From San Francisco later that night comes my sister's urging: "Come here as soon as you can."

But at the moment, I am alone. At the university in Wisconsin, Young Gene responds to the phone call he had dreaded for months. The operator's voice clips across the wires: "I have a long distance—" Gene interrupts, his voice breaking huskily, "Mom? I'm coming. Hold on, I'm coming." But at the moment, I am alone.

From those whom Gene had for fifteen, twenty, thirty years called "my comrades and co-workers" came not a word that night. And I lay alone in the dark with Gene's stricken accusing eyes staring at me, his hand clutching mine, and we are drowned again and again in the eruptive stream of blood.

V

The elements did not mourn gently that week before the public funeral. Snowstorms blanketed most of the nation. Air, rail and bus traffic stopped. Subway trains stalled. Abandoned cars lay like humped igloos under snowdrifts. Delivery trucks could not get through and neighborhood shops ran low on food supplies. In the worst blizzard in its history, New York City became a beautifully hushed, sparklingly clean, officially-declared disaster city.

Each day I plow along Riverside Drive, snowflakes clinging to my eyelashes, dry snow spilling and melting into my boots. And two long strides ahead of me, the image of Gene walks, laughing at my puffing efforts to keep up. His white hair almost invisible in the falling snow, his broad shoulders swinging in that characteristic forward thrust that appeared to be pushing obstacles right and left out of his way. His booted, large footsteps leave deep impressions for me to follow.

Something was terribly wrong back at the apartment, and although I fled its reality by tramping alone in the snow, the question "Why?" beat on exposed nerve-ends. Official couriers came each day to inform me of decisions for the funeral arrangements. No one—except Elizabeth Gurley Flynn and Gene's friend Morris from Chicago—came to sit and talk and seek comfort at the loss of their friend.

True, the four years factional fight had left deep wounds. Animosities still sparked. Jostling for top positions still crackled, in fact they intensified in the few days since Gene's death. But surely, I pondered as I brushed the snow from my eyes, behind it all there should be some residue of simple, uncomplicated human feeling for a comrade so closely worked with in a Party that was no ordinary ballot designation on election day. Was there no one to mourn the man without first weighing the political consequences, or to reach out in friendship to their comrade's wife and son? Instead, the funeral was being planned as efficiently and matter-of-factly as a political rally.

On the first morning I had told them, "No funeral. Gene and I had an agreement on that. A memorial meeting later, if you wish." No, there must be a public funeral. Especially now, they said. People would draw harmful political conclusions if Gene were not accorded proper respect.

On the second day, I said, no burial. During our 1959 summer in Maine, one dawn as we beachcombed and death seemed eons of years away, Gene had said, "When I die, scatter my ashes over Penobscot Bay, or better yet, back home over the Pacific Ocean. Turn me free and loose, heavenly thought!"

I was over-ruled. Not to include him in the Party's burial plot at Waldheim cemetery in Chicago with other Party leaders, they said, would arouse political speculations the organization could ill afford at this time.

Each day additional names were added to the long eulogy speakers' list carefully selected for proper ethnic, racial, political status. I laugh too loudly at the latest additions. I ask sarcastically, "What are they going to do there, raise the Iwo Jimo victory flag over his coffin?" No one laughs with me. Young Gene digs his fingers into my shoulder as he stands behind my chair. The solemn reply, "A symbol of our much-needed unity." Over Gene's dead body. Gurley Flynn, exasperated, objects particularly to two names, comrades who had hated him and bitterly fought him. They are reluctantly withdrawn.

On the third day I hide behind the morning *Times* as the honor guard list is discussed. Young Gene, who had moved unobtrusively through the past few days, silently buffering, easing, protecting, now said hesitantly, "I would like to stand honor guard." The comrades look surprised. They had not even considered him. This quiet eighteen-year-old had no political status, no special élan to bring to their funeral-show. I laugh too loud and retreat to walk alone in the snow. Downtown emissaries do not listen, so I stop talking.

As I walk, I wonder at my response. Party widows I had known sought every prestige they could from the event. They watchdogged each detail, demanding every expression of political homage due their dead husbands. What was wrong with me? I seek more than that official eulogy praise. Because of the long years of in-fighting the formal accolades ring false from these particular people. I want, instead, the simple embrace, the words,

"I miss him, too;" "I have lost a friend;" "Let me weep with you."

On the fifth day of that interminable interlude, I startle everyone, including myself, when I suddenly say in response to still another guise of consulting me about the scenario, "Do whatever you want. It's your show. I won't be there anyway."

Pandemonium erupts. Horrified couriers come scurrying. They attribute to me the only motive they know—politics. "You must be there! Don't be vindictive. You must stand with us and show your unity with the new leadership." From the moment the surgeon had pronounced the death sentence eight months ago they had turned him into a pawn for their politicking. They were incapable of conceiving that I was neither politically vindictive nor conniving. They could not fathom simple grief, nor the bewildered hurt at their calculating callousness.

On the evening before the public funeral Young Gene answered the phone as he had been doing all week, prepared once again to ward off those who persisted in warning me I must show at the funeral. Instead, he called, "Long distance operator for you, Mom." Over the wire came a tentative, "Mama?" I hesitated and then puzzled, "Tim?"

The words stumbled over each other. "I am in Montreal, Mama. The funeral is tomorrow, yes? I will be there. I have only just arrived from Moscow. There are no planes flying to New York, also no trains or buses. Everything is prevented by the snow. But there is a man here also impatient to get to New York. We will rent a car. I will be there."

At five o'clock in the morning Young Gene opened the apartment door and the two brothers meet for the first time. Tim explains, simply: "I merely asked the American Embassy in Moscow for an emergency visa to attend my father's funeral. They asked me many questions and then said they would have to cable Washington. They did and I got the visa within a few hours."

So simple and ordinary an act dissipated twenty-five years of impossibility. At noon, with Gurley Flynn's salty overriding of the objections of those who had banished him three months earlier, Tim stood honor guard with his brother at their father's coffin.

Unaccountably, during the week he stayed with us those who in October had forbidden him to remain now fawned over Tim. He was officially entertained and showered with expensive gifts by the Party leadership circle. Each vied to assure him of their special friendship with his father.

Unaccountably, too, no reporters rang doorbells or telephoned to get confirmation that Eugene Dennis' Moscow-raised son was truly back in New York. News accounts of the funeral recorded without comment that Gene's two sons were among the honor guard.

The speedy visa from Washington. The absolute lid put on media publicity. The solicitous attention from Party leadership. Suddenly the impossible had become possible. Too late. Why now? I was too withdrawn, too confused, too hurt, to seek answers.

VI

Fifteen hundred people stomped their way into the Riviera Casino in mid-Manhattan for the funeral on February fifth. How they got there was not quite clear. Most subways were still not running. Disaster-city regulations were still in effect. All cars, including those planning to travel to the crematorium in Queens, had to get special permits to be on the streets. Hundreds across the country telephoned and wired they could not get to New York for the funeral because planes, buses, trains were not operating.

The eulogy speakers downtown paid fine tribute to Gene's Marxist leadership, his life devoted to the struggle against imperialism and to world peace, his staunch commitment to Soviet-American friendship, his tireless work for socialism.

I sit alone in the gratifyingly empty apartment, coffee mug in hand, and seek to warm the outer edges of the deep numbness by deliberately conjuring up more personal images.

The Puerto Rican mother and her four babies in the ground-floor apartment, greeting me on the day he was taken to the hospital for the last time: "I lit a candle for him, Mrs. Dennis. He is God's man among us, so kind, always a word for me and the children. God should spare such as he."

Our postman, a slight, tired man who climbed the six flights the morning after the television and radio announced Gene's death. His mail bag at his feet, he embraced me: "I had to come. He was a big man, he was for little people like me."

Barry, the neighborhood street-gang leader. In the last weeks Gene had often insisted on going alone to sit on the Drive. Emaciated, walking slowly with a cane, he impatiently accused me of nursemaiding him. I was uneasy because of the spreading stories of rising incidence of senseless youthful violence on the Drive. Barry, lounging on the front stoop one morning, greeted me: "Glad to see Mr. Dennis out again. Don't worry about him. Word is out, no one touches him. A guy that goes to jail for fighting the lousy system don't get touched by us. Don't worry, Mrs. Dennis, we'll watch out for him."

Our beery, loquacious building superintendent had come upstairs, grasped my hand: "I think he was a fanatic wasting his life on people who don't give a damn. But, you know, we need people like him, even when we don't know we do."

Behind the counter in the little shop on Broadway where Gene had bought his newspapers and cigars and cigarettes and pipe-tobacco each morning, the large Black woman cried softly: "He was such a gentle, gracious man. He was for my people. He will be missed, yes, indeed, he will be missed."

Downtown the formal speeches drone on and I wander about the empty apartment. I refill my coffee cup. I empty ash trays. I leaf through some of the telegrams, letters, hand-written notes sent on from Party headquarters. The pile is high and I pull them out at random.

From Wisconsin—". . . his uncanny ability to translate the abstract ideals of young people like me into the realities of politics, his ability to turn slogans into movements of people—"

A Baltimore housewife—"He was the only leading comrade I knew who made me feel that my opinion was important to him."

From Alabama—"I never knew your husband, but I know he lived for us."

From Chicago—"More than to anyone else, we owe to Gene the continued existence and unity of our Party."

Paperclipped with a pencilled "V.I.P." notation made downtown, a London cable from Paul and Eslanda Robeson—"We have lost a treasured friend."

Dr. William E.B. DuBois and his author wife Shirley Graham—"Our sympathy and love go out to you."

Socialist Party leader Norman Thomas—"Sharply as he and I disagreed on important matters, I never doubted the sincerity of his devotion to the achievement of a better world. . . . I know by experience what it means when death breaks up a marriage as happy as I think yours was."

Pacifist peace leader Rev. A.J. Muste—"Though I differed strongly with him in some matters, I respected his determination and his courageous faithfulness to his convictions."

Roger Baldwin of the Civil Liberties Union, despite his anti-communist prejudices, wrote—"You have my sympathy in the passing of a man whose integrity of purpose and independence of thought distinguished him even among those who, like myself, did not share his political philosophy. Character knows no politics and it should be a satisfaction to you to have had as husband and companion in public life a man who sought in his own way only the welfare of his fellow man."

A note to Young Gene, one of many from his wide circle of friends from Downtown Community school, Bronx High School of Science, the University of Wisconsin and his various political groups over the years. This was from a girl he had dated heavily in high school and had not seen in over a year. She wrote in a firm, prim, rounded hand: "Remember, Gene, you used to tell me, the world belongs to us? In your grief for your father, do remember now that he spent his whole life trying to make it a better world for us to take over."

I wander about the quiet rooms, seeking something that is not there. My fingers pass lightly over the top of his desk, neatly facing mine. His pipes lay cold in the large ceramic bowl. The recliner-chair dominates the small room. We had bought it only a few weeks ago, when the agony in his back and shoulders drove him from a bed of pain. We had sat, night after night, wrapped in blankets in the icy apartment. Often I read aloud. Sometimes we talked, quietly and slowly of things personal and things political.

Hesitatingly, now, I slide into that chair, angle the recliner sharply, slowly relax my rigid back. I pull his brightly plaid blanket, neatly folded on the footrest, up to my chin and release myself into the protective hold of the arms of his chair.

Far off the droning of eulogies and condolences rises and falls like billowing waves in the distance. I lay quietly waiting. I know in my mind the day will come when I will feel and live again. The night will come when I will sleep again. The moment will come when I no longer see the now-inerasable still-life of Gene clenching my hand, his eyes accusing me, his blood cascading, drowning us both.

I know I will work my way back beyond these last four painful years and recent horror-filled months; I will reclaim the thirty-three years of our life together. I know I must first deal with the anger and resentment and guilt and fury. Anger at him for leaving me. Resentment of Nature's omnipotent death cycle. Guilt from being alive and having failed him somehow. Fury at those he had for some twenty, thirty years called "my comrades and colleagues."

I know that some day I will unfreeze, some day the future will intrude and for the first time in my life I will go on, a woman alone.

Twelve:
A WOMAN ALONE

I

Fifteen years after Gene died, I resigned from the Communist Party. In early June, 1976, I severed ties with the organization that had shaped and dominated my life and opinions since childhood. For fifty years I had believed the Party to be the only vehicle through which a commitment to radical activism and socialism could be pursued. I no longer believe that, while my commitment to radical activism and socialism remains intact.

Approaching what for me was a momentous decision, I walked for hours day after day on the fishing pier at the Berkeley marina and tossed at night, restless and tense, a torrent of questions roaring through my head. Uppermost was the question: why now, after fifty years, and I found the answer rooted in the fifteen years since Gene's death.

They had been complex, fast-moving years in which the social fabric of our society had been challenged, its stability badly shaken. It had been an era of anger, frustration and militant fighting in which many hundreds of thousands became politically aware and active for the first time. It was a time of significant changes within the international Communist movement and in the relationships between its many sectors.

For me, as for anyone, all of these events were sifted through my own experiences and my independent responses to them. As a Communist, it became decisively important to me how my Party reacted to the social and political phenomena of the new decade and a half.

Within a week of Gene's death in January, 1961, I made my

first independent decisions in thirty-three years. Without his political and personal needs to consider and ignoring the procedure of getting my Party's permission, I decided to leave New York immediately, and permanently. I accepted the invitation Tim had extended from the central committee of the Soviet Communist Party that Young Gene and I be their guests for the summer. Preliminary thoughts about future Party activity centered on a desire to join the staff of the Party's West Coast weekly, the *People's World.*

These were not the calm decisions of a competent widow firmly taking hold of her life. They were blind, intuitive, gut decisions that seemed to surface from my subconscious.

I had to run away from the New York national leadership milieu in order to save my relationship with the Party. The accumulated anger and bewildered hurt I felt toward Gene's "comrades and co-workers" threatened to poison my attitude toward the organization unless I could separate the two. To do this I had to get away.

Also, my organizational relationship had to be redefined. Without Gene, it was different. I was on my own, responsible to express opinions without worrying how they might reflect on Gene in his work; responsible now to undertake my own activity without concern that it fit into Gene's scheme of things. No longer his wife, I needed to guard against being made his perennial and ceremonial widow.

In all our travels and during the twenty-three years in New York, California had been home to Gene and me. That is where I wanted to go now. I needed, too, to be with my sister Mini and brother-in-law Albert, who offered love with no political strings attached.

Papa had died a few years earlier, as quietly and unobtrusively as he had lived. Determined not to become a family burden, Mama had gone into the Jewish Home for the Aged out on Silver Avenue in San Francisco, near where Mini and Al lived. In a short time Mama had lapsed into a gentle form of senility and she died in 1963, quietly and alone during the night.

I arrived in San Francisco in mid-February, two weeks after Gene died, and for the next four months I lived in what was for me a sheltered cocoon. Mini and Al had created for themselves a comfortable life spiced with avid memories of the activism they had discarded twenty years earlier, and surrounded themselves with stimulating political conversation each day during cocktails and dinner.

My only problem in this pleasant hiatus were the nights. I did not sleep. Each night I lay frozen as there unrolled a slow-motion replay of Gene's last year. Mesmerized, I watched, unable to stop my eye's camera.

As the last scene began, each night I broke out in a clammy sweat. Gene in his hospital bed, his hand clinging to mine, his eyes questioning, accusing. His blood erupting like a volcano and the feel of that blood's warmth as I held onto him. Daylight came and with it the family sounds in bathroom and kitchen. Only then did I sleep for an hour before resuming my pleasant, lazy, daytime routines.

Even as I drew sustenance from Mini and Al and their lifestyle, I knew I needed the politically active life. I phoned Al Richmond at the *People's World* and we met for lunch. At the time we knew each other only by name. Before I left for my summer abroad I had become the paper's new foreign editor, scheduled to report for work in September. Although I suffered certain doubts regarding my abilities, it felt good. I had planted a root.

II

The return to Moscow that summer was a highly-charged, emotional pilgrimage. At the airport to meet us was the grown son I had brought to the Soviet Union thirty years earlier as a sixteen-month-old toddler. With him was his Russian wife, a charming stranger who, upon embracing me, thrust a key into my palm saying, "Our home is always your home."

I had last seen my friend Molly in 1941, when I had left a Moscow under siege. Now, twenty years later, she greeted me in her clipped British manner, "Well, m'dear, we meet again," and our tears flowed as we clung to each other.

My hosts from the central committee warmly greeted me with flowers and embraces, saying, "Welcome home, comrade Peggy, welcome home." Later, at his summer camp, I was to meet my five-year-old grandson, Ghenya, who insisted he was named after the young uncle he immediately adored, rather than the grandfather he would never know.

For eighteen-year-old Young Gene it was an exciting summer of rapidly widening political horizons. He spent eighteen days at the International Youth Camp on the Black Sea coast working, playing, talking with young workers and students from the Soviet Union, Western and Eastern Europe, Africa and Asia. He attended the week-long First World Youth Forum in Moscow where young Cubans, Vietnamese and Latin Americans made the revolution a living reality. Sometimes with Tim and sometimes with the young interpreter assigned him, he roamed the streets and campuses in Leningrad, Moscow, Odessa, met with Young Communists in their factory canteens, and danced in the youth cafes of Kishinev. In the first days of our arrival our hosts extended him the tantalizing invitation to remain in the Soviet Union to study at any university or institute he chose.

Throughout the summer Tim urged Gene to accept, while I waited silently for his decision. Tim said, "If you stay, Mom will stay and we can finally be together, a real family." As for me, I knew my life had to be resolved back home, not in Moscow.

At the end of the summer, Gene told us he was going home. He said that the very insights and political growth he had experienced compelled him to go back. "My commitment is to my own generation back there. I must be a part of all that they will experience in the next years. I can't isolate myself from them."

For Tim the summer was a confusing experience. We needed to get to know each other. It was too late to recreate the mother-child relationship, but we hoped to become good friends.

He had a mercurial, fascinating personality. He strutted excitedly like a bantam rooster. His gestures were broad, his face animated, his words raced to keep pace with his soaring ideas. He was a creative thinker and, despite his youth, he was already making his mark in his chosen political career.

Thoroughly a Party man, Tim's life and views were determined by Party authority, as mine had been for so long. In New York he had been shocked at my rejection of political protocol and he had been stunned at the primary emphasis I placed upon personal considerations.

Now in Moscow he watched his brother and mother warily. Over the weeks his neatly defined and wholly politically-determined scheme of things cracked a little under our impact. I embarassed him at times, although as the summer wore on he learned to laugh in the re-telling of some of the incidents. He got himself assigned in charge of my tour-program so we could be together.

In Odessa and Leningrad Tim squirmed when I showed

little interest in the new factory machines of which the Soviet comrades were so proud and I asked, instead, to be shown the effects that machinery had on improving the everyday life of the people.

He apologized to local comrades when I cut prepared tour schedules to allow hours for us to wander alone on the streets. He kicked my leg under the table when I interrupted a convoluted answer regarding Soviet Jews. I told the Soviet comrades I was not interested in statistics about synagogues and *matzos*. I am a Jew, I explained, and I have never been inside a synagogue in my life. Why do the Soviet comrades, like so many Israelis, persist in placing The Jewish Question solely as a religious issue?

In Kishinev, capital of the Moldavian Republic, Tim elbowed me when I asked government officials about the effects of Stalin's process of Russification of the republics and how these distortions were being rectified.

At a banquet in Tbilisi, the capital of Stalin's native Georgia, Tim flushed and tried to mistranslate my response to the persistence of Georgian Party leaders that I drink a toast "to Comrade Stalin, leader of us all." I insisted upon changing the words, saying: "I drink to the good he has done—as to the great harms he inflicted, history must judge him."

Despite getting unsatisfactory replies to many of my questions, these incidents did not disturb me. They were problems that I believed would eventually right themselves. Instead I viewed everything I saw with Rip Van Winkle-like enthusiasm. I defended the inadequate from the complaints of young people. In typical old-generation style, I regaled them with descriptions of what life had been like in the early days of my life in Moscow. I wandered through the shops and neighborhoods alone and with Molly. I compared everything to the past and I liked everything I saw.

I visited the family's friends in their new apartments and was told that the improvements in life—the massive housing construction, the availability of a larger but still insufficient variety of food, clothing and household items in the shops—had come only since "The Old Man died." Stalin was eight years dead but people spoke as if it were yesterday. Relatives and friends were still returning from camps and prison. Certain freedoms were being cautiously tested; no one seemed to quite trust how far they could safely go with them.

III

I was deeply moved throughout the summer by the expressions of personal sympathy I received and by the frequent voicing of political appreciation for Gene's contributions to the movement. At a state farm sixty miles out of Leningrad, the farm chairman met me with a little speech about having "Comrade Eugene Dennis' books on my shelves at home. . . . The Soviet people know of Eugene Dennis' courage in face of capitalist persecution," he said, "and of his courage to fight for the very life of the American Communist Party when it was torn with dissension."

The woman director of a textile factory in Tbilisi embraced me saying, "I grieve with you. I too am recently widowed. I know your pain." Later in a formal meeting in her office with department managers, Party and trade union personnel, she offered a toast: "to the memory of your husband and to our fraternal Communist Party which is now consolidating itself on the basis of his ideas."

A young translator in Leningrad told us that his post-graduate thesis at the Foreign Languages Institute had been a translation into Russian of Gene's book, *Letters from Prison*. He explained, "To do this I studied again and again those letters so I could transmit into translation the quality of the man. As a result, I feel that I know each of you as though you are my own family."

At the rest home on the Black Sea where I vacationed with Tim, I walked into the dining room on my first morning and some twenty foreign Party comrades crowded about, embracing me. An Arab comrade murmured, "Your loss is our loss." A Bulgarian comrade began to cry, "He was the comrade-in-arms of our Dimitroff. Both are missed."

At a reception by the editorial staff of *Rabotnitza (Woman Worker)* in Moscow, I was presented with a framed facsimilie of a page in their newspaper. It was one of my articles titled "Four Long Years," published back home in 1953 during the prison years. They had translated and reprinted it shortly thereafter.

In a working conference with the editors of *Soviet Woman,* an international magazine published in sixteen languages, I was officially welcomed "as the co-worker of our beloved comrade Eugene Dennis to whom all humanity owes a great debt for his dedication to the interests of all peoples. But we greet you too as a woman in your own right whose voice and pen is known to us and to women everywhere."

If these comrades, from Leningrad to Tbilisi, had been briefed by advance agenting on the specifics of the Dennis family, this was a significant indication that the Soviet Party leadership wanted such tributes made. It was not done merely to feed my bruised ego, but was related to their concern for the still precarious situation inside our Party back home.

I received frequent letters from Elizabeth Gurley Flynn during the summer, forwarded from Moscow to wherever my schedule had taken me at the moment. Chatty and full of political gossip which always made her letters a delight, Gurley continued to emphasize that which she had talked about during my ten days in New York en route to Europe.

Many comrades had come singly to my room at the Chelsea Hotel on West 23rd Street during that time. Each felt the need to tell me of their concern for a Party leadership still in deep disarray, of continuing factionalism by remnants of the old Foster-Davis group now being joined by those already disillusioned with Gus Hall, whom so many had welcomed as the new savior at the 1959 national convention.

Gurley Flynn, who had loved Gene as the son she had lost, came to my room every day and we talked for hours. She warned me that the name of Dennis—"Gene's and now yours," she said—was being used as rally point for further dissent. Former opponents were now defenders, weeping crocodile tears over us. She urged that I not let myself be used. Laughing, I reassured her, I was out of all that now. It was her problem, no longer mine.

In Moscow, my hosts from the International Department of the central committee had come to my hotel room. They said I had impeccable credentials with them that went back over some thirty years. They had followed the internal struggle in our Party closely, and were concerned that it was still in a leadership crisis. Gene was sorely needed, they said, but unfortunately the Party had to go on without him.

I listened intently. On the surface the words sounded like a second welcoming speech. However, as they talked I realized their words tied in with what had occurred during my stop-over in New York. They asked many questions about our internal situation, seeking my opinions regarding individuals. They told me that Foster, from his death-bed in a hospital *dacha* set up specially for him outside of Moscow, was demanding that the Soviet comrades, in ways not too subtle, display their support of

Foster's original political views and of Ben Davis as top Party leader.

All this questioning made me uncomfortable. I emphasized only the need to consolidate the Party and put an end to any manifestations of factionalism continuing around the issue of personalities. I expressed concern that our Party couldn't take any more dissension at this time, and also my belief that our 1959 convention contained sufficient basis for much-needed unity. The old tensions I had escaped in leaving New York two weeks after Gene died once again engulfed me and I was relieved to rush off to Leningrad with Tim and Gene a few days later.

IV

Returning from the Soviet Union in September, Gene went on to Wisconsin for his sophomore year and I travelled on to San Francisco. Once again home was with Mini, Albert and my teen-aged niece, Laura. I settled into my old room and reported for work.

The special quality and character of the *People's World* bore the imprint of the team of Al Richmond and Steve Murdock. Al captained a tight operation with a light hand while Steve was always tense and impatient. Al assumed top grade work from us; Steve was a hard, explosive taskmaster. Both were fine craftsmen and despite their many years in the Party and on the paper, both retained a biting scorn for the cliché. They demanded objectivity from us and we were encouraged to seek out and emphasize the new and the controversial.

Our foreign news coverage offered factual details, background history and analysis of the world's crisis spot of the week. For years I daily devoured numerous diversely oriented magazines and newspapers, reading them with scissors, pastepot and note pad in hand. I acquired a master file bulging with folders on every country in the world and cross-files on every major political, economic, and social issue in each country.

For more than a year I worked until dawn each week preparing my week's article. With time I mastered the effort a little more, but it never became easy or routine. I no longer was plagued with my nightly nightmare of re-living the circumstances of Gene's death. I was too exhausted, too immersed in the problems of my work.

Sometimes an article I worked on evoked personal memories. Writing on the Soviet Union, thoughts of Tim, his wife Elena, my grandson and Molly would intrude. Writing on Berlin, I wondered where my friend Gr. of the 1930s might be, had he survived the Hitler holocaust and the war? Writing of China, the sound and smell of Shanghai enveloped me. Trying to disentangle the complicated news from the Mideast, I recalled the comrades I had met in Tel Aviv and Cairo—they had not been on warring sides.

The Cuban missile confrontation became a personal reality as I sat late at my typewriter one night during the week-long crisis of October 22-29, 1962. The phone rang and I rushed to answer it so the family would not awaken. It was Gene calling from Wisconsin. I learned later that all over the country many parents had received similar phone calls from sons and daughters away at school.

"Mom, if there's a war . . . a lot of us are planning . . . we're in touch with other campuses . . . there are ways . . . I've got to do this, Mom . . . Cuba is our Spain . . . if there's war . . . we have plans . . . you of all people will understand . . . I will call you. . ."

I went back to my typewriter, badly shaken. Once again the day's headline touched my life very personally, now through the son as it had for thirty-three years through his father. My prayer that night that Krushchev and Kennedy resolve the Cuban crisis quickly took on a very subjective urgency.

V

In addition to the weekly foreign page, I wrote human interest features, took my rotating turn at writing an opinion piece for the Staff Column, went out on "live," action stories—covering conferences, demonstrations, meetings, interviews.

From this expanding contact with all that was happening in and around the movement, and as a result of having to formulate my views into my writing, I found that my growing disagreements with a number of national leadership policies agreed with those of Party comrades who came to similar criticisms from their organizational activism.

Through ineptness or design, the national leadership from the beginning of the 1960s placed the Party in isolation from practically every new form of struggle that erupted in the ghettos, on the campuses and in the street. It placed the Party in competitive opposition to practically every new trend within the

Left which began to emerge after the silent Fifties. It zig-zagged from Right to Left, always ending up isolated. The popular term for it in the movements was "irrelevant."

Enclaves within the Party, particularly the Northern and Southern California organizations, battled throughout the 1960s to reverse this situation. The differences sharpened steadily and climaxed at the 1966 and then again at the 1968 national conventions.

Early in the 1960s the national Party leadership opted to transform small local youth DuBois Clubs, which in only a very few cities, notably San Francisco, were deeply involved in militant struggles, into a national "socialist-oriented" organization. This placed our young comrades in competition with, instead of cooperation with, the new Students for a Democratic Society (SDS), which in its formative years was a broad-based national rallying-point for white radical youth. The DuBois Club members became immersed in the daily problems of maintaining a national structure. The organization proved to have short-lived staying powers, and meanwhile the weaknesses of SDS, which our young comrades possibly could have helped overcome if they were in that movement, resulted in its eventual demise. And the Party glibly moved on to organize still another narrowly-based national youth organization.

Black youth began to move militantly, expressing their national racial pride in unorthodox ways, including the right to armed self-defense and forms of separatism. Our national Party leaders were horrified, calling the emerging Black Panther Party a "neo-Negro" organization, and charged the young militants with being national chauvinists and "Maoists."

By contrast, we in the San Francisco Bay area related favorably to this new Black movement from its inception, and established good working relations with it. Both the local Party organization and the *People's World* were under critical fire from the national leadership for this.

National electoral policy see-sawed throughout the decade from Right to Left. In 1963 Gus Hall committed the Party to support the Johnson administration, assuring the President we Communists were "the responsible Left." Both the act and the phrase reminded too many of us of Browder's assurance to the Roosevelt administration that, after the war, we Communists would be the "loyal opposition."

The national leadership used the word "coalitions" in its

speeches and reports, but in practice it proved itself incapable or unwilling to actually seek out and help create coalition relationships. It dug moats instead of building bridges between itself and all potential allies for struggle. By 1972 the leadership raised this inability or refusal to high principle by officially enunciating a 180-degree turn to the sectarian left, calling it the exercise of the independent role of the vanguard.

In the international arena, too, the differences were evident. In the *People's World* I reported factually the charges and counter-charges that Moscow and Peking were hurling at each other. I reported factually the issues, historical and current, in the China-India border disputes. I reported factually, quoting from documents and newspapers of other Communist Parties, the growing differences surfacing within the international Communist movement. These centered on the need for independence from Moscow's hegemony, avoidance of a break with People's China, the development of national roads to socialism based upon the circumstances in each country, and concern about limitation of political democracy in the socialist countries and its reflection upon the Communist movements abroad.

Gus Hall time and again charged the *People's World* with being "neutral" and "objective" in situations where there could be, in his view, only one correct position: Moscow's. As the struggles of the new movements became sharper in the second half of the Sixties, so did the debates within the Party; but mid-decade I left the home scene for eight months.

VI

In May I proposed that I take an investigative journey through the Eastern European socialist countries. No Party journalist had done what I suggested and I was uneasy at my audacity for proposing it, yet I persisted. Financially and logistically the plan had to be approved by Moscow and arranged with the countries involved. I was pleased when the idea was endorsed in record time.

I was restless even while my work at the paper still fascinated me. I had finally, with some trepidation, moved away from the family and had been living alone for the last two years. I was coping rather well.

It was not loneliness but aloneness that I found difficult. I did not need company to fill social hours, but I did feel keenly the absence of a pivotal person on whom to lavish my capacity to love. I missed that one person to whom I was all-important and with whom to share my nights and thoughts and talk.

On the third anniversary of Gene's death, Young Gene had written from Wisconsin:

"The change that has taken place in you is really wonderful and amazing to witness. It is an affirmation of yourself, coming out of the context in which you functioned for thirty-three years. [*Had I really mastered the mask so well?*] At first you seemed to work hard at forming a new life for yourself totally apart from what your life was before Dad's death. [*Had he been disturbed by the early absorption into the politically inactive life of Mini and Al?*] Then you apparently realized that the new life you build cannot be divorced from the old. Then too a part of what you were before your life changed with Dad has now come forth again. [*Had he actually listened when I talked about my radical youth in Los Angeles?*] All these things are the things which make up you and are no longer repressed."

In June, Gene and his wife of a few months, Jackie, moved to San Francisco, and four days later I left for Europe. My first stop was the World Congress for Peace in Helsinki. Behind the color of national costumes and many races, behind the pageantry of comradeship among 1,400 delegates from ninety-two countries, speaking many languages, there were two difficult stories I had to cope with in the articles I sent back to San Francisco and New York. One was the role of the Chinese delegation; the other was about the American delegation.

Involved was the time-worn problem of one's attitude toward coalition tactics. Does one alienate and lose the broadest possible diversity of motivation in the struggle movements in order to force through a formal adherence to an advanced ideological position?

The Chinese delegation to the peace congress, supported by the Indonesian and some African delegates, aggressively insisted that commitment to anti-imperialism was the only acceptable basis for the world peace movement. A few young Party delegates from the DuBois Clubs pushed through such an anti-imperialist commitment by a majority-minority vote in a formal statement of the U.S. delegation of one hundred—the largest, most diverse contingent at the congress. Where there had been mutual respect for the different views within the delegation, now debate became acrimonious. Some argued that at that time, mid-June 1965, the anti-imperialist sector was not the dominant feature of the U.S. peace movement, nor of the delegation; that the group had to view itself in relation to the struggle back home, not here at Helsinki; that the solution was that no consensus viewpoint be attempted and no statement be issued. This lost by a small margin. Our young comrades were jubilant at achieving the delegation's anti-imperialist statement, but the group lost its tolerance of diverse opinion which ranged from anti-imperialist to humanist to pacifist. Older Black community and white labor delegates and clergy abstained from voting and left the delegation.

Although the *People's World* featured my reports, in New York the comrades believed I should have portrayed only the pageantry, that I should not have reported the controversies.

VII

From Helsinki I went to Moscow and within the week I left with Tim, Elenya and Ghenya for a month's vacation on the beaches of the Black Sea. At our resort I spent a delightful evening with the Soviet social satirist Arkady Raiken. The small Chaplinesque actor is not a stand-up comedian but a master artist, able to contort his rubbery face and fluid body motions into the various characters he portrays in his one-man show. Popular throughout the Soviet Union and Eastern Europe, Raiken depicts the idiocies of pipsqueak, pompous bureaucrats and the little people caught up in their catch-22 machinations.

Sitting in my room overlooking the gardens edging the Black Sea, Raiken explained mildly, "I am no advocate; I put a mirror to the everyday realities of our life. People respond as they wish." At the crowded performance I attended, the howls of laughter and foot-stomping applause that greeted each Raiken vignette indicated that the mirror images touched the Soviet audience very individually.

Returning from the south, I went with my interpreter to Volgagrad for a number of days while my Soviet hosts prepared my Eastern European trip. Known then as Stalingrad, the city and its regions had been destroyed in the two hundred and one days' battle in 1942. After the war it was rebuilt by young people from all over the Soviet Union who came to construct the new modern buildings, build the hydroelectric power station, plant green parks on a soil covered with layers of broken shrapnel shells.

Now in Volgagrad a group of eleven editors of the youth newspaper *Young Leninist* describe to me how, in some ways, their problems today are greater than the rebuilding of the city. The twenty-eight-year-old editor-in-chief informs me that such practical mundane goals as achieving high scholastic grades and realizing factory production norms are "not the stuff of which young people's dreams are made."

Back in Moscow we agree that a more extensive Soviet program would be worked out on my return around Christmas. Now I would proceed with my three and one-half months of travel into East Germany, Poland, Hungary, Czechoslovakia and Yugoslavia. First I was to go to each of these countries' embassies in Moscow and there, with the sponsorship of the Soviet comrades and the strength of my own Party credentials, arrange for the unique character of the explorations I sought.

It had been ten years since the 1956 upheavals in Hungary and Poland and the steps taken toward correction of the Stalinist repressions, yet those events still cast a long shadow over everything the Party and the socialist state organs said and did in Eastern Europe. Unlike in the Soviet Union, where the steps at de-Stalinization had come from the leadership, in Eastern Europe the people had forced those changes upon the leadership, and the difference was evident everywhere I went.

Despite different economic and political circumstances at the time of the socialist takeover, each of the socialist countries were grappling in 1965 with identical economic difficulties, and each was seeking to overcome them in identical ways. From Moscow to East Berlin and from Warsaw to Belgrade all attention and effort was on what was termed The New Economic Reforms. Common to all the countries was a relatively low productivity, extensive rather than intensive industrialization, poor quality products that had difficulty competing on the foreign markets of the West, and a too-slow satisfaction of the consumer needs and demands of the population.

All of these problems existed, however, against a unique background. I sat in the Press Box as the premier of Hungary, Gyula Kallai, emphasized this fact in his address to the national parliament. And I heard it mentioned in sessions with chief economists in each of the countries I visited. While each of the socialist countries lag behind the industrialized capitalist countries in the rate of labor productivity, the socialist countries appropriate the (relatively) highest budgets in the world for their people's economic security and social needs—all of which is guaranteed by law.

VIII

As I went from country to country, government and party leaders explained, in almost one voice, that ideological and political questions are rooted in the solution of the economic problems. Economics decide everything, they insist, because socialism is only as successful as its ability to meet the people's economic needs. However, in Hungary, Czechoslovakia and also in Poland, I found some post-1956 re-thinking that broadened this concept somewhat.

In Warsaw a group of Party ideologists told me the 1956 strikes and demonstrations against the socialist government were caused by the Party "pushing too hard... [using] illegal and repressive measures to achieve economic tasks. ... We were too busy with our state plans to listen to what the workers thought of our methods of work."

In Hungary I was told by Party editors that the 1956 rebellion was caused by the Party's mechanistic adoption of the Soviet experience and Stalinist methodology. The people were pushed to a breaking point and an atmosphere was created whereby the remnants of the Horthy fascists and Cardinal Mindzenty reactionaries had room to operate.

"If socialism functions well," I was told, "there is no climate for counter-revolution and there should be no need for repression."

Central committee members defined the relaxed atmosphere so notable in Hungary as being based, in large part, on the abandonment of the old Stalinist edict, "All who are not with us are against us." In its place the leadership had adopted officially the post-1956 view that "All who are not against us are with us." This has subtly changed the relationships between the people, the Party and the socialist state.

Czechoslovakia has one of the highest standards of living among the socialist countries, and the country had developed industrial processes and a democratic form of government before the 1948 socialist consolidation. Yet Czechoslovakia's Communist leadership followed the same blueprints as Moscow in economic policy and political repressions based upon a centralized Party control of all phases of industrial, public and social life.

Now in 1965 three central committee members of the Party's ideology commission sat in a private lounge of the Party hotel in Prague explaining to me for a day and an evening the fundamental changes that had to be made to assure the effective growth of the socialist society. These were necessary, they said, not only to correct past mistakes, but because society must remain a constantly changing process or it stagnates into a mutation.

In Prague, and among these ideologists, I found an emphasis on the role of the individual in the socialist society. They agreed with the concept that there is no *class* conflict of interest between the individual and the socialist state, but they saw as "greatly over-simplified" the Stalinist view of "the automatic unity of interests" of these component parts.

Contradictions between individual needs and wants and needs of the Party and the socialist state are inevitable, they told me. Manifestations of these contradictions are not to be seen as opposition to the socialist organs but as a healthy expression of what the people demand from their socialist leadership. "People must have individual rights as well as social rights and responsibilities and these rights require free channels for expression," they said. The Party must at some stage in the development of the socialist society relinquish to the individual and the people's organizations the actual control of all socialist life, economic as well as political. Reluctance to do this becomes a serious deterrent to further development of the economic resources no less than to all other aspects of socialist life. These discussions took place three years before the 1968 Czechoslovakian crisis.

In Belgrade I found Party and government leaders considered Yugoslavia far in advance of other socialist countries because of their system of workers' management control of all institutions and factories. I was told that the new economic reforms would not work in the Soviet Union or in any other socialist country unless political reforms accompanied these changes. I could not get a satisfactory answer, however, to my question as to why then was the political and economic situation in Yugoslavia not appreciably improved over those in the other socialist countries.

After a month in Moscow, I flew home, exhilarated by my political impressions of the new thinking in the socialist countries. But in New York no one expressed the slightest interest in my months of investigations. Not a single comrade, officially or personally, asked a single question as to where I had gone and what I had experienced. Nor did anyone mention why they had refused to publish my articles from abroad in the Party's east coast newspaper.

IX

Two family crises confronted me the night I arrived in San Francisco. That morning my sister had been told that a fifteen-year-arrested cancer had reactivated. Driving in from the airport, Gene told me he had lost his draft deferrment, and he and Jackie were considering a move to Canada.

Over the years that followed that day her cancer reactivated, Mini transmitted to each of us close to her an appreciation of each moment of prolonged life. Ten years later she still lives each day with courage, humor and vitality even as she has had to retreat slowly from the use of a cane to a crutch to a wheelchair to almost total bed confinement, coping with side-effects of chemotherapy and radiation treatments, measuring good days only in comparison to bad days. I agonized over each recurring crisis and was exuberant at each partial victory over the years; at the same time I was shocked at my resentment that, by comparison, Gene had had only eight months in his struggle with the dread disease.

In those first weeks of my return in 1966, while frightened at Mini's illness, I routinely went back to work on the *People's World,* and faced, too, the alternatives open to Gene and Jackie. Actually, there were none. Gene would of course not report for induction, but neither would he select prison over exile.

"Dad was a fool to go to prison for six years. What purpose did it serve?" he asked bitterly.

I reminded him of his father's effort to avoid prison in 1951 and go underground. Gene chuckled, "Well, this time I'll make it for him."

I suggested they might go to Moscow, pick up on that offer to study there, be with Tim and the family. They rejected the idea, saying that would be an individual way out. In Canada they'd still be part of the struggle against the war, they'd be active in the U.S. exile community.

We came up with one last effort at deferrment. Gene wrote a political statement to his draft board, giving also his record of past radical activities, his own and family commitment to revolutionary concepts. He enclosed copies of articles he had written on the new youth rebellion since joining the *People's World* staff while I was in Europe.

While waiting for the board's response, Gene wrote a series of articles for the *People's World* on the problems of draft evaders and deserters, and the paper sent him to Canada to do a series on the U.S. exile community there. His week up north was an emotional dry-run of what he and Jackie could soon be facing. And I silently went about my work, wondering whether our internationally divided family was now to be further atomized. From Moscow to San Francisco to Vancouver or Montreal or Toronto. Gene's documents and clippings brought results, however. Without making reference to them, his draft board gave him a permanent deferrment.

X

During the eight months I had been abroad, the early stirrings at the beginning of the decade began to erupt into what many soon called "The Youth Revolution."

With the Vietnam war as catalyst, white youth attacked the citadels of corporate and government power. Black and Third World young people from campuses and ghettoes took to the picketline and the streets fighting fiercely for a voice in their own future. Tens of thousands of young people staged demonstrations in front of induction centers shouting "Hell no! we won't go!" and "Stop the Draft!" A new breed of women, of all colors and all walks of life, challenged every specific manifestation of sexism in traditional American life, including those within the Left movement itself.

Anger and resistance changed the climate of the country, touching practically every American home in fear or support or curiosity. Kent State University in Ohio, Jackson State in Mississippi, Berkeley in California, Black Panther Fred Hampton in Chicago—each became a symbol of the violence with which the repressive agencies of the government responded to this new wave.

Living in Berkeley at a time when one young man was murdered and another permanently blinded by police fire over the right of young people to plant flowers on a vacant lot was a frightening time. Living in a Berkeley occupied by Gov. Reagan's

National Guardsmen patrolling in battle readiness, prepared to shoot to kill in order to prevent young people from building a community people's park was to live with the feeling that "Vietnam" had indeed come home. At the same time, I felt the exhilaration of people's power when some 75,000 persons, many of them white families from the fashionable hills area, marched in our small university town in support of the young people, demanding the removal of troops from our streets.

Within this ferment and struggle sweeping the country, there grew an inner core of revolutionary awareness. Never before in our history had there been such open talk of revolution and socialism among so many. Everyone argued new ideas, challenged old ones. The Black movement explored its different roads to freedom—nationalism, separatism, pan-africanism, black-white unity, integration, self-imposed segregation. From various directions white youth converged, parallel to the Black movements, towards an anti-imperialist, anti-capitalist viewpoint.

Confused, without continuity of background experience, without an ideology or sustained organizational forms, these struggles and actions exploded, floundered, re-grouped, exploded again. What an opportunity and what a responsibility for the single most experienced organization on the American Left, the Communist Party, to provide through direct participation, the leadership and ideology to help unite this angry, militant, and strongly anarchistic movement into a cohesive, organized force.

Instead, the majority of the Communist Party's older generation and especially its leadership, with notable exceptions, did not understand this youth explosion, and was repelled by the unorthodox rhetoric and free-wheeling forms. The national leadership chose to place our Party in angry opposition to the most significant political events of the period. The white youth fighters were labelled "petty bourgeois kooks" and the young Black militants were "Maoist nationalists."

The Party leadership held out for "economic factors" as the only catalyst for struggle at a moment when reality had brought to the fore the broader social contradictions of capitalism. It counterposed a narrow concept of the industrial worker at the point of factory production against the Black and white youth generation which was in explosion. It pitted Black factory worker against the new Black youth militancy and posed black-white alliance against the national liberation aspirations inherent in the Black Power demand. It denied the Leninist precept that the character of the national liberation movement of an oppressed people transcends class lines even while the working class core remains intact within the broader struggle. Similarly, the leadership isolated our women comrades from the massive liberation movement under the guise of a purist class view. As with the national liberation struggle, the Party leadership denied the cross-class lines character of sexist exploitation which makes the women's movement a broad, all-inclusive one in which working women retain their own interests and needs.

Those of us who sought for years to inaugurate change in leadership policy avidly read the views of other Communist Parties, although these views were not reported in our Party newspapers or magazines.

For example, at the 1969 international conference of Communist Parties, Gus Hall devoted a couple of sentences in his formal speech to the youth rebellion, saying only that we had to overcome its "petty bourgeois" character. By contrast, Santiago Carrillo of Spain credited the youth struggles in Europe and the U.S. with "playing a role in awakening class consciousness of working people," and said the Communists' attitude to this youth "phenomena" was "decisive for the revolutionary consolidation of the Party of the working class."

Enrico Berlinguer of the Italian Communist Party emphasized that the Party had "to include within its line and policy all the revolutionary motives which induce [the youth] to rebel and fight." He urged "an alliance" between "youth, the working class, intellectuals and the Party to struggle to remake society."

By the time of our 1968 national convention nearly forty percent of the delegates, with those from Northern and Southern California in the lead, were challenging the leadership's attitudes. Many issues were involved, but the attitude to the current Black and white youth struggles and our relations with those moving toward socialist thought independently of the Communist Party remained the key to the re-thinking we were urging in all areas of activity and analysis.

Pacing in the back of the convention hall during one heated session, Black party leader James Jackson turned on me. "Gene Dennis would turn over in his grave at what you are lending his name to here."

Surprised, I retorted, "It's my name, too, Anyway, Gene's activity all his life was devoted to avoiding the very negative sectarianism towards non-Party mass movements that you comrades here are defending."

The leadership did respond fulsomely to the one form of struggle it was familiar with, the massive anti-war demonstrations. Also, as the brutal police repressions against the young Black and white activists intensified, the Party leadership came to the defense of what it called "these misguided victims." And the Angela Davis case inadvertently reflected well upon the Party.

The issues were dramatic. Angela was Black, young, a woman, an activist in support of the radical prison movement, and recently had been strongly influenced by the Black Panther Party. That she was a member of the Communist Party, having joined only two years before her arrest in 1970, was incidental to the symbol she became. However, many of her young defenders joined "Angela's party."

The debates concerning the revelations of the Stalin crimes, which devastated the international Communist movement in 1956, occasioned, at the same time, positive re-thinking of many old concepts. A number of Communist Parties in the capitalist countries slowly broke with time-worn dogmas.

The 1968 crisis in Czechoslovakia, triggered by the Soviet military invasion of that socialist country, led to a re-examination of many theoretical concepts by the Italian, Spanish, Australian, British and Japanese Parties; and, to some extent, by the French Communist Party. In the U.S., however, the Czechoslovak events froze the Communist Party leadership into a new decade of dogmatism and sectarianism.

In no other Communist Party in the western capitalist world were the facts so deliberately misrepresented as in our country. And nowhere else was discussion of this event so deliberately falsified and restricted.

Ironically, the C.I.A. and our Party agreed that a counter-revolutionary attempt had been made in Czechoslovakia to restore capitalism. So the C.I.A., of course, deplored the Soviet military invasion. By the same reasoning, the U.S. Communist leadership supported the Soviet action. Meanwhile, well-meaning liberals confused the situation further by claiming what was involved was bourgeois-democratic "individual freedoms."

Obviously no one paid attention to what the Czechoslovak government, Communist Party, trade unions, news media and the majority of the people said they were trying to achieve when an enraged and/or frightened Soviet leadership sent in military troops and tanks. Actually what was involved were the problems I had found throughout Eastern Europe in 1965. The Czechoslovak leadership had moved to resolve difficulties rooted in the old political dogma that was straitjacketing socialist growth.

Eight years after the event, Czechoslovakia still haunts the world Communist movement. Many Parties learned well the lessons of that event. The U.S. Party learned the wrong lessons and launched a renewed era of "ideological purity," one of sectarian "we-alone-ism." Yet Gus Hall recently admitted that his defense of the Soviet invasion was indefensible; but he did this in private and not for publication. During the petition effort in the 1976 presidential campaign he told the Party members that they should not try publicly to defend the Party's support of that Soviet invasion. Instead, he urged them to change the subject as quickly as possible. He also told that meeting that the comrades should not try to defend socialist democracy either, but always to turn the subject into a condemnation of capitalist democracy. Hall's cynical admonitions were marked "not for publication" in their mimeographed form. When his report was later published, that portion of it was cleaned up.

XI

The four years between the end of the 1968 national convention and the summer of 1972, when I went to Moscow for a three-month visit, were difficult years, yet on the surface they were almost routine.

I had been separated from the *People's World* foreign editorship in late 1967 at a moment when editor Al Richmond was under heavy flack from "New York" for foreign news coverage that still emphasized facts and quotes from all sources. However, within a few months I was doing a weekly factual column, "Scanning the Globe," without re-joining the staff. My emphasis on the controversial intensified, particularly after the Czechoslovak events and the 1969 international Communist Parties' conference in which the differences sharply surfaced once again.

Most of my time, however, was devoted to beginning work on this book, although I did digress for six months to put together another book, a compilation of Gene's writings on the united front and coalition politics from the 1930s until his death in 1961. This had been requested by the national leadership. However, upon completion the book was rejected without any discussion with me, without allowing me an opportunity to rework it if I should be willing to do so.

By 1970 conformity had officially silenced all who had tried to update Party policy and methodology during the decade. Dorothy Healey resigned from her years-long post as leader of the Southern California Party organization, refusing to take positions of responsibility because of her differences with the national leadership. Others claimed they would remain silent now in order to fight another day. However, their silence stretched into years and they gave tacit support to the things which they claimed, in private, they opposed.

A number of young comrades, particularly young activists, (Gene among them), left the Party in frustration. In order to not confront my own frustrations openly, I took a protracted leave of absence and later changed this to a member-at-large status. My Party clubs, first in San Francisco and then in Berkeley, had been dull, routine gatherings of comrades engrossed in collecting items for the annual bazaar, while around us the confrontation-struggles were exploding.

I withdrew from the club structure when our national chairman, Henry Winston, confronted me with a notebook containing verbatim reports of what was supposed to have been critical views I had expressed at a number of club meetings. He was calling me to task for what he called my "anti-leadership" comments, but he took as natural the practice of monitors for the national leadership inside local Party clubs.

My column for the *People's World* ended when Richmond, Murdock, and our cultural editor, Nancy Scott, left the paper. They were indirectly forced out by the pressures from "New York." Carl Bloice, who apparently had no difficulty on this score, became editor.

By the summer of 1972 I needed to get away. I wanted to touch my second-home base. I was tired politically, exhausted emotionally, and for the first time I was grappling, too, with some painful, although not basically serious, health problems.

XII

I arrived in Moscow in mid-July, during the hottest and most humid summer on record. My Soviet hosts said they were puzzled by a cable they had received from the national leadership in New York, specifying that I was on a purely private family visit and I was not to be afforded any official courtesies.

"This cannot be," they said, "You are our guest, we will not consider anything less."

I was housed in the Party hotel, as in the past. An interpreter and car were assigned me and arrangements were made within a week for me to go to a luxurious resort on the coast of Latvia for three weeks' vacation and medical care for my painful back. Molly was sent with me, as interpreter, and Tim joined us for part of the time.

I was puzzled but grateful for this display of official acceptance in a country where everything is determined by protocol—especially at a time when my relations with the leadership at home were sorely strained.

Each day at lunch in the Party hotel dining room two comrades from the central committee whom I knew from my earlier visits asked questions about the movement and our Party back in the States. With one I got into constant arguments, while the other sat silent, nodding as I argued.

I expressed contempt for my Party's idiotic claims that President Nixon's visit to Moscow had been a brilliant Soviet "blow for world peace," while Nixon in Peking was a Maoist sellout to U.S. imperialism. I hotly defended the intent of the youth efforts around the McGovern electoral campaign and emphasized the importance of the reform movement inside the Democratic Party as an expression of the kind of upsurge we should not contemptuously discard as "liberal." I discoursed on the strong heritage in our country of the liberal, democratic and progressive ideology and I defined its positive, if limited and vacillating aspects for the social and class struggles.

In Latvia, I alternated between beach-lolling and following prescribed medical treatments with guided tours of the capital city of Riga, where I heard and felt the strong national pride of the Latvian people contained within the socialist character of their society.

Upon returning to Moscow, I told my hosts I wanted to leave the Party hotel and I wanted no tour programs, interpreters or cars. I moved into Tim's home and for the next six weeks lived within the daily family routines, and concentrated upon being *babushka* to my grandson.

I looked up old, retired, Comintern friends I had not seen on earlier, more hectically official visits. I visited leisurely in their homes and with them visited their families and their friends. Because of these personal contact experiences, and because of the different stage of Soviet life at the time, I became increasingly confused at the contradictions I found.

The material advances made in the six years since my last stay were evident everywhere. Everyone I met seemed to have just moved into a new apartment whose most prized feature was its private kitchen and bathroom. Television sets, tape recorders, refrigerators, new furniture had become newly-acquired "necessities" and now the goal was possession of the privately-owned automobile.

Unlike 1931 or even 1965, Tim's housekeeper kept the refrigerator stocked with eggs, butter, pasteurized milk in bottles, and we had meat or chicken every day. The queues were still long, however, and one could not plan a shopping list because one did not know what would be available that day.

As on each return, I marvelled at all I saw in the shops, but my friends scornfully passed by the Soviet-made consumer goods, queuing instead in slow-moving, blocks-long lines to buy products from the other socialist countries.

Back home I had rejected the concept emanating from Peking at the time that socialism equates with austerity. I had been impatient, too, with middle-class, white radicals decrying "Soviet consumerism." Yet in 1972 in Moscow something bothered me. The economic base for socialism was secure. Education, jobs, medical care, leisure facilities, old-age pensions—all these were assured in varying degrees of quality. And yet the socialist norms of the quality of life were still being measured, as they were forty years ago, in comparison to Western capitalist material possessions.

Time and again, whenever I asked about "a socialist quality" to everyday life beyond personal goals to acquire an automobile or build a private *dacha*, I was indulgently called "the oldtime Comintern idealist." Shrugs greeted my efforts to discuss the definition and whereabouts of that "socialist man" (*sic*) one no longer heard or read about.

I found, too, a self-conscious and cautious political conformity among the Party and government activists I had known in the past. Instead of the lively discussions over tea and wine we had in 1965-1966, I now evoked heavily clichéd responses to the simplest questions and abrupt changing of the subject with an almost pleading admonishment, "You don't understand."

In one instance I was told that de-Stalinization, limited as it was, "had been a big mistake." No one would discuss Czechoslovakia, except to say, "We should have shot them all, as Stalin would have done."

In casual exchanges of non-political subjects among these circles of upward-moving Party activists, I heard strange phrases, all the more disturbing because they were said so nonchalantly. Referring to a mutual acquaintance of those present, one says and the others agree, "For a Jew, he's quite a good fellow." At another time I am told, "You can appreciate how capable he is, he holds such a responsible position even though he is a Jew."

Among these bright, political career-minded persons, none can give me an answer to the question why blatantly anti-semitic articles appear repeatedly in popular Soviet magazines, in the form of book reviews, when a *glavlit*—an official government censor—has to approve everything that appears in print.

Away from this political milieu, I glimpsed the everyday life of ordinary people. I met no dissidents. I met no Jews who seek emigration to Israel or to the West. The persons I visited with are fiercely proud of their country's achievements, yet they are cynically aware of the dichotomies that exist between official Party rhetoric and the realities of their lives. They shrug off the rhetoric and concentrate upon coping quietly and deviously with the anti-semitism boldly expressed in little ways on the street and on the job, with the inequalities and elitism so manifest in their society. This is their life. It is much better than it has ever been. Their material gains are still new enough to be all-important. Whether that is all there is to the socialist society, no one is asking at the moment.

I returned home in mid-October, confused by the many contradictions I had experienced. I wrote an article based on my Moscow stay that was published in the Party journal, "Political Affairs," and then reprinted in a popular Soviet mass weekly. I limited its scope to challenging the charge of consumerism against the Soviet people, a subject still popular within the New Left. I believed strongly in what I did write, but I had not written everything about my impressions of my three months' stay. I was not ready to confront publicly those issues which disturbed me.

I believed that the Soviet problems and inconsistencies were essentially the responsibility of the Soviet people. If they and the peoples in the other socialist countries could live with the contradictions in their lives and with the shortcomings of their socialist society, that was up to them. My concern was how the U.S. Communist Party leadership and the sectors of the American Left responded to events in those countries. I decided to deal with this as specific occasions arose within the U.S. movement. That moment came soon enough.

XIII

In June 1973, an article of mine in the independent *Guardian* newspaper in New York evoked a blistering attack from Gus Hall and Henry Winston at a central committee meeting. Hall's charges were printed later in *Party Affairs,* a journal sent to all Party clubs. As in the past, those charges were not discussed with me at any time.

Their objections centered primarily on the fact that I had written in a newspaper which was critical of the Communist Party. Also, according to Hall and Winston, I had downgraded Stalin and I was a national chauvinist because I urged the New Left to not revert to the ways of the Old Left, seeking blue-prints in Moscow, Peking or Havana. Instead the American experience and heritage should be the base for the U.S. movement.

(Three years later Winston castigated Santiago Carrillo, head of the Communist Party in Spain, for being a national chauvinist because in an interview with the *New York Times* he had said, "I am a Spaniard, not a Russian.")

Since Hall's accusations had circulated throughout the Party, I replied to the criticisms in a letter I requested be sent to the Party clubs. My request was denied.

In that letter I explained that my article had been a polemic with the *Guardian* editor who in numerous columns had eulogized the worst aspects of Stalinist methodology as a guide for the American socialist movement. Surely, I wrote, neither Hall nor Winston supported such a revival.

I urged that our Party leadership abandon its paranoia and competitiveness in relation to other Left groupings. We should be in the middle of all debates and explorations, trying to influence the thinking and political searchings going on, instead of forbidding Party comrades to participate.

I charged that it was reprehensible and in violation of

Marxist thought to term as national chauvinist emphasis on the need to establish deep roots in the reality of one's own country and to apply Marxism-Leninism creatively to one's own historical and cultural experience. To deify the Moscow or Peking or Havana experience and viewpoint as a blueprint is to expose the isolation of the deifiers from their home scene. Such deification distorts the true meaning of internationalism. It also does a disservice to efforts to popularize achievements of the socialist countries which must be understood on the basis of their indigenous situations, not as blueprints for us.

My document was buried in official silence.

A few weeks later Al Richmond and Dorothy Healey resigned from the Party. As with my *Guardian* article, the leadership officially castigated in Party journals and at Party meetings Richmond's just-released autobiography, *A Long View from the Left*. Like myself, he was denied the right to reply. In his resignation letter Richmond wrote,

> "In these circumstances, to remain silent and to remain in the Party means, in effect, to tacitly accept the vile characterizations and to acquiesce in their outrageous consequences."

In Southern California, Dorothy Healey had been for forty years the Party's most effective publicist. Even now she conducts a popular radio talk program noted for its exhilarating controversy. She allied herself with the political directions of the Richmond book and my article and refused to accept the local decree that every Party member had to publicly support the official condemnation of both. She resigned from the Party in protest at this latest display of "lack of Party democracy."

Afraid of the impact of Dorothy's action, and under the guise of a campaign for "Party purity," the Los Angeles leadership carried through a number of expulsions and censures. Though deeply upset, I did not leave the Party. Instead, I removed myself still further from the point of friction, although my actual physical contact had been practically nil for some time.

At age sixty-four, for the first time I applied for a job in the "outside" or "straight" world, and I was surprised and terrified when I got it. Adjusting to this wholly new experience—physically as well as to the job-related economic and social relations with the predominantly young Black, Asian, Chicano and white women—became my chief preoccupation. I began to write political reviews of books for national magazines, which enabled me to comment on various Left issues. I also followed more closely developments and debates within the groupings of the New Left.

At the end of 1975 I sent to the Communist Party's journal *Political Affairs* an article titled "Learning from History." It was a sharp polemic against the trend within the New Left to distort and reject the role and achievements of the Communist Party in the 1930s and 1940s.

The article was rejected, however, as being "anti-leadership." In my concentration upon polemicizing with the New Left in defense of the Party, I had forgotten that in 1972 Gus Hall had justified the Party's present sectarianism by unilaterally declaring that the Party's coalition policies of the thirty years prior to his leadership had been wrong. Unwittingly, my article disproved Hall's claim.

By reminding readers of our past achievements based upon a practical know-how in building sophisticated coalition relationships and movements, I had exposed the paucity of the current leadership. I had shown that the highest levels of Party and mass people's organization, struggle and practical achievements had been in those years in which the Party had boldly displayed the ability to build bridges of cooperation with the most diverse elements in our country.

I had written the article out of a real concern to reach the radical, socialist-oriented young people who were pitting their commitment to socialism against coalition tactics of struggle. In a somewhat changed format that article was published in early Spring, 1976 in the New Left quarterly *Socialist Revolution*.

XIV

This latest experience with the Party bureaucracy and censorship finally compelled me to face the unfinished business in my life. I had to stop beating my head against the wall behind which the leadership encased me. Either I had to become silently acquiescent, as others had become, or I had to place my life in unity with what I believed had to be said and done.

It is not because my opinions are so important to the movement that I was compelled to act; it is because the movement is so important to me, and I could not silently accept leadership viewpoints without the right to discuss, debate and exchange opinions inside and outside of the Party.

In addition to the cumulative effects of my experiences directly inside the Party during the previous fifteen years, an additional factor influenced me greatly.

I noted in my letter of resignation the important fact that in our country today there are many serious Marxists and Marxist-Leninists outside the Communist Party. There are dedicated revolutionary activists not willing to join the Communist Party for various reasons. There is a growing socialist trend independent of and outside of the Communist Party. Internationally there are responsible and more influential Communist Parties than that of the U.S., whose views and policies are different than those of the current leadership of the U.S. Party.

There is nothing in history nor in the record of achievements of the current U.S. Party leadership to justify its claim of divine-rights franchise over the class struggle, the movement for socialism or the vehicle through which these will function. Nor has that leadership ordained powers to read out of the struggle and out of the movement all those who do not agree with it or who refuse to accept its hegemonic omniscience.

Each year the problems, issues and struggles have become more complex. Difficulties exist that were unimaginable to our simplistic view of the world back in the 1920s.

In these fifty years the character of the problems, issues and struggles have changed, as have the component sectors considering themselves the revolutionary movement. And most important, we have not truly come a very long way towards resolving the new needs of our country and our people.

In 1957 Gene had sought to move his Party away from its internalized factionalism and back into the mainstream struggles of the American people. He reminded his Communist comrades that while they fought amongst themselves:

"We still have poverty, unemployment and a rising cost of living in the midst of plenty. Millions of Americans, especially millions of Negro Americans, are ill-fed, ill-clothed and ill-housed. A staggering technological advance does not foreshadow a second industrial revolution, nor bring capitalism a second blooming, nor resolve the crisis-breeding contradictions inherent in the profit system. The anti-monopoly forces have not yet merged into an anti-monopoly coalition capable of curbing the monopolists who, through their mergers, are tightening their grip on the nations' political and economic life. Imperialism still breeds war and reaction and engenders aggression and social retrogression. . . ."

These gargantuan tasks and responsibilities still face the movement today. As Lenin warned, the road to social change, to revolution, to socialism, is a long road that turns and twists and detours. And on this journey all are needed, for as long or short a distance they can travel and for whatever reasons their needs momentarily coincide with the greater struggle for liberation and socialism.

I am reminded of a story Gene used to quote often, the last time during a debate with Norman Thomas and Roger Baldwin at Carnegie Hall in 1956. Persistently countering their anti-Communist baiting with an appeal for unity-in-struggle, Gene told the story of our eighth president of the United States and the conservative anti-slavery leaders. The latter complained bitterly to the President that the movement against slavery had to be disassociated from the radical abolitionists and the Marxists. Van Buren listened patiently, then told them, thirty years before the Civil War:

"You must be very strong if you are already picking and choosing. I had supposed we wanted every man [sic] who is opposed to the expansion of slavery."

From the podium, Gene told the audience, Thomas and Baldwin, "It is in this spirit that I offer my views tonight."

It is in this spirit, too, that I offer this view of a half-century devoted to the winning of recruits into the struggle against capitalist exploitation and racism. In our country at this moment no one group can claim hegemony over the movement, the struggle or the American people. Surely, the real champions of the best interests of our people and our nation are myriad and still need to combine forces in the struggle for that new and better society we call socialism.

Appendix:
LETTER OF RESIGNATION FROM THE COMMUNIST PARTY, U.S.A.

June 7, 1976

Dear Winnie and Gus:

(Although I address you familiarly through years of habit, this is a formal letter and I send it to each of you in your respective capacities as chairman and general secretary of the Communist Party, U.S.A.)

I write to inform you that with this letter I am terminating my fifty years-long membership in the CP U.S.A. A lifetime's loyalty and commitment to the organization I served as a fulltime revolutionary since my graduation from the Young Communist League at age sixteen in Los Angeles is not easily discarded. Yet resigning at this time is not the trauma it would have been many years ago. Too much has happened to ignore any longer the accumulated effect of developments at home and abroad.

The lessons of the Stalin crimes revelations for our Party here in the U.S.A. have never been learned by the current leadership. Instead since 1960 the leadership has rejected those lessons and has continued much of the internal methodology rooted in that past. The achievements and decisions adopted during the 1956-1960 struggle within the Party against doctrinaire sectarianism were reversed by the current leadership after

1960. The American Party leadership supported the violent crushing of the Czechoslovak events initiated by the legal and official Czechoslovak government and Communist Party; the leadership here forbid serious examination within our organization of the issues involved and categorized as "counter-revolutionary" and "anti-soviet" those in the Party who sought such examination. For the past fifteen years the current Party leadership here substituted declaratory denunciations or serious analysis of the new conceptual ideas being discussed in other Communist Parties and within the international Communist movement. Discussions within the Party of these new theoretical and ideological questions (which go beyond merely the pragmatic clashes between Moscow and Peking alone) were not allowed in our organization.

Throughout the 1960s decade the current Party leadership placed the organization in opposition to and in isolation from practically every new form of struggle that erupted in the ghettoes, on the campuses and in the streets. Only the anti-war demonstrations were a familiar form of struggle to the Party leadership and therefore acceptable to it. Blinded by the inexactness of the new rhetoric of the Black and white youth militants and by the sometimes erroneous and often strongly anarchist ideas in their ranks, the Party leadership proved incapable of understanding this new movement and the deep-going social crisis it engendered. The Party leadership slowly modified its opposition under the impact of the struggle waged inside the Party (particularly by the organization in Northern and Southern California, Boston, and partially in New York) by those comrades who sought to put the Party in friendly, cooperative relations with all that was happening outside of and independently of the Communist Party. The current Party leadership finally adopted a condescending posture of concern for the young Black and white resistance fighters as "misguided victims of repression," still denying them the decisive catalyst role for struggle these young people were throughout the decade.

Despite its rhetoric favoring coalition and unity, the current Party leadership continues, as it has since 1960, to prove itself incapable or unwilling to work within the mainstream for building coalitions of struggle or to act as a unifying factor within the decimated Left. On the contrary. The current party leadership has taken the Party backward into a pre-1930-like sectarianism; it exacerbates rifts between itself and the various levels of possible coalition allies; it gloats over the disarray within the Left, and sees itself in competition with any and all socialist searchings not contained within the Party itself. The current leadership legitimizes its attitudes with the sweeping declaration, without prior examination and discussion by the membership, that all of the pre-1960 years in which the Party achieved its most intensive mass activity, its highest level of influence among the mainstream and its unprecedented organizational growth were "years of error" and "days of opportunist abdication."

Primarily as a result of its own errors and inadequacies the current Party leadership has been unable or unwilling since 1960 to re-establish the Party into the dynamic factor for effective mass struggle and the decisive catalyst that it was in the 1930s-1940s. Today there are serious Marxists and Marxist-Leninists outside the CP U.S.A. and there are dedicated revolutionary activists not willing to join the CP U.S.A. Outside of the Party though all these may be, they are not The Enemy as dogmatic Party ideologues claim. Internationally, too, there are responsible leaders of Communist Parties in Europe and Asia and elsewhere whose views on a number of important questions affecting their political directions are different than the views held by the current leadership of the CP U.S.A. This fact does not make these fraternal Communist Parties and their leaderships any less Marxist-Leninist than, say, a Gus Hall and the opinions he enunciates for the CP U.S.A.

In my fifty years in the Party I have experienced at home and abroad the rise and fall of too many Communist leaders and participated, upon official instruction, in their cultist glorification and then in their condemnation, to any longer be impressed with any more ukases from any current Party leadership that it alone is the receptacle of all Marxist-Leninist wisdom, that no Party member may examine, question or discuss any idea or concept unless it is pre-digested and sanctioned by leadership, that any viewpoint not so officially sanctioned is, ipso-facto, "anti-Party," "anti-soviet," "anti-socialist."

Yes, of course, there is only *one* side for a revolutionary in the class struggle. However the question "Which side are you on?" flung at those who seek serious analysis and debate of old precepts and practices in light of new social phenomena, is demagogic and intentionally intimidating. It is deliberately intended to obscure the simple fact that one can be a Marxist-Leninist on the only valid side of the class struggle and in the movement for socialism without accepting the claim of the current leadership of the CP U.S.A. that it has divine-rights over the struggle and that movement, that it alone has sovereign franchise to operate the locomotive of history and to chart its direction. Lenin noted the classic fact that only the masses in struggle can acclaim its vanguard on the basis of performance. On this score, the current leadership has caused the Party to lose ground over the years.

An almost inevitable extension of these political attitudes of the current Party leadership into the organizational realm has been the punitive administrative measures taken to silence those in the Party who sought to effect positive change and to intimidate others from listening to views not officially sanctioned by the leadership. Only a few more glaring examples of such administrative actions include: the ouster of Al Richmond as editor of the Pacific Coast *People's World* after twenty-five years, and of myself as foreign editor after eight years—punishment for our reportage of the facts about the Czechoslovak events and about the substantive differences that surfaced in the international conferences of the Communist Parties; the scurrilous distortions of the Richmond book (*Long View from the Left*) and more personal attacks upon him both in central committee meetings and in a review of the book in *Political Affairs,* and the denial to Richmond of the customary author's privilege to reply in the magazine, unless his reply was acceptable to the editor who had written the original review! Party committees around the country had to endorse the campaign against Richmond and in Southern California an over-zealous committee instructed its membership they had to publicly defend the leadership's characterization and criticisms of Richmond and his book. A somewhat ludicrous note was sounded around this whole affair when the current Party leadership expelled Dorothy Healey and Al Richmond four months after they had publicly resigned from the Party. Sometime later, long-time Party members Ethel and Angelo Bertolini were expelled because they participated in a public non-Party meeting to hear George Wheeler (American economist for twenty-five years with the Czechoslovak government) and again to hear two visiting comrades from the fraternal Italian Communist Party. In each instance these persons came with first-hand experiences and viewpoints which the current Party leadership in Southern California, abetted by the national leadership, did not want known.

My own experiences with this prevalent political and administrative mentality of the current Party leadership had a somewhat different twist. Periodically over the years I was criticized by Gus Hall and sometimes by Henry Winston in national central committee meetings in New York and in various regional conferences in Chicago, San Francisco, Los Angeles, and in the *Party Affairs* magazine for specific viewpoints I expressed in articles written in the *People's World* and in non-Party Left press—*but this criticism was always made in my absence and never in discussion with me.* My requests that I be allowed to respond were denied. Articles I submitted to the discussion section of *Political Affairs* were rejected with the claim they were "anti-leadership" because they "deal with Party mistakes" and "other matters still unresolved in the Party." So an already distorted concept of democratic centralism practiced within the organization was now further emasculated to mean a Party member may not even raise for discussion any question not already decided upon by leadership. Obviously, ours not to reason why, ours only to carry out leadership decisions.

I was let go as foreign editor of the *People's World* without discussion with me; my request at that time that I work on the west coast part-time for the *Daily World* on "non-sensitive" subjects other than foreign affairs was rejected, without discussion. On the day I returned to New York City after eight months abroad, Gus Hall invited me to attend a Political Committee meeting to hear his criticism of the Northern California Party's involvement with New Left and Black Panther struggles. That meeting also heard a report from another male comrade who had just returned from some congress in Havana. However I was not asked to report on my eight months in Europe where, as correspondent for the *People's World*, I had gotten first-time interviews with Party leaders in each of the socialist countries, interviews in which they candidly discussed the new ideological and economic problems they were grappling with—problems which erupted two years later in Czechoslovakia. But in New York the Party leadership did not want to know; it did not discuss with me why it had refused to publish these articles from abroad; it did not refer to the fact that it had sent a message during my travels that I was to return home immediately, nor the fact that I had ignored that instruction.

The manuscript of a book I had submitted, at the request of the national leadership, was rejected *without discussion with me* so I could not re-work it to please them even if I wanted to. This same manuscript, however, was criticized by Gus Hall in a central committee meeting where the majority of the comrades present had no idea what he was talking about, once again in my absence. Having heard I was working on a different book, the national leadership sent an emissary, once again not talking directly with me, to warn me that I could not express opinions different than those of the leadership, I could not write about anything the current leadership has not yet taken an official stand on, I could make no political evaluations of my husband's role, work or contributions during his thirty-five years in national and international Party leadership, because only current Party leadership had that right.

The political meaning of these examples of incidents that occurred constantly over the years are self-evident. However, there is, too, another element here. These attitudes are rooted in an explicit, deliberate and reprehensible sexism. My independent activism and political views were consciously contained by the current leadership into a personalized, subjective status. I was "handled" as the "difficult" widow of the former general secretary of the CP U.S.A. whom the leadership would patiently tolerate "for old times' sake" in a relationship which bypassed all political essence. But as a political trend my views were to be condemned, without my participation in any discussions and without my ever being present. This same sexism was apparent as well in the unexplainable concern the top Party leader showed over the years concerning my political relations within the international Communist movement. He intervened on numerous occasions to reduce those relations to purely courtesy gestures to the widow status channeled through his permission. Actually my international relations were rooted in my record of activity abroad for the Comintern in 1931-1935, 1937, 1941, and cemented in later years through my political writings during the 1950s and 1960s which were well-known and often reprinted in Party magazines in a number of countries. My travels abroad in 1961, 1965-1966, and 1972, which the leadership here at home insisted were purely personal in character, however verified once again the political character of those relations. I am aware, of course, that in accordance with procedures followed by some Communist Parties abroad, my leaving the CP U.S.A. will undoubtedly affect some of those long-time relations. I wish this were not so.

It has been a long process by which I come to this moment. Periodically over the years there had been moments of high hope (particularly at the end of 1959, again around the national conventions of 1966, 1968 and even 1970) that the efforts of so many who tried would at some point have a positive and salutatory effect changing the Party's political policies and administrative methodology. Thus, step by step and year by year, I found myself together with other Party comrades accepting that which finally for me at least has become unacceptable and untenable. Perhaps, too, it took this long to reach the moment of decision because in recent years personal problems loomed larger than political ones. Plagued with physical health problems, I was simultaneously confronted with the difficult adjustment at age sixty-four for the first time in my lifetime as a fulltime Party activist with the need to find, adjust to and hold on to the formal job outside the movement I now have—a realistic need I share with countless others who cannot subsist on a minimal social security allowance.

On the other hand, working these last three years on the job with Blacks, Asians, whites, mostly women of all ages, organizing with them around job grievances, coping with complex work and social relations among them arising out of affirmative action effects, encouraging exchanges of views on community and national issues—all this helped the process of realization of how far removed is the current Party leadership from real America and how inconsequential is its rhetoric.

However, I do believe that under the impact of events, circumstances and necessity, the leadership of the CP U.S.A. will be propelled to re-examine and re-adjust—with the same boldness and independence displayed in 1956-1960 but hopefully with none of the destructive factionalism of that time—those of its precepts and concepts which are outmoded and restrictive, those of its methods and practices which are rigid, undemocratic and cultist, those of its policies which are sectarian and ineffectual—all of which, taken together, tend too often to repel rather than attract, to divide rather than unify, to undercut rather than expand the Party's potential and thereby weaken the potential of the class struggle and the movement for socialism in our country.

Meanwhile outside of the Party I will continue to use my fifty years accumulated knowledge of Marxism-Leninism to participate in the exploration of all issues being debated and challenged in this freewheeling, divided, often confused, frequently wrong, but vitally searching movement that characterizes the present moment in our country and abroad.

Comradely yours,
Peggy Dennis

Index

NOTE: *No entry appears here for* Dennis, Eugene *or* Dennis, Peggy. *Highlights of the Dennis chronology are outlined under each chapter in the Contents, and virtually every page in the book focuses on their individual and collective attitudes.*

Abraham Lincoln Brigade, 110, 111
Abt, John, 197, 248
Agricultural Workers, 44, 45, 46, 56, 58, 60
Agricultural Workers' Industrial League, 46, 51
Alabama Federation of Labor, 168
American Civil Liberties Union, 45, 242
American Federation of Labor (A.F.L.), 29, 31, 35, 92, 93, 94-95, 104, 106, 139
American League Against War & Fascism, 92, 103
American Youth Congress, 92, 127
Anglo-American Children's School (Moscow), 66, 67
Arlen, Michael, 21
Arrests (1930), 40, 41, 42, 45, 47, 48, 51
Atlanta Federal Penitentiary, 195-197, 198, 199, 200-201, 202, 203, 215

Baldwin, Roger, 216, 230, 256
Baltimore Afro-American, 171
Barbara and Bernie, 194, 207
Bennett, James V., 197, 199, 200, 201
Berger, Meta, 93, 102, 107-109, 110, 128, 132
Berlin, 74-76, 87
Berlinguer, Enrico, 277

Bernard, Rep. John, 128
Billings, Warren K., 25
Bittleman, Alex, 195
Blair, Fred, 89, 93-94, 98, 106
Bloice, Carl, 280
Bob and Valerie, 64, 65, 113, 116, 137
Bock, Mini Carson, 18, 19, 21, 22, 23, 24, 36, 39, 142-143, 207, 250, 259, 260, 265, 269, 274
Bock, Albert (Al), 18, 19, 39, 259, 260, 265, 269
Bock, Laura, 265
Bogue, Judge (1930), 49
Boris and Musa, 64, 113, 116, 137
Bridges, Harry, 156, 217
Bridges, Nancy, 217
Broun, Heywood, 103
Budenz, Louis F., 177
Bukharin (also, -ism), 70
Bunting, Rebecca (So. Africa), 73

Cacchione, Pete, 156
Carlson, Oliver, 14, 16
Carnegie Hall, 143, 220, 288
Carrillo, Santiago, 277, 284
China, 39, 61, 64, 89, 93;
   Comintern group in, 83, 84
   Communist Party of, 80, 82, 83-84, 90
   Khruschev on, 246, 247
   Long March, 90
   Mao Tse-tung in, 84

297

Red Armies of, 83, 84
Soviet Provinces in, 80, 83, 84
Christoffel, Harold, 95
Churchill, Winston, 35, 160, 166
Civil Rights Congress Bail Fund, 211
Columbia University, 185
Communist Parties:
  Britain, 120-121, 233
  France, 90, 233
  Germany, 75-76
  Italy, 233
  Los Angeles, 44, 48, 51
  Wisconsin, 88, 89, 93, 96-97, 98-100, 104, 105, 106, 110
Communist Children's Movement, 13, 23, 24, 25, 38
Comintern (Communist International), 32-33, 34, 59, 60, 61-62, 65, 67, 70, 71-72, 73, 74, 76, 77-78, 79, 83-84, 85, 86, 90-91, 113, 114, 115, 116, 117-118, 120, 144, 146, 148, 149, 151, 160
Communist Party, U.S.A., 13, 14, 24, 26, 29, 30, 31-32, 35, 91, 97, 98, 104, 119, 120, 123, 127-128, 129, 135, 136, 139, 140, 154, 155, 157-158, 159, 160-162, 163-164, 167, 168, 174-175, 203-205, 208-209, 221-222, 222-224, 226-236, 230-231, 234, 236, 248, 249, 251-253, 254, 264-265, 266-268, 277, 278, 279, 280, 281
Communist Youth Organization (Young Communist League), 13, 22, 24, 25, 26, 35, 38, 40, 42
Congress of Industrial Organization (C.I.O.), 94-95, 103, 123, 139, 172, 175
Costello, Emil, 95
Crockett, George, 180
Crouch, Paul & Trumbull, Walter, 25
Cuba, 266
Czechoslovakia, 272-273, 278-279

Daily Worker, 21, 34, 139, 158, 189, 220, 225, 230, 236
Dangerous Scot (by John Williamson), 192

Davis, Angela, 278
Davis Jr., Benjamin (Ben), 156, 170, 181, 182, 199, 217, 227, 236, 237, 238, 239, 240
Davies, Helen, 70
Debs, Eugene V., 121
Democratic Party, 96, 97, 105, 122, 123, 124
Dennis, Jr., Eugene (Young Gene, Gene), 153, 169, 184, 185, 186-189, 190, 192-193, 194, 198, 202, 206, 207, 210, 211, 215, 220, 241, 242, 245, 247, 249, 250-251, 252, 253, 256, 259, 260-261, 265, 266, 269, 274-275, 280
Dennis, Jackie, 269, 274
Dickerson, Earl, 171
Dies, Martin, 127, 140
Dimitroff, George, 76, 85, 90, 114, 124, 145, 150-152
Downtown Community School, 187
Dreiser, Theodore, 21
DuBois, Dr. William, and Graham, Shirley, 255
DuBois Youth Clubs, 267, 269, 270
Duclos, Jacques, 162, 163, 231
Duncan, Katherine, 110

Eastern Europe, 268, 271-274
Eisenhower, Pres. Dwight D., 214
Elena, 266, 270
Elmer (Lockner), 89, 98, 106
Emery, Lawrence, 40, 46, 54
Emmerich, 68, 69
Engels, Frederick, 70, 99
Erickson, Oscar, 54
Ethiopia, 122
Eva, 65, 66, 67
Evangelista, Crisanto, 72, 119

Families of Smith Act Victims Committee, 211, 212-215, 216, 217, 220
Far Eastern Section (Comintern), 60, 85, 116
Far Eastern University (Moscow), 64
Farmer Labor Progressive Federation 95, 96, 97, 104, 105, 106
Father Coughlin, 97

Federal Bureau of Investigation
   (F.B.I.), 137, 140, 178, 179, 180,
   186, 187, 203, 206, 208, 209, 212,
   213, 245
Federal House of Detention (West St.
   Prison, New York), 192-193
Federal Social Security Act, 127
Feinglass, Abe, 216
Field, Frederick Vanderbilt, 212
Fight Against Cancer, 241-243,
   249-250
   Gene's death of, 250
   reactions to death, official, 250, 252
   personal, 254-256
   Mini's life with, 274
Fine, Fred, 235
Fifth Amendment, 169, 193
First Amendment, 53, 193
First Five Year Plan (Soviet), 59, 67
Fishermen's Union, 15, 217
Flynn, Elizabeth Gurley, 165, 237,
   251, 252, 253, 264
Foreign Specialists' Food Store (Moscow), 63, 66, 69, 117
Foster, William Z., 32, 34, 86, 120-124
   passim, 129, 130, 145, 155, 158,
   160-165 *passim*, 174-176 *passim*,
   204, 222-239 *passim*, 264
Fourteenth Amendment, 170, 172
France, 90, 157
France, Royal W., 215-216
Frankfeld, Phil, 195
   and family, 212
Friends of New Germany, 97

Gallagher, Leo, 45, 49
Garland, Judy, 172
Gates, John (Gates Group), 179-180,
   195, 201, 220, 226, 227, 230, 231,
   234, 236
George, Harrison, 39
Ghenya, 260, 266, 270
Gillette, Sheriff Charles L., 45, 54
Gladstein, Richard, 178
Gr. (Berlin), 75, 79, 266
Grace (Arnold), 65, 66, 67
Green, Gil, 163, 179, 181, 209, 237
Green, William, 168

Gromyko, Andrei, 245-246
Guardian, 284, 285

Hall, Gus, 209, 236-239, 240-242, 264,
   267, 268, 277, 279, 284, 286
Hammett, Dashiell, 211, 212
Haywood, Big Bill, 121
Heald, District Att'y Elmer, 51
Healey, Dorothy, 217, 235, 236, 280,
   285
Helsinki World Peace Congress
   (1965), 269-270
Hiatt, Warden (Atlanta prison), 195-
   196, 198, 200, 201
Hiroshima, 158, 166
Hiss, Alger, 173
Hitler, Adolph (Hitlerism, Nazis),
   75, 76, 90, 108, 122, 127, 138, 147,
   148, 150
Hitler-Stalin Pact, 109, 132-137, 140,
   160
Hoan, Mayor Dan (Milwaukee), 96,
   97, 108
Hollywood, 172, 206
House Un-American Activities Committee, 28, 126-129 *passim*, 156,
   167-169, 170-172, 173, 184, 186,
   188, 206
Hunton, Dr. Alpheus, 212
Houston, Charles, 171
Horiuchi, I., 54
Hughes, Langston *(Weary Blues)*, 21
Hungary, 230, 233, 272
Hynes, Lieut. Wm., 47, 49, 53, 55

Imperial Valley Agri-Struggles, 44-
   46, 51-54 *passim*, 86
Industrial Workers of the World
   (I.W.W.), 25, 28-29, 37-38, 104
International Children's Home
   (Comintern), 78, 87, 125, 147
International Communist Movement,
   71-72, 258, 268, 278-279
International Labor Defense, 49
International Lenin School (Moscow), 60, 69, 70, 77
International Publishers, 220

299

Jackson, James, 217, 244, 277
Janney, Dr. (Atlanta), 200, 201
Japan, 90, 157, 158
Jewish Arbeiter Ring, 20
Jones, Claudia, 190, 217

Kerensky, Alexander, 20
Khruschev, Nikita, 71, 226, 244-246, 248
Khruschev Report (on Stalin), 224-226, 229, 233-234
Krumbiegel, Dr. Stanley, 200, 201

Labor (organizing, unions, working class), 35, 38, 93-95, 99, 103, 155, 166-167, 174, 175, 204
LaFollette, Gov. Phil, 96, 97, 103, 104, 110
Leavenworth Federal Prison, 199
Lenin, Nicholai, 14, 20, 29-30, 34, 70, 99, 175, 288
Lenway, Clyde, 111
Lewis, John L., 141
Lewis, Sinclair, 21
Lewisburg Federal Prison, 192
Lightfoot, Claude, 228, 236, 237
Lima, Mickie, 236
Lovestone, Jay, 31, 32, 34
Luxe Hotel (Comintern, Moscow), 59-60, 62, 63, 66, 80, 85, 113, 115, 117, 118

McCabe, Louis F., 171
McCarran-Walters (Alien Registration) Act, 141
McCarthy, Sen. Joseph / McCarthyism, 166, 167, 190, 203, 204, 206, 217, 221
McGohey, U.S. Prosecutor John F., 177, 178, 182
McMahon, John, 68, 69
McNamara brothers, 25
Manuilsky, Dimitri, 60, 85, 86, 114, 124, 145
Marcantonio, Rep. Vito, 128, 171, 176, 197, 200
March, Frederic, 172
Marsh, Herbert, 216

Marshall Plan, 166, 174
Marine Workers' Industrial League, 35, 39, 46
Marx, Karl (Marxism-Leninism), 14, 29, 31, 70, 99, 161, 162, 174, 177, 223, 226, 230, 288

Medina, Judge Harold R. (Smith Act), 177, 178, 179, 180, 181, 182, 183, 184, 189, 194
Millay, Edna St. Vincent, 21
Miller, Dr. (Spanish Anti-Fascist Committee), 193
Mine, Mill, Smelter Workers' Union, 216
Mingulin, 115, 116, 137
Molotov, Foreign Minister, 136, 146
Molly, 68-69, 78, 113, 114, 118, 119, 144, 145, 148-151 *passim*, 260, 262, 266, 281
Mooney, Tom, 25
Moore, R.P. (Growers Ass'n), 46
Morford, Rev. Richard, 193
Moscow Daily News, 66, 117
Mount Sinai Hospital, 241, 243, 249
Murdock, Steve, 265
Muste, Rev. A.J., 216, 256

Nagasaki, 158, 166
National Committee to Win Amnesty for Smith Act victims, 211, 214, 215
National Farm Labor Party, 123, 124
New Deal, 96, 97, 103, 105, 106, 122, 123, 124, 127, 128, 140, 141, 166, 167, 173
Newspaper Guild Strike, 103
New York Times, 168, 224, 284
Nixon, Richard M., 171, 281

Olga, 65, 66, 67, 69, 78
Old Doc (Milwaukee), 100

Pacific Coast Marxist Summer School, 13, 14-17 *passim*, 26, 31
Palmer, Fred, 110
Pan-Pacific Monthly, 39
Parents (of Eugene Dennis)
father, 26-28, 30, 31

mother, 27
stepmother, 27, 28, 30, 31
  (and sister), 27, 28
Parents (of Peggy Dennis), 17-22
  passim, 25, 36, 37, 39, 40-43, 47, 54,
  55, 57, 131, 207, 259
Pearl Harbor, 152, 153
People's World, 259, 260, 265, 267,
  268, 270, 274, 275, 279, 280
Perry, Eleanor, 185, 186
Perry, Pettis, 217
Perry, Rose, 215
Philippines, 39, 61, 65, 72-73, 86
Piaf, Edith (songs of), 118
Pierce, Mark (L.A. Police), 48
Pine, Judge David, 172, 188
Poer, Dr. Ernest, 200, 201
Poland, 135, 157, 233, 272
Pollitt, Harry, 120
Porter, Mayor John C. (L.A.), 48
Potash, Irving, 68, 69, 199
Profintern (Red Int'l Labor Unions),
  39, 67, 68, 69
Progressive Party
  of Wisconsin, 93, 96, 99, 104, 105,
    106, 110
  national, 1948—, 173, 174, 175
Political Affairs, 283, 286

Raiken, Arkady, 270
Rankin, John E., 170
Remington, William, 199
Republican Party, 96, 97, 172, 173
Richmond, Al, 260, 265, 279, 285
Riverside Church Nursery School,
  185-186
Robeson, Eslanda, 119, 120, 255
Robeson, Paul, 119, 120, 244, 255
Robeson, Pauli, 119, 120
Rojas, Danny, 54
Rothstein, Ida, 45
Roosevelt, F.D. (Administration), 74,
  86, 91, 92, 97, 105, 110, 111, 112,
  122, 124, 127, 135, 137, 139, 140,
  142, 143, 148, 154, 160, 162, 165,
  166, 172, 173
Roosevelt, Eleanor, 127, 130, 168, 214
Rosenberg, Ethel & Julius, 206, 210

Ryan, Tim, 54, 61

Sacco and Vanzetti, 25
Sacher, Harry, 178, 182-183
S.F.—L.A. (a contrast of), 39-40
San Pedro, 37, 38, 48
Second Five-Year Plan, 117
Second Front (Europe), 157
Section 7a (N.R.A.), 91, 92
Schneiderman, William (Bill), 13, 17,
  19, 26, 37, 39, 140, 156, 216
Scott, Nancy, 280
Shanghai, 76, 77, 80-84, 87
Shingle Weavers' Union, 15
Sig (Eisencher), 89, 98
Sinclair, Upton, 21, 38
Sklar, Carl, 49, 51, 52
Smith Act
  indictment, 173
  trial, first, 175-183, 184, 186, 189,
    192, 194
  political prisoners of, 198, 199, 211,
    213
  defendants of, 203, 211, 212
  amnesty campaign for, 215,
    216-217
Sobel, Morton, 206
Social Democratic Party, 75-76
Social Democracy, 33, 90, 91
Socialist Party, 20, 29, 35, 93, 96, 99
  105-110 *passim*
Sokolsky, George, 248
South Africa, 61, 65, 73-74, 86, 93
Soviet Union (and leadership), 26, 29,
  58, 71, 74, 89, 107, 117-118, 119,
  133, 136, 139, 140, 146, 148, 154,
  155, 158, 164, 166, 174, 224-226,
  228, 230, 233, 234, 259, 260, 264,
  281
Spain, 90, 109-115 *passim*, 122, 127
Spector, Frank, 49-50, 51, 52, 54
Stachel, Jack, 182
Stalin, Joseph, 34, 59, 65, 70-71, 91,
  99, 117-119, 133, 147, 148, 160,
  262, 284
Shein, Sid, 235
Stone, I.F., 172, 205
Strong, Anna Louise, 119

Students for a Democratic Society (S.D.S.), 267
Studer, Norman and Hannah, 187
Subversive Activities Control Board, 219, 221
Sun Yat-sen, Madame, 83

Taft, Rev. Clinton, 45, 48
Taft-Hartley Act, 167, 173
Teheran, 160, 161, 163
Terre Haute Federal Prison, 199
Thomas, J. Parnell, 168, 169, 172
Thomas, Norman, 97, 216, 230, 255, 288
Thompson, Robert (Bob), 163, 179, 186, 195, 199, 209, 237
Tim (Dennis), 40, 42, 51, 52, 54, 100, 101, 113-115 *passim*, 118-119, 120, 121, 125, 132, 144-147 *passim*, 153, 244-249 *passim*, 253, 259, 261, 266, 270
Time magazine, 28, 29, 168
Trade Union Unity League (T.U.U.L.), 35, 48, 51, 68, 131
Trotsky (-ism, -ites), 70, 217
Truman, Pres. Harry S., 162, 164, 166, 172-174

Unemployed Struggles, 34, 41, 46-50, 92, 103-104, 155
Unfinished Woman (by Lillian Hellman), 212
United Auto Workers, 168, 172
U.N. Soviet Mission, 245, 247, 248
U.S. concentration camps, 157
U.S. Supreme Court Decision, Smith Act Convictions, reactions to, 205

Van Buren, U.S. President, 288
Vengeance Upon the Young: Story of the Smith Act Children (by Albert Kahn), 213, 216
Volgagrad (1965), 270, 271
Voorhis (foreign agent) Act, 141

Waldron, Frank, 13, 14, 28, 29, 30, 46, 61
Wallace, Henry, 172

Weinstone, Will, 63, 65-66, 67
Williamson, John, 163, 192, 227, 228-229, 231, 232, 233
Winston, Henry, 179, 181, 209, 217, 280, 284
Winter, Carl, 179, 181, 212, 236
Wisconsin Central Labor Councils, 95
Wisconsin Communist Party Full-time School, 98-100
Wisconsin C.I.O., 92-93, 94-95
Wisconsin Workers' Alliance of Unemployed, 92, 103-104, 106
Women's Commission, C.P.U.S.A., 190, 191
Woman's Page, *Sunday Worker*, 190, 191, 192, 193
Woman Question, personal grappling with, 36-37, 41-42, 56-57, 62, 77, 89, 100-101, 130-131, 190-191, 215, 259, 268-269, 277

"Youth Revolution", 1960's decade, 267, 268, 275-278
Yugoslavia, 157, 233, 273